D1107862

NIKOLAI MIKHAILOV

ACROSS THE MAP
OF THE U.S.S.R.

**V. I. Lenin and J. V. Stalin discuss the Plan for the
Electrification of Russia (the GOELRO plan)**

Painting by A. Andreyev

"EACH DAY OUR PEOPLE RISE HIGHER AND HIGHER. WE ARE NOT THE SAME TODAY AS WE WERE YESTERDAY, AND WE WILL NOT BE THE SAME TOMORROW AS WE ARE TODAY. WE ARE NOT THE SAME RUSSIANS WE WERE BEFORE 1917, AND RUSSIA IS NOT THE SAME, AND OUR NATURE IS NOT THE SAME. WE HAVE CHANGED AND GROWN ALONG WITH THE VAST CHANGES THAT HAVE COMPLETELY CHANGED THE FACE OF OUR COUNTRY."

A. A. Zhdanov

CONTENTS

I

THE HANDWRITING OF HISTORY

A MAP is hanging on the wall. Let us go up to it as we would to an open window: through the grid of latitudes and longitudes we see the entire country. On the coloured surface, in three dimensional space, we see spreading plains, and towering mountain ranges. Thin, winding lines expand into broad rivers, and small circles into cities teeming with life. In the North, the ice pack crunches against the sides of ships. In the South the hot sand trickles down the dunes in fine streaks. We can almost feel the wind from those distant open spaces breaking through the map and beating in our faces. The whole of the boundless Soviet Union lies before our eyes!

But there is also a "fourth dimension" in the picture that is spread before us: this is to be measured not in terms of latitude and longitude, or height above sea level, but in years of human endeavour. The rivers have been curbed, the roads explored and the plains ploughed up. Steel drills have bitten into the earth and have brought up from the depths an inexhaustible stream of wealth. Metal and concrete in the shape of pitheads, factory buildings and the latticework of bridges have broken the eternal silence of the ancient landscape. . . .

The strokes on the map tell us the story of the creative labour, the life and the heroic deeds of the people. Like a sensitive photographic plate, the map records the march of time, the birth and death of cities, the destiny of states. The lines and signs of the map indicate the path history has traversed.

Thirty years ago mankind reached the steepest and highest mountain pass in its history. Lightning lit up the earth—the October Revolution thundered in Russia. A red line appeared on the map of the world, marking the boundary between two eras, the boundary between the past and the future.

That red line tells us that a new world has been created on a sixth of the earth's surface, the world of Socialism; a state, the first in history, in which power is wielded by the working people, the first country in the world in which there are no parasitic classes, no exploitation, no enslavement of man by man.

For thirty years our great Soviet Union has been steadily growing stronger. A commonwealth of equal republics has been founded and consolidated on a huge area stretching from the Carpathian Mountains to the Bering Strait. Under the leadership of the Communist Party, the Party of Lenin and Stalin, the peoples of our country have built up socialist society in fraternal unity and are now victoriously marching onward towards Communism.

More than once during these three decades rapacious imperialists tried to obliterate that red line from the map of the world, tried to destroy the Soviet system, to enslave and partition our country. On each occasion, however, the people of the Soviet Union, strong in their unity and patriotism, defeated and expelled the invaders. Our people emerged victorious from the struggle against the foreign interventionists and Russian whiteguards in the years of the Civil War. They heroically bore all the hardships and tribulations of the Second World War, the Great Patriotic War of the Soviet people. In grim battles in defence of their socialist motherland and of the great achievements of the October Revolution they broke the back of the fascist beast. In liberating the peoples of Europe from fascist slavery they enhanced still further the world importance and glory of the world's first socialist state.

From Pechenga to Kaliningrad, from Kaliningrad to Ismail, from Ismail to the Kuril Islands there runs a red line that marks the sacred frontiers of the Land of Soviets. This is not only the frontier of the greatest country in the world—it is a line which injustice, tyranny and oppression cannot cross. On the other side of the line, in the capitalist countries, reign darkness and slavery, the power of money, violence against the masses. On our side, the Soviet side, we have free citizens of a free land, the joy of creative labour, the gigantic scaffolding of Communism.

The October Socialist Revolution released the creative energy of the people, and this energy has revealed itself in all its strength. Following the route outlined by Lenin and Stalin, the Soviet people have, in a short space of time, transformed our country. They have thrown off the shackles of ancient backwardness and have broken the heavy fetters of economic slavery with which foreign capital bound old Russia. They have built up a powerful socialist industry and a collective-farm system in which agriculture is more highly mechanized than in any other country in the world. We have transformed our country into a mighty power that is advancing at the head of progressive mankind.

Socialism has opened up tremendous opportunities for the development of the productive forces of our society. The country teems with new riches created by the labour of Soviet people.

The country has changed. Its economic geography has changed too. A wise plan has redistributed both the wealth and the efforts of its people, has given the country's regions and territories a new aspect and has set up new economic relations between them.

The political and economic development of the capitalist world proceeds unevenly. Some regions and some countries of this world develop and grow rich by ruining others. The economic might of the imperialist countries rests upon the exploitation of the workers at home and on the enslavement and plunder of the colonial peoples.

In our Soviet land there is not and cannot be any enslavement of some people by others, nor can there be any backward colonial regions. All the regions of our country grow and develop, every nation has the opportunity rapidly to develop its economy and culture—this is one of the basic principles of the Lenin and Stalin national policy.

The old industrial centres of the U.S.S.R. have grown and have changed beyond recognition. At the same time new industrial regions have sprung up, many of them in places that only recently were a wilderness. New cities have been built in the Soviet Union, new railways and motor roads have been laid across the country. New bridges, new dams and new navigable canals have been built. Rivers have been deepened. Agriculture has spread to regions where it had not existed before, and the distribution of the country's crops is different from what it was before. New crops are now being grown. Artificial streams now irrigate formerly arid wastes. Poor soils have been enriched. Swamps have been drained over a vast area. In some places forests have been cleared, in others they have been newly planted.

New territory of an area as large as that of the biggest countries in Europe has been explored and newly mapped. Our knowledge of our country's mineral kingdom has grown to such an extent that this kingdom too may be regarded as a newly-discovered land.

Old Russia knew only the anarchic form of development. Factories, mills and mines were built by private enterprise. Profit drained swamps. Hunger felled forests. This was not a planned and wide-scale operation. Human effort was dissipated by competition. In the race for profits forest lands and mines were exhausted. Avarice was accompanied by waste—both of natural resources and of human labour.

Today, capitalism, with its anarchy of production and crises, with its unemployment and predatory wars, is confronted by a new and far more perfect social system. By converting all the wealth of the country into the property of society as a whole, the Socialist Revolution greatly enhanced the strength of the people in their struggle to conquer nature.

The old economic geography of the country took shape in a haphazard way. Today, our country is organizing its economy consciously and purposefully. Throughout these vast expanses of territory work is carried on in conformity with a single plan, and no crises, nor the selfish interests of capitalists, hinder this work.

The country has changed. And much of what has appeared in it since the Soviet system was established is to be seen on the map.

The map of old tsarist Russia told the story of the poverty of the huge backward country, the story of the chained forces of the people, of golden opportunities unused. The map of the Soviet Union tells the story of vast economic and cultural progress, of the country's renovation, of the growth of her might, and of the new socialist way of life.

Verily, Russia is no longer what she was! Not what she was before October 1917. Our country has grown and has become renovated; her face has changed.

Together with the country the people have changed. In transforming the world around them they are transforming themselves.

The Soviet system and the Communist Party have imparted splendid new qualities to the people—a fervent love for their socialist country, profound loyalty to the cause of Communism, courage and perseverance in struggle, and ability to overcome all obstacles. These splendid traits of the Soviet people have made themselves manifest both in the sphere of labour and on the battlefield. And in the sphere of labour and on the battlefield, their titanic strength has grown.

Everything that has strengthened and elevated our country, everything that has made it powerful and prosperous, is the result of the tireless labour of our people, the embodiment of the ideas and the energy of the Communist Party.

In March 1918, shortly after the inception of the Soviet State, the great Lenin announced the inflexible determination of the Bolsheviks "to see to it that Russia ceases to be wretched and impotent and becomes mighty and abundant in the full meaning of the word. . . ."

"In our natural wealth, in our stores of man power, and in the splendid impetus which the great revolution has imparted to the creative powers of the people," wrote Lenin, "we have the material for the creation of a truly mighty and abundant Russia."*

The eagle eye of the leader, the creator of our state, saw far ahead. And those prophetic words of his have come true.

Brick by brick are we building our house, our state. The face of the country has been changed according to Stalin's plan. The plans outlined by the genius of Lenin and Stalin are being embodied in the wonderful creative achievements of the hands, minds and hearts of our people. The Soviet people are led by the Communist Party, which directs the efforts of millions into one single channel. Stalin shows us the way forward, to new victories. He is building the happiness of the people. It is he who inspires the Soviet people to perform great deeds of labour and heroism. The might and glory of our country, which is holding aloft the great banner of Communism, were created by Lenin and Stalin.

---

* Lenin, *Selected Works*, Two-Vol. ed., Vol. II, Moscow 1947, p. 309.

II

UNDER THE SOVIET FLAG

WHEN the sun sets in the Kuril Islands it is just rising in Kaliningrad. When night falls in Kaliningrad, dawn is breaking in the Kuril Islands. These two points lie on different sides of the globe. But both are on Soviet territory. The scarlet flag of the Soviets waves proudly over Kaliningrad and over the distant Kuril Islands.

Our country is immense; no other country equals it in size. The Soviet Union covers one-sixth of the habitable surface of the earth.

The great Soviet revolution marched triumphantly across a vast expanse—to the Pacific coast, to the Pamir Mountains, to the rivers Dniester and Niemen. Scores of nationalities rallied under the banner of the revolution. They gained their freedom and a homeland, and they established their own national states, which united in an invincible union of republics.

Beyond the frontiers of our great country, however, there remained millions of dispossessed people, our kinsmen in blood and language.

The lands of Ukrainian Galicia remained under the yoke of Austria-Hungary. The peasants of Transcarpathian Ukraine remained groaning under the oppression of the Hungarian landowners. And when the ramshackle Austro-Hungarian Empire collapsed under the strain of the First World War, the Entente imperialists used these countries as counters in the game of reshuffling the map of Europe. Such was the situation in the West. In the Far East, ancient Russian lands, discovered and settled by bold Russian explorers, fell under the rule of the Japanese. The Japanese samurai built their war bases in Southern Sakhalin and on the Kuril Islands.

During the stormy years of the Civil War the German and Anglo-French imperialists, with the bayonets of their armies, set up reactionary bourgeois governments in the Baltic countries. The western regions of the Ukraine and Byelorussia were appropriated by the Polish squires, and Bessarabia by the Rumanian boyars.

For many a long year our brothers suffered in separation from their mother country. Only now have the disunited peoples been brought together again. Lake Chudskoye (Peipus) is no longer a prohibited frontier separating Russians and Estonians —it now unites them. The Byelorussian peasants of Polesie no longer bow to the Polish squires, the squires have gone; and the lands they once seized are now ploughed by tractors sent from Stalingrad and Kharkov. The Ukrainian woodsmen of the Transcarpathian Ukraine, the Ukrainian miners of the Donets Basin, the Ukrainian collective farmers of the Poltava Region, the Ukrainian fishermen of Ismail, the Ukrainian academicians of Kiev are all now citizens of one state.

The wisdom of Stalin and the might of the Soviet State restored to us our ancient lands; historical justice has triumphed. We have returned to the banks of the Danube and to the free expanses of the Pacific Ocean.

IN THE NORTHWEST

In the extreme Northwest of our country, beyond Murmansk, the territory of Pechenga is now included within the Soviet frontiers. Russian people have lived on the ice-free banks of the Varanger Fjord from time immemorial. This territory was within the borders of the land of Russia as far back as the reign of Prince Yaroslav the Wise.* That

---

* Grand Prince of Kiev, 1019-1054.—*Tr.*

Tallinn, capital of the Estonian S.S.R.

Gedimin Street in Vilnius, capital of the Lithuanian S.S.R.

ST. MARY'S
COLLEGE LIBRARY
CALIFORNIA

The Liberty Monument in Riga,
capital of the Latvian S.S.R.

Lenin Street in Kishinev,
capital of the Moldavian .S.S.R.

Petrozavodsk, capital of the Karelo-Finnish S.S.R.

distant Arctic shore was peopled by the descendants of the bold men of Novgorod—the "pomors," or maritime people. They fished in the stormy Barents Sea and traded with Norwegian merchants. In the 16th century Russian monks founded the Pechenga Monastery here.

During the Civil War the former rulers of bourgeois Finland secured the inclusion of the Pechenga district within the domains of Finland. In conformity with the Armistice Agreement signed at the end of our Great Patriotic War, Finland restored Pechenga to the Soviet Union. These new Soviet lands now form part of the Murmansk Region of the R.S.F.S.R.

The restitution of the Pechenga district, up to the Potso River, enhanced the security of Murmansk, our gate to the Atlantic and the Arctic. We now have a second ice-free port in the Northwest—Pechenga. On the rocky coast, amidst stony hills and turbulent rivers, lie rich deposits of nickel ore. The mines and refinery of Pechenga have already been rehabilitated.

The territory to the north and west of Lake Ladoga was brought within the boundary of the Soviet Union somewhat earlier, in 1940. Before that date, the frontier of the Soviet Union on the Karelian Isthmus lay within gunshot of Leningrad. With the view to ensuring the security of the City of Lenin, the Soviet Government made provision in the peace treaty concluded with Finland in 1940, for the shifting of the frontier a few dozen kilometres further west. Part of the new territory went to the Karelo-Finnish S.S.R. and part to the Leningrad Region of the R.S.F.S.R.

The town of Vyborg, which lies within this territory—and which Peter the Great called a "strong bolster for St. Petersburg"—has now become a frontier outpost of Leningrad. Lake Ladoga, our ancient Russian Ladoga, has become an inland lake: it is surrounded by a ring of Soviet railways. The pinewoods and sandy beaches of the Karelian Isthmus, formerly scarred by the fortifications of the Mannerheim Line, are now at the disposal of the people of Leningrad for rest and recreation. The collective and state farms that have been organized on the Karelian Isthmus are already supplying Leningrad with vegetables, meat and milk. Paper mills have been built. The Pitkäranta region supplies us with non-ferrous metals, the Sortavala region supplies us with beautiful marble and the turbulent Vuoksen River provides us with abundant water power. The Vuoksen power stations, which the German invaders destroyed, have now been restored and a high-voltage transmission line now runs through the forest cuttings, carrying current to Leningrad.

These are the changes that have been made in the map of the frontier regions of the Northwest.

IN THE WEST

Southwest of Leningrad run the maritime frontiers of the U.S.S.R. On the shores of the Baltic Sea lie the lands of the Estonians, Latvians and Lithuanians.

For centuries the peoples of the Baltic were closely bound to the peoples of our country, primarily to the great Russian people, by strong ties of friendship. Side by side with the warriors of Russia they fought the German invaders. It was across this territory that Alexander Nevsky pursued the German cur-knights after the Battle on the Ice.

For about two centuries the Baltic countries formed part of Russia. Close economic relations between them and the other parts of our country were established long ago. The industries of Latvia marketed about two-thirds of their output in the provinces of Russia. About a third of all Russia's exports passed through the Latvian ports of Riga, Liepaja and Ventspils. Estonian manufactured goods found a market in Russia, and Estonian dairy farmers sold their produce in St. Petersburg.

The working people of the Baltic countries fought side by side with the workers and peasants of all Russia against

tsarism, against the landowners and the capitalists. As Lenin
stated, during the 1905 Revolution the Latvian proletariat occupied one of the first and most important places.

In November 1917 the red banner of the Socialist Revolution was hoisted over the Baltic countries as it was over
the rest of Russia. The working people of the Baltic overthrew
the oppressors and won their freedom.

Soviet government did not, however, endure long in Latvia,
Estonia and Lithuania. These countries were soon occupied
by German troops. The descendants of the cur-knights came
to plunder, kill and burn. The ancient soil was drenched with
the blood of the working people.

But in December 1918, the flames of the revolution again
burst out on the shores of the Baltic. Soviet government—government by the working people—was again established in
those countries. The heroic "Red Rifles" put the satraps of
the German occupants to flight. The puppet governments
swayed and collapsed.

The Entente imperialists, however, came to their rescue.
They helped the bourgeoisie of the Baltic countries to regain
their lost power. For twenty years bloodthirsty reaction reigned
in Latvia, Lithuania and Estonia.

Against the wishes of the working people, the Baltic countries were separated from Soviet Russia. The "independent"
bourgeois republics became a "cordon sanitaire" for the imperialists on the borders of the Land of Soviets. The French
Minister Clemenceau called them "a barbed-wire fence."

Under the yoke of West-European imperialism the national
economy of the Baltic countries fell into decline and desolation.
Isolated from the Russian market, their industries dwindled.
Factories were closed one after another. The engineering industry lost its former importance. The weaving sheds of the
Krenholm Textile Mills in Narva became deserted; of the
fourteen thousand workers formerly employed, only two
thousand remained. The number of workers employed in Estonia's biggest shipbuilding yards was reduced to one-tenth.

2*

The gigantic yards where ships and railway cars were built passed to the manufacture of combs and cotton reels. In Lithuania four thousand enterprises closed down. All three Baltic states, Estonia, Latvia and Lithuania, became the backwoods of Europe, a farming and raw materials appendage of the western countries.

Unemployment and poverty became the lot of the working class in the Baltic countries. The poor peasants and farm labourers groaned under the yoke of bondage to the rich farmers. The land of fifty per cent of the peasant holdings in Latvia accounted for only ten per cent of the total farmland of the country. During the last ten years of the Latvian bourgeois republic, thirty thousand peasant farms were sold by auction.

The bourgeoisie of the Baltic states took stern measures of repression against the masses of the working people. Thousands of splendid proletarian fighters languished in gaol. But the workers and peasants continued their revolutionary struggle; their confidence that they would again liberate themselves from oppression never left them.

Their hopes proved justified. In 1940 the working people of the Baltic countries overthrew their reactionary governments and again hoisted the flag of the Soviets. Latvia, Lithuania and Estonia were declared Soviet Socialist Republics. These republics petitioned the Supreme Soviet of the U.S.S.R. to incorporate them into the Soviet Union. The petition was granted.

The peoples of the Baltic rejoined the united family of Soviet peoples. The national economy of the Baltic republics became an integral part of the constantly growing economy of the Soviet Union. The working people of Lithuania, Latvia and Estonia began to play their part in the great task of building Communism.

The days of oppression, poverty and decline passed away. The Baltic republics ceased to be dependent on foreign capital, which had held these small states in bondage. An era of prosperity began for the awakened and renovated Baltic countries.

Unemployment, the scourge of the working class under the rule of the capitalists, disappeared forever. The Soviet government provided land for the landless peasants and additional land for those whose holdings were inadequate, and also rendered them generous assistance in the way of farm machinery and funds.

Culture began to make rapid progress. Each of the three Baltic republics established its own Academy of Sciences.

Socialist construction in the Baltic was temporarily interrupted by the Nazi invasion. The German occupation caused colossal damage to the national economy of the republics. In Latvia alone 785 industrial enterprises and five cities were wholly or partially destroyed, and over 100,000 horses and about 500,000 head of cattle were slaughtered or driven off to Germany. Tremendous damage was done to the cultural institutions and art treasures of the cities of all three republics.

When victory over Nazi Germany was achieved, the economy and culture of the Baltic republics revived with added vigour. The whole Soviet Union is helping to rehabilitate and further develop the economy of the Soviet Baltic.

As regards the Baltic republics, the Stalin postwar five-year plan is first and foremost a plan of socialist industrialization. Factories are being built, mineral wealth is being tapped; the industrious peoples of the Baltic countries are now devoting their skill and energy to the extraction of gas and lubricating oil from combustible shale, the manufacture of wireless sets, shipbuilding and the production of chemicals, high-class textile fabrics and paper.

The new, Soviet Baltic still retains and is further developing its most important industry—animal husbandry; but at the same time it is becoming an important region of large-scale socialist industry. The new industries are beyond all comparison with the old, both in scale and importance. They belong not to capitalists but to the people. They are developing according to plan and are safeguarded against economic crises as well as against the caprices of the world market. The factories do not work up imported raw materials as they did in the past, they obtain their supplies at home.

Until 1940 the waters of the Baltic Sea washed the shores of the Soviet Union only at the base of the Gulf of Finland. Today, the whole eastern coast of the Baltic—from the Gulf of Finland to the River Niemen—lies within the borders of the Soviet Union. The Klaipeda Region, which the Nazis seized from the Lithuanians in 1939, has now been restored to Lithuania and provides that republic with convenient access to the Baltic Sea. The Estonian islands of Saaremaa and Hiiumaa stand guard over the Gulf of Finland and the Gulf of Riga. The ports of Tallinn and Riga are icebound for a shorter period of the year than Leningrad, while the ports of Ventspils, Liepaja and Klaipeda are quite ice free, so that the Soviet Union now has communication between the Baltic and the seas of Western Europe all the year round.

After the Great Patriotic War, in addition to the eastern coast of the Baltic, part of the southern seaboard—from the mouth of the Niemen and the Kurisches Haff to the Frisches Haff—was incorporated in the Soviet Union. This territory now forms the Kaliningrad Region of the R.S.F.S.R. The long sandy spit opposite the town of Pillau is the westernmost point of our country.

In ancient times this territory was inhabited by Slavs. The Germanic tribes annihilated part of them and enslaved and Germanized the remainder. East Prussia, with its chief city of Königsberg, became a dagger thrust into the heart of the Slav lands. More than once the German land-grabber stretched forth his hand from here towards our country; and more than once evil and avaricious hordes set out on their conquests from here.

This hotbed of German aggression has now been destroyed forever. Slavs have again settled on the ancient Slav lands. Soviet people from Smolensk, Bryansk and Penza have permanently settled in the region; collective farmers plant rye and flax, lumberjacks float their timber down the Niemen, workers stand at their machines in engineering works and paper mills, Soviet dockers handle cargoes in the ice-free port. Königsberg is now Kaliningrad. Insterburg is now Chernyakhovsk. Friedland is now Pravdinsk, and Tilsit is now Sovietsk.... This region is the Soviet frontier guard on the distant approaches to Minsk, Riga and Leningrad.

South of Kaliningrad Region lie the territories that were incorporated in the Byelorussian Soviet Socialist Republic. These territories are inhabited by Byelorussians, but for a long time they were under the rule of the Polish squires, who treated them as a backward and oppressed colony. On one side of the frontier, in Soviet Byelorussia, factories were built, collective farms prospered and the Soviet national culture flourished. On the other side of the line Byelorussians lived in dire poverty, with no rights, oppressed by the Polish landowners. Here agriculture was poor and backward, conducted with the most primitive implements; in some of the villages in the depths of Polesie the stone axe was still employed.

Today all these lands, from Molodechno to Grodno, from Minsk to Brest, form part of Soviet Byelorussia. In 1939 the great Soviet people stretched out the hand of help and friendship to their Byelorussian brothers and liberated them from the oppression of the Polish landowners and capitalists. The treaty concluded in 1945 with fraternal democratic Poland definitely fixed the Soviet-Polish frontier. The Byelorussian people are now completely united in their Soviet national state. The lands that were once a colony of the Polish squires now enjoy the free Soviet life that all Byelorussia enjoys.

Look at the map. You will see that Minsk, the national centre of the Byelorussian people, once stood close to the frontier. Today Minsk stands in the centre of the united Byelorussian lands. All around—on the gigantic peat beds near Orsha, on the new Dnieper-Bug Canal, on the drained

marshlands of Pinsk and near Byelovezha Forest—the constructive work of the postwar five-year plan is well under way.

Soviet Byelorussia is successfully healing the wounds of
war and is marching forward to a new era of economic
prosperity.

IN THE SOUTHWEST

Still further to the south lie the Ukrainian lands. They
stretched far to the west also in olden times, in the days of
Kiev Rūs. It was said of Prince Yaroslav Osmomysl,* that
he closed the gates of the Danube and "ruled and dispensed
justice up to the Danube."

The fertile lands of the Western Ukraine long ago attracted
the attention of avaricious conquerors.

Hungarian princes, Polish woiewodas and German knights
all coveted them. For four centuries fighting raged in Galicia
and in the foothills of the Carpathians. Our warriors fought
with great courage and more than once put the invaders
to flight. But the struggle was an unequal one. The Mongol
yoke lay like a black cloud over the land of Russia. Weakened and bled white, Russia was unable to strike the final
blow and repel her enemies on the west. They swarmed like
ravens over the Ukrainian lands in the endeavour to rend
them, to peck them to pieces. Ukrainian Galicia became the
domain of the Polish squires, Transcarpathian Ukraine fell
under the yoke of the King of Hungary. The Turkish Jani-
zaries drove into the Danube steppes and Bessarabia became
the prey of the Sultan.

Years passed. The foreign overlords changed. The map of
this tormented corner of our homeland was reshuffled over
and over again. The conquerors forbade the Ukrainian people
to speak their native language, they stifled the national culture,
they tried to convert the people into Germans and Poles. But

---

* Prince of Galich, 1152-1187.—*Tr.*

in their hearts the Ukrainians, separated from their brethren, always retained hopes of freedom and reunion with their motherland.

Those dreams have come true today. The Ukrainian lands, like those of the Byelorussians, have been united in a single Soviet state. After centuries of tribulation the Ukrainian people have acquired state unity. The population of Soviet Ukraine has increased by over ten million. Today, not counting the R.S.F.S.R., the Ukraine is the largest state in Europe.

Part of the new territory passed to Soviet Ukraine from Poland. Western Ukraine was incorporated in the Soviet Union in 1939. Thanks to the fraternal help of the great Soviet people, the population of Western Ukraine was liberated from the yoke of the Polish squires. The western frontiers of the Ukrainian Republic have now been definitely fixed by treaty with democratic Poland. On the map of the U.S.S.R. we now see the ancient Ukrainian city of Lvov, the fertile fields of Volhynia and Podolia, the chain of oil fields in the Carpathian foothills, and the potassium and salt mines and coniferous and beech forests in the folds of the mountains. Another part of the new territories passed to the Ukraine from Rumania. This part includes mountainous Bukovina with its dense forests and highland pastures, and the busy city of Chernovtsy, the hot district of Ismail with its lowland pastures and narrow inlets of the Black Sea teeming with fish. At Ismail, famous for the fortress which Suvorov stormed, the Soviet frontiers again reach the Danube.

The reunion of the Ukrainian people was completed in 1945. By a treaty concluded between the Soviet Union and friendly Czechoslovakia, Transcarpathian Ukraine passed to the Ukrainian S.S.R. For centuries the Ukrainians beyond the Carpathians had dreamed of reunion with their motherland; this dream also has come true today.

The Soviet frontier was shifted across the Carpathian Mountains. Down wooded slopes and through the valleys of rushing mountain rivers, it descended to the banks of the

River Tisza which flows through the broad Hungarian plains. The central section of the Carpathians, the high barrier that once separated the Soviet Union from the countries of South-eastern Europe, is now within our borders. This serves to strengthen our ties with the Danube and Balkan countries.

Soviet Ukraine suffered terribly under the German occupation. The Nazis destroyed cities, blew up factories and laid waste the flourishing Ukrainian fields. But, under the leadership of the Communist Party, and with the fraternal help of the great Russian people, the Ukrainian people have already done much to wipe out the dismal traces of war from their land. Intensive creative work is now in progress in the new Soviet lands, as it is throughout the Ukraine. Industry is being restored and expanded. The farms, emancipated from the rule of the landlords, are applying the latest achievements of scientific farming. The entire Soviet Union is helping the Ukraine to develop the economy and culture of the new territories. Lvov is becoming a big industrial centre. The ciscarpathian oil fields are being extended, new gas wells and coal pits are being sunk, and lumbering is being developed in the mountains. Machine and tractor stations are being organized in the villages. A Ukrainian university has been opened in the Transcarpathian town of Uzhgorod.

Between the Dniester and the Pruth lies the region of vineyards and wineries—Bessarabia. The Moldavian population of these parts has had close ties with the Russians and Ukrainians since ancient times.

At the beginning of the nineteenth century Russia liberated the Moldavians from the Turkish yoke. In 1918, however, Bessarabia was again subjected to foreign occupation—the country was seized by the Rumanian boyars. The Soviet people never recognized this annexation. On our maps Bessarabia has always been printed in the same colour as our country. Only the dark shaded lines indicated that Bessarabia had been temporarily severed from us and lay under a foreign yoke. In 1940, on the demand of the Soviet Government, Rumania restored Bessarabia to the Soviet Union. The greater part of the country, where Moldavians constitute the majority of the inhabitants, was incorporated in the Moldavian Soviet Socialist Republic.

Once again the frontiers of our country, shifting westward from Odessa, run along the Pruth. Once again the fertile Byeltsy steppe, the vineyards and orchards of hilly Kodry, sultry Budjak and the thickets of the Dniester backwaters have come within the borders of our country. Once again Kishinev, Orgeyev and Benderi are our cities.

But life in these parts is not what it was in old Bessarabia. For the first time in history the Moldavian people have acquired national sovereignty and the opportunity freely and rapidly to develop their economy and culture. They are building their way of life on new, Soviet foundations. They no longer know need and oppression. In the towns of this once purely agrarian region factories are being built: the Stalin postwar five-year plan brings with it industrialization. For the first time the Moldavian fields have learned what scientific farming is. For the first time Moldavian school children are receiving instruction in their native language. The free Moldavian people, in fraternal unity with the other peoples of our country, are marching forward along the road of Socialism, the road of prosperity.

IN THE EAST

The map also records changes in the eastern frontiers of our country.

In distant Siberia, around the sources of the Yenisei, in the very heart of Asia, live the Tuva people, a people related to the Khakassians, Oirots and Yakuts. Before the revolution Tuva was the most poverty-stricken and backward corner of Central Asia. Manchurian conquerors, local lamas and the noyon princelings reduced the Tuva arats (herdsmen) to slavery.

In 1921, the working people of Tuva, assisted by the great Russian people, expelled the invaders, overthrew the feudal rulers and set up a people's revolutionary government. Tuva was proclaimed a People's Republic.

The fraternal help of the Soviet people enabled the free Tuva people to introduce reforms which brought the country closer to the socialist way of life. In 1944 the Tuva people entered the friendly family of Soviet peoples; at her request Tuva was incorporated in the Soviet Union. It is marked on the map of the U.S.S.R. as the Tuva Autonomous Region of the R.S.F.S.R.

The frontiers of our country shifted farther to the south, beyond the Tannu Ola mountain range. The whole of the River Yenisei, from source to mouth, now flows through Soviet territory.

Soviet Tuva is a region of wooded mountains rich in fur-bearing animals and valuable minerals, a region of grassy valleys containing extensive pastures. Here numerous herds roam, herds which now belong to the arats, collective farms, and cooperative cattle-breeding and agricultural societies. The young industry of Tuva is growing. The people who formerly had no written language are now developing their national culture. In Kyzyl, the capital of the region, books are printed and a theatre has been opened. The number of general schools, special vocational schools, libraries and reading rooms is growing from year to year.

The Soviet frontiers in the Far East have also been changed. The victory over imperialist Japan rectified a long-standing historical injustice. The southern half of Sakhalin and the long chain of the Kuril Islands—stretching for over a thousand kilometres from Hokkaido to Kamchatka—have been restored to us.

As early as the seventeenth century Russian explorers brought back home—to the "mainland," as they called Russia proper—news of an island lying opposite the mouth of the Amur. Later the island was named Sakhalin, which means "crags of the black river." Half a century later Russian people settled on the Kuril Islands for the first time. Undaunted by difficulties, they developed these distant islands, "made drawings" of them, built homes, raised cattle and hunted sea animals.

In 1875 the cunning and treacherous Japanese samurai inveigled the tsar's ministers into a commercial transaction. Completely renouncing their alleged "rights" to Sakhalin, the Japanese received "in exchange" complete and absolute possession of the whole of the Kuril chain. With the Kurils as their base, the Japanese began to control Russia's exit to the Pacific Ocean.

After the Russo-Japanese War of 1904 Southern Sakhalin was left in the hands of the Japanese samurai. A wide cutting was driven through the forest right across the island at 50° North Latitude and frontier posts were erected along it.

For a number of decades the Japanese were complete masters of this territory, which our ancestors had explored and developed. Southern Sakhalin was in their hands for forty years, the Kurils for seventy years.

But the hour struck, and the Russian people again returned to their historical frontiers. As a result of the defeat of imperialist Japan, Southern Sakhalin and the Kuril Islands passed to the Soviet Union.

Southern Sakhalin and the Kuril chain no longer form a barrier separating our country from the Pacific Ocean, they are no longer the outposts of the Japanese pirates threatening the Soviet seaboard. The Soviet Union now has a free outlet to the Pacific Ocean. Sakhalin and the Kuril Islands have become a direct connecting link between the Soviet mainland and the ocean and constitute our first line of defence against foreign aggression.

We have firmly established ourselves here. Once again Russian is spoken in the whole of Sakhalin. Again our vessels are moored in the ports of the Kuril Islands. New, Russian, city names have appeared on the map of the Far East:— South Sakhalinsk, Korsakov, Nevelsk....

The new Soviet lands are being settled by Soviet people—builders, factory workers, collective farmers, fishermen, woodsmen. For a long period houses of plywood and cardboard, with sliding walls, rice straw mats and tall earthenware chimneys, predominated on the islands. In the fields and on the low-lying coves of the seacoast Russian people are now building solid log houses, are tilling the soil and catching fish. New buildings are being erected in the cities. Timber is sawn, paper and canned goods are produced, coal and sulphur are mined. At the foot of the volcanoes and hills new factory chimneys are rising up, Soviet automobiles travel the roads, flotillas of cooperatively-owned fishing vessels put out to sea. New, Soviet lighthouses send out their beams from the rocky shores of the Pacific Ocean.

III

NEW TERRITORIES ON AN OLD MAP

THE EXPLORATION
OF THE COUNTRY COMPLETED

THE BOUNDARIES of the Land of Socialism have changed, they have shifted outwards. New territories have been included within them. Territories which had been forcibly severed from us by our enemies have again become an integral part of the Soviet Union.

But there are territories which have always been within the boundaries of our country, but which may still be called "new." We have only just discovered and explored them, and are now developing them. They have been marked on the map of the U.S.S.R. for the first time.

The appearance of new mountain peaks, new islands and new lakes and rivers on our map is due to the growth of Soviet economy and culture, to the development of Soviet geography.

In old, pre-revolutionary Russia, the economic development of territory proceeded slowly and unevenly. The remote parts of the country, those far removed from the industrial centres and commercial routes, remained for a long time almost unexplored. Their exploration entailed heavy expenditure and did not offer the capitalists and landowners a quick and certain profit. The economic backwardness of Russia was also expressed by the blank spaces that figured on the map.

There were many distinguished geographers in Russia, but the tsarist regime prevented them from applying their abilities to the full. Russian geographers were obliged to conduct their scientific work with wretchedly small funds. Explorers boldly penetrated into unknown regions, but their field of activity was restricted compared with the huge areas that were awaiting exploration. In area Russia is equal to whole continents—to two Europes, a half of Asia or three Australias. There was no planned exploration of the country, however: the tsarist government lacked both the desire and the funds to promote this work. By arduous toil enthusiasts laid the foundations of the scientific exploration of their beloved Russia.

Russia, the country of Afanasy Nikitin, Semyon Dezhnev, Przhevalsky and Semyonov Tien Shansky, had witnessed great feats of exploration. Nevertheless, there were huge gaps even in this initial and superficial investigation of the country.

Right up to the October Socialist Revolution the map of the remoter parts of Russia contained numerous "blank spaces," indicating the places where no geographer had ever been. The territories lying far off the beaten track, far from populated centres—corners of the Far North, the depths of Northeast Siberia, of the Kara Kum Desert, of the Tien Shan Mountains and of the Pamirs—were never explored.

It was only under the Soviet government that our people set to work to complete the geographical investigation of those parts of the country which hitherto had been unexplored. The era of great labour and cultural progress in our country also became the era of large-scale geographical investigation.

The country soon learned to know itself. The sites for the works of socialist construction were quickly and systematically explored. Year after year, from spring to autumn, the white tents and campfires of exploring expeditions dotted the distant parts of the country. The science of geography helped

Khan Tengri, the second highest peak in the Tien Shan range
(6,992 metres above sea level)

The Pamirs. Meteorological station on the Fedchenko Glacier
(4,300 metres above sea level)

Hall of Culture in Magadan, a new city built on the shore of
the Okhotsk Sea during the Stalin five-year plan periods

to spread the new social relations, the new, Soviet culture, to the remotest corners of the Soviet Union.

Formerly, expeditions were often conducted by individuals who had had the good fortune to find a patron who valued science. Soviet expeditions, however, are complex organizations set up by the state for the systematic investigation of the whole country, step by step, in conformity with a single plan.

The Soviet Government provides generous funds for the geographic investigation of the country. One after another, scientific expeditions, well-equipped with tools, instruments and everything else they need, are fitted out by the state.

These expeditions do not, as a rule, consist exclusively of topographers or geologists; Soviet expeditions are combined expeditions. They consist of topographers, geologists, soil scientists, hydrologists, biologists, economists, and ethnographers. A new region is investigated in all its aspects. The topographical survey serves only as the basis for a more detailed, all-round investigation.

In addition to expeditions, a new method of investigating the country is being practised: permanent geographical stations, which may be called "nature laboratories," are being established.

The country has provided Soviet geographers with new equipment. They cross the sands of the Kara Kum Desert on powerful automobiles, they map the roadless wastes of Chukotka from the air, they explore the glaciers of Novaya Zemlya by means of tracked automobiles and plumb the Arctic waters from the decks of icebreakers.

This has eased the important and difficult task that confronts Soviet geographers, viz., of completing the exploration of the most distant and inaccessible parts of the country.

IN THE SOUTH

Deep in the heart of Asia where, surrounded by bound-less deserts, the Hindu Kush, the Kuen Lun and the Tien Shan form a tangle of mountains, tower the Pamirs. Ridge after ridge, the rocky masses rise higher and higher, far above the forest level, beyond the eternal snow line. Between them lie lifeless valleys filled with the faint smell of dry and dusty herbage. The rocks are covered with the brown crust of "desert sunburn." The snow-clad peaks glitter in the rays of the daz-zling, scorching sun.

The Pamirs were "the end of the world." Unpopulated expanses. A half-ruined mountain outpost with a fire of dried yak dung. Occasionally, the tent of a nomad. The sac-rificial rags torn from the clothing of superstitious travellers flutter in the wind at the highest point on the mountain pass.

In the middle of the Pamirs, beyond the steep wall of mountains that rises into the heavens, beyond the icy barrier of the glaciers, lay the unexplored region. Across the ridge that rises above the clouds and divides the Eastern from the Western Pamirs, through the middle of the huge ice cap, lay the legendary passes. Tales were told of a savage tribe who killed everybody who penetrated there from the outer, already "discovered," world.

On the map of Asia there was a "blank space" that looked like a flaw in the printing.

The attack on the unexplored Pamirs began at the time of the First Stalin Five-Year Plan. This was called for both by the development of Soviet geography and by the economic progress of Central Asia. Glaciers melt in the mountains, the waters pour down into the oases and irrigate the cotton plantations. It was necessary to know the laws that govern the melting of the glaciers, the laws that govern the changes in the weather in the mountains.

The attack was continued year after year. Camel caravans were fitted out at Osh. Loaded with the equipment of the expeditions, they crossed first the Alai and then the Transalai ridges. The scientists' base camps advanced up the Kyzyl Su River to the Kara Kul and then on to the snow-clad slopes of the Academia Ridge. Triangulate points were plotted and maps were drawn, names were given to new peaks and new glaciers.

The explorers' faces were sunburned, the skin peeled, their feet froze, the heavy theodolites bruised their shoulders; but the Soviet explorers pressed on and on. At last, the intricate tangle of snow-covered peaks was unravelled.

They crossed the "blank spaces" in all directions. They took measurements of the almost eighty-kilometre Fedchenko Glacier—a broad, slowly creeping, white ribbon, scarred by black stripes of moraine; this is the biggest valley glacier in the world. They found the mysterious passes of Kashalayak and Tanymas. They determined the height of the highest point in the Soviet Union, Peak Stalin, and climbed it—7,495 metres above sea level.

The scientific conquest of the Pamirs was consolidated by the construction of an Ice Observatory on the Fedchenko Glacier, 4,300 metres above sea level.

The observatory contains separate rooms for every member of the staff, a common room, a radio laboratory, meteorological and photographic rooms and an electric power station. This is the highest human habitation in the Soviet Union.

To the northeast the Tien Shan (Celestial Mountains) form a junction with the Pamirs. In the form of a cluster of extremely high ridges they extend from the Syr Darya, in Soviet Central Asia, to the distant Gobi Desert. The Tien Shan ridges are welded together into a gigantic tangle by a massive icecap. This majestic massif rises up beyond the Issyk-Kul depression, beyond the roaring, seething Sary-Jas on the very frontiers of China. It is a tangle of gigantic

3*

ST. MARY'S COLLEGE LIBRARY CALIFORNIA

glaciers, impenetrable canyons and steep mountains covered with snow almost to the foot. From the midst of this chaos rises the marble peak of Khan Tengri, like a sharp, glittering wedge thrust into the sky.

The region lying around Khan Tengri, an area of hundreds of square kilometres, was for a long time unexplored. White snow on the mountains, and a white space on the map.

Now, Soviet expeditions go to Khan Tengri almost every year. On the shores of Lake Issyk-Kul they pass the monument on the grave of Przhevalsky—a bronze eagle on a grey stone pedestal—they travel on horseback up to the mountain passes, cross watersheds, ford swift rivers, scarcely able to resist the pressure of the water which is almost girth high, they establish base camps in the valley where one of the tongues of the Southern Inylchek Glacier is melting, and pitch their tents in the last copse of slender Tien Shan firs. From there they drive the sharp points of their climbing irons into the steep, slippery ice slopes.

Bold and inquisitive Soviet explorers have driven their pack horses across the countless cracks and crevices of the Southern Inylchek, right up to the Khan Tengri Mountain. To penetrate the "blank space" of Northern Inylchek, they rode in an inflated rubber boat, in places climbing the overhanging cliffs of the riverbank with all the weight of the body hanging on the fingers, crossed Lake Merzbacher, the biggest ice lake in our country, and mapped all the twists and turns of the valley, the steps of the glacier and the ridges of the mountain chains. They also climbed to the very summit of Khan Tengri, the "King of the Spirits."

They climbed it in order to uncrown the King. To the south of Khan Tengri they saw another peak still more majestic, rising above the dishevelled clouds. It took several years to reach this new peak. They climbed on to its icy shoulders. They took observations of it from the surrounding heights. They mapped it from an aeroplane at a height of nearly ten thousand metres—a barely perceptible silver dot in

the blue sky over a wild sea of ice and rock, leaving in its wake a white streak that was blown away by the wind.

The new peak was found to be over five hundred metres higher than Khan Tengri—it was 7,440 metres above sea level. It, and not Khan Tengri, is the highest point in this mountain system. The mountain chains and the glaciers radiate from it. It is the focal point of the Tien Shan, and one of the world's highest mountains. This mountain was discovered during the war and named Victory Peak.

IN THE NORTH

In tsarist times the remote northeast corner of Siberia was almost inaccessible. Mountains covered with dense forest and valleys filled with swamps barred the road to this huge unexplored region. Thousands of kilometres separated it from big towns; few people, travelling by the rivers of Siberia, big and small, and along almost impassable bridle paths, had ever reached that hidden taiga region.

Pre-revolutionary geographers had but a hazy idea of what lay within the rocky arc of the Verkhoyansk, Kolyma and Anadyr mountain ranges. Explorers confined themselves to interrogating local inhabitants and compiling maps from the information they supplied—blue lines for the assumed courses of rivers, and brown ones in the places where the mountains probably were. These unchecked drawings went into the world's atlases.

In 1926 a Soviet expedition, headed by Sergei Obruchev, penetrated this region after an arduous march through swamps and over barriers of fallen trees. They were the first to describe this tremendous mountain system, which is over a thousand kilometres long, three hundred kilometres wide and nearly three thousand metres high. The old maps had to be altered. It was discovered that the mountains within the great arc formed by the Verkhoyansk, Kolyma and Anadyr ranges do not radiate from the arc and do not run between the upper reaches of the rivers as had been indicated on the old maps; they run parallel to the main arc, and the rivers Kolyma and Indigirka cut across them through narrow canyons. It was discovered that the Kolyma Range does not form a sharp barrier between the upper reaches of the River Kolyma and the Okhotsk Sea coast. The River Kolyma flows much nearer to the sea than was formerly thought to be the case.

The map of this huge territory, equal in area to France, was redrawn.

The new range of mountains was named the Chersky Range, in honour of the scientist of that name. Exiled to distant Siberia by the tsar, Chersky engaged in geographical research. He died on one of his travels—in his wife's arms in a boat.

In this region, until recently quite deserted, an extensive mining centre, with new towns and automobile roads, has sprung up; and for the first time in these latitudes, agriculture is being developed.

Not only the Kolyma, but other rivers of Northeastern Siberia were wrongly plotted on the maps, sometimes as much as 200 kilometres out of place. New instruments for determining longitude have enabled explorers to map the courses of the Siberian rivers with complete accuracy.

The investigations of Soviet scientists also made it necessary to alter the Siberian isotherms and to shift the world's "cold pole" from Verkhoyansk to Oimyakon.

Quite recently a new discovery was made near Oimyakon. The heavy summer floods on the upper reaches of the Indigirka seemed strange. They could have been caused by the melting of glaciers. But were there any glaciers in these regions? The dry climate had forced scientists to conclude that there were not. It was only during the recent exploration of the Suntar Hayat Range that glaciers were found. Unexpectedly, one of the biggest ice masses in the Soviet mountains was discovered—in places the ice here is 250 metres thick.

During this same investigation explorers discovered the highest mountain peak in Northeastern Siberia—it is over three thousand metres high.

Soviet geographers have done most in the region that is the hardest to explore—the Arctic. They helped to open up the Northern Sea Route.

In the autumn of 1913 the *Taimyr* and the *Vaigach*, the ships of a hydrographical expedition, pushed their way through the ice north of Cape Chelyuskin and reached the shores of an unknown land. On the shore, at the foot of frowning, snow-clad hills, they hoisted the Russian flag. The oncoming Arctic winter, however, compelled the expedition to leave. They only had time to map a part of the newly-discovered coastline.

On maps of the Arctic Ocean two winding lines appeared— the uncertain, dotted outline of an unknown coast. What was situated here? A few small islands? Or, perhaps, a large archipelago? The land discovered by the sailors of the *Taimyr* and *Vaigach* remained unexplored.

In 1930 a Soviet expedition reached the shores of this mysterious land on an icebreaker. Four men stayed behind to winter on the island that had been named Domashny. These four men explored the area and found that it was an archipelago with an area larger than that of Holland. They named it Severnaya Zemlya. Exploration continued for two years, during which the expedition travelled over three thousand kilometres with dog sleighs, crossing snow and ice fields, driving through Arctic blizzards. The new country was explored in every detail and plotted on the map.

Soviet scientists have discovered many other islands in the Arctic Ocean, such as Sergei Kirov Island, Arctic Institute Islands and Izvestia Islands. Some of these discoveries provide examples of scientific prediction. Charts of the Kara Sea had long shown the dotted outlines of the "problematic land of Vizé." Professor Vizé, a Soviet scientist, discovered this island by theoretical calculations made in his study. He studied the drift of a certain icebound Arctic vessel, noted the deviation of the sea currents and concluded that somewhere they must meet with an obstacle that diverted them from their course—the obstacle could only be a huge sandbank, or an island. The 1930 expedition showed that Vizé Island actually existed, and that it was precisely at the spot the scientist had said it was.

Other assumptions have been disproved by geographers.

In 1810, Yakov Sannikov claimed that he had seen land on the horizon to the north of the Novosibirsk Islands. "Sannikov Land" was sought for a long time: this search prompted Academician Obruchev to write his scientific novel *Sannikov Land*.

In recent years this part of the Arctic Ocean was traversed by Soviet vessels. They did not find any islands there. In 1944, at Academician Obruchev's request, aircraft were sent to this part of the ocean, but they too failed to find anything. It must be assumed that "Sannikov Land" does not exist.

It is possible, of course, that this island existed here formerly. Scientists are of the opinion that it could have been formed from mineral ice which was later washed away.

Soviet scientists have made many discoveries in high latitudes. The Soviet Union has laid bare the secrets of the Central Arctic.

We are accustomed to look at pictures of the globe from one side, from the side of the equator; consequently, we always see the polar countries on the edge of the map, far from inhabited continents, away from the world routes. It is possible, however, to depict the hemispheres with the equator as the edge, that is, we may look at them from the direction of the poles. We would then see the Central Polar Basin as the centre of the northern hemisphere. It is surrounded by developed and inhabited countries, but the centre that separates them is a "blank space," the unexplored and desert region of the Central Arctic. World routes wind around it, and are therefore much longer than they need be.

A geographical expedition camp near an iceberg in Red Army
Strait, Severnaya Zemlya

Soviet merchant ships off the shore of the Kola Peninsula

Mount Klyuchevskaya, Kamchatka's biggest active volcano

Mail arrives for Arctic winterers on Dickson Island

But a country came forward which proved capable of filling in the blank space in the centre of the northern hemisphere.

For the first time in history the U.S.S.R. joined up the East and West by the shortest air route across the pole.

As long ago as the summer of 1937, the Soviet airmen Chkalov and Gromov made their transarctic flights. A scientific station was set up right on the North Pole.

This was an event of tremendous scientific and historical importance; it was the last link in a chain of great geographical discoveries: the North Pole was investigated by modern scientific methods.

Soviet aircraft took a party of four explorers, headed by Papanin, to the North Pole, "the top of the world." The red flag was hoisted over the white, icy waste.

The scientific station encamped on an ice floe over three metres thick. The ice floe drifted rapidly from the North Pole towards the Greenland Sea. There it was broken up after a storm lasting six days. The explorers, however, continued their scientific observations on a piece of the ice floe until the Soviet icebreakers *Taimyr* and *Murman* reached them and took them on board.

Papanin's party spent 274 days on the ice floe and drifted a distance of about 2,500 kilometres.

It was known before this expedition that the ocean here was no less than 2,742 metres deep—the depth at which Peary's line broke off when he took his soundings at the North Pole in 1909. The Papanin Expedition was the first to ascertain the real depth of the ocean at the Pole; it found it to be 4,290 metres. Thus, the Arctic Ocean proved to be very deep. This finally refuted the assumption that there is land in the vicinity of the North Pole.

Nansen already knew that the waters of the Atlantic reach the Polar Basin. He was of the opinion, however, that they turned to the right at Spitzbergen and flowed along the shores of the mainland. The Papanin Expedition discovered a deep

stratum of warm water several hundred metres below the
surface at the North Pole itself. This shows that water heated
by the sun in the Gulf of Mexico reaches the North Pole.

Many people were of the opinion that the central part of
the Arctic Basin was devoid of life. The Papanin Expedition
found life at the very pole. In the water, even at a depth of
three kilometres, they found seaweed and various living crea-
tures—molluscs and larvae. In the depths of the Arctic they
saw sea gulls, seals, and polar bears with their cubs.

It was formerly assumed that there is constant high pressure
at the pole and that, consequently, the climate there underwent
very little change. It has been proved that strong cyclones
reach the vicinity of the pole, causing variations in temperature.

Formerly, scientific Arctic stations were established round
the rim of the Arctic Ocean. Only ten years ago the whole
central part of the Arctic had still been unexplored. The work
performed by the Papanin Expedition filled in this gap.

Soviet science succeeded in doing what the scientists of
other countries had failed to do: they were the first to investigate and describe in detail the most inaccessible parts of the
North Pole region.

The way in which the Soviet scientific expedition to the
North Pole was organized provided the whole world with
another example of the Bolshevik style of work—wide scale
of operation combined with efficiency. A broad and bold idea
was put into practice with calm, planned precision.

The Sedov Expedition continued the work begun by Papanin. In the autumn of 1937, when the Papanin ice floe was
already drifting south, the icebreaker *Sedov* began its northward drift from the other side of the Arctic, from the New
Siberian Islands. A damaged rudder had prevented the vessel
from putting into port for the winter. Fifteen polar explorers
remained on board the icebound *Sedov* and drifted slowly
with it. They converted their forced drift into a great scientific
exploit.

The *Sedov* remained in the grip of the ice for over two years. All this time, day after day, its crew continued their scientific observations. They discovered a second magnetic pole —we call it the Sedov Pole—and in the depths of the ocean they discovered dozens of new species of animal life. Their log line reached a depth of 5,180 metres; this is the greatest known depth in the Arctic Ocean, if we exclude the measurement of about 5,440 metres made by Wilkins with a sonic depth finder and, therefore, not quite reliable.

Drifting with the ice field into which it was firmly caught, the *Sedov* passed within four hundred kilometres of the North Pole. Our knowledge of the Central Arctic was still further enhanced.

The Pole has divulged its secrets. Our airmen fly over it in winter as well as summer. One night, in 1945, an aeroplane piloted by Titlov left Cape Chelyuskin. Making observations throughout their journey, the crew flew as far as the North Pole, cast overboard a buoy with a portrait of Stalin attached, and then returned to their base. Guided by his instruments, the pilot returned to the appointed spot on the Soviet Arctic coast. After a flight of fifteen hours in darkness and inclement weather, Titlov landed safely by the light of bonfires at the mouth of the Indigirka.

The Pole divulged its secrets. But the geographical pole is the centre of the northern hemisphere and not of the Polar basin. That part of the Arctic Ocean that is farthest from the coast, the central part of it that had been little explored, is also called the pole—it was called the "Pole of Inaccessibility."

It was not until 1941 that man first set foot on this part of the earth that is so difficult to reach. The first people there were our Soviet people, the envoys of Stalin.

The weather was comparatively warm, slightly more than twenty degrees below zero, centigrade.

The explorers made a complete series of oceanographical and geophysical observations: they measured the depth of the ocean, the velocity and direction of currents and winds, and gravity; they examined planktons and took samples of water for chemical analysis.... The whole series was repeated three times: after spending five days on the ice, the expedition returned to Wrangel Island and then flew off again to another ice field. Sometimes they spent two hours circling round in search of a smooth place to land and at last would land on a film of new ice formed over an old water channel between the floes.

In this way a new type of Arctic expedition came into being, an expedition that hops from floe to floe.

The inaccessible had become accessible, the unknown had become known.

* * *

During the thirty years the Soviet system has been in existence something new has been discovered about every part of our great country.

It was formerly believed that Mount Telpos-Iz was the highest point in the Urals. Priority has now passed to Mount Narodnaya. Contrary to expectations, glaciers, small ones, it is true, have been found in the Urals. The formation of an ice sheet in the Koryak Mountains has been discovered. The boundary between the sands of the Kara Kum and the clays of Ust Urt has been shifted. New glaciers and lakes have been found in the Altai Mountains.

A short time ago geysers were for the first time discovered on the territory of the U.S.S.R. They were found in Kamchatka, in the Kronotskoye Reservation. At definite intervals, a low rumble begins deep down in the earth: the noise increases rapidly and suddenly a mighty stream of boiling water, surrounded by clouds of steam, breaks out of the bowels of the earth with a deafening roar and spurts into the air to a height of tens of metres.

During the past thirty years hundreds of thousands of square kilometres of territory in the U.S.S.R. have been newly explored. Soviet scholars have made a big contribution to science and have filled in gaps in the maps.

The very dimensions and shape of the earth have been calculated anew by our scientists. It has been established that the earth is not only slightly flattened at the poles but also at the sides. The roundest meridian passes through Honolulu and Prague and the flattest through Irkutsk and Philadelphia.

These measurements of the curvature of the earth's surface help geographers to compile more precise and accurate maps.

The successes Soviet geographers have achieved have enabled them to compile a large and complete State Map of the Soviet Union. It has a scale of 1:1,000,000 and is done in colours. Its 180 sheets, making a total of 54 square metres, cover the entire Soviet Union, the biggest country in the world. The pages of this map show the whole of our country—its mountains, forests and rivers, its towns and villages.

The only part of the entire Soviet Union that has not yet been entered on the map is a small piece of the interior of the Taimyr Peninsula. This area is being explored by a scientific expedition. The last "blank space" will be removed from the Soviet map. Only in the distant Arctic waters are there still a few places that Soviet scientists have not explored.

The country is the people's house. Today we have an accurate plan of our house.

We know our country much better than the rulers of pre-revolutionary Russia knew it. The new territories, the vast new regions, have not only been explored, they have been brought into the sphere of the creative activity of the Soviet people.

IV

NEW SOURCES OF MINERAL WEALTH

SEARCH

THE SURFACE of our country is shown on the map on a scale hundred of thousands or millions of times reduced. The height of a locality can be seen from the density of the yellowish-brown colouring. The lowlands are coloured green. The winding, serpentine lines are rivers. The blue patches are lakes.... We have seen how this map, the map of our country, has been revised and made more accurate during the period the Soviet system has been in existence.

But, in addition to the geographical map, we have another map of our country, a geological map. This map shows us what is hidden from our eyes in the depths of the earth. A whole rainbow of colours and a collection of conventional signs tell us of deep-lying strata ranged one above the other, of minerals hidden in the bowels of the earth, of deposits of valuable minerals.

This map, the map of the subterranean wealth of our country, has been almost completely remade during the period the Soviet system has been in existence. By placing the working people in power, the October Revolution gave our country a wise and zealous master. The new master of the land, the people, has taken stock of his domains, has registered all the riches that belong to him and has placed the newly-surveyed mineral raw material at the service of his socialist motherland.

The mounting figures of the mineral deposits discovered in the U.S.S.R. are not only the measure of the great wealth that is stored in the earth, they are also the measure of the culture and energy of Soviet society that is making fuller and fuller use of nature's riches.

What has changed in the bowels of the earth during these past thirty years? The amount of peat in the bogs may have increased: springs may have broken through to the surface in some places and have ceased to flow in others; in caves stalactites and stalagmites may have grown together to form complete columns. The formation of a coal vein, or of other mineral deposits, however, takes millions of years. But compare the former mineral map of the U.S.S.R. with the present one. How many new symbols have been placed on the map! Each of these symbols is a record of the labour of Soviet people, of their indomitable will, of many years of search, of failure overcome, and of the triumph of the human intellect.

Tsarist Russia was not poor in minerals but in its knowledge of them. Nine-tenths of the country had not been surveyed by geologists—it was like an unexplored continent. So little was known that old Russia was credited with only one per cent of the world's supply of iron ore, only one per cent of the world's phosphorites and only three per cent of the world's coal. The deposits of nickel, potassium, borax, sulphur and bauxite were not explored at all.

It is bitter to have to admit that the country which had given birth to the far-seeing mining experts of the Urals, to such distinguished geologists as Karpinsky and Chernyshev, to the founder of the science of crystallography, Fyodorov, to the founders of the science of geochemistry, Vernadsky and Fersman—that this country was mentioned in small print in the geological tables of the world.

The age-old backwardness of the country made itself felt. The ruling classes in old Russia were unable to surmount this backwardness. They opened wide the doors to foreign imperialists and thereby only helped to keep Russia in the position of an economically backward and dependent country.

The capitalists of Britain, France, Germany and Belgium regarded Russia as their colonial possession. They started their own enterprises in Russia, and billions of rubles found their way abroad in the shape of profit. They bought timber, hemp, flax, wheat, furs and other raw materials they needed at ridiculously low prices and sent them abroad. The development of Russian home industry was hindered; it was unable to obtain its raw materials at home.

The raw materials used by the Russian industries were mostly imported from abroad; they were purchased from foreign firms.

Home supplies of coal were inadequate; the St. Petersburg factories obtained their coal from Great Britain.

There was a shortage of phosphates—they were brought from Morocco.

There was a shortage of potassium—it was bought in Germany.

There was a shortage of raw material for nitrate fertilizers— Chilean nitrates were imported.

And not only industrial raw materials. Even stone for building purposes the Russian capitalists preferred to import from abroad! The buildings on the Nevsky Prospect in St. Petersburg were faced with sandstone brought from the quarries of the Rhine. Theatre Square in Moscow was paved with stone blocks imported from Sweden.

This paid the foreign businessmen who held Russia in their grip; the shortage of raw materials in Russia protected them from competition and ensured them huge profits.

There had long been rumours about deposits of coal on the banks of the Pechora River. This would have been a veritable treasure for the industries of St. Petersburg. But instead of seeking and developing this coal deposit, Russian merchants made contracts with the coal merchants of Cardiff.

It was also known that there were deposits of sulphur in the Kara Kum Desert. But instead of sending a geological

Academician *A. E. Fersman,*
mineralogist and geochemist

Academician *V. I. Vernadsky,*
mineralogist and crystallographer

A trainload of apatite arrives at the refinery.
Kirovsk, beyond the Arctic Circle

Karaganda, in the Kazakh S.S.R., the third largest coal field
in the Soviet Union. Open workings

expedition to the Kara Kum, the tsarist authorities sent orders for sulphur to Italy.

Even the mineral wealth that was known slipped out of the hands of the feeble Russian bourgeoisie. The rich mines in the Altai and in Kazakhstan were operated by British capitalists. French and Belgian capitalists operated the coal mines in the Donets Basin. The Baku oil fields, the iron mines of Krivoi Rog and the manganese mines of Chiatury were also largely operated by foreigners.

Thirty years have passed since the people became masters of their land and its minerals. They threw off the shackles of capitalist slavery and took the government of the country— and with it its economy and the rich gifts with which nature had endowed it—into their own strong and capable hands.

Liberated Russia freed herself of her medieval backwardness. The Soviet system put an end to economic dependence on foreign countries, refused to rely on foreign industry and foreign raw material. It opened up wide prospects for the development of the forces of production and brought new, untold wealth to light.

Socialist industrialization was undertaken in the U.S.S.R. This called for tremendous supplies of mineral raw materials that were scarce in old, tsarist Russia. Soviet industry, however, obtained these materials. In a short space of time it was ascertained that the known mineral sources were larger than had been assumed, and hundreds of new sources were discovered.

New factories of the most diverse types sprang up in the Land of Soviets, and geological surveys provided them with everything they needed, from ordinary coal and iron to the rarest metals, such as the factory owners of tsarist Russia had only read about in foreign catalogues or, in many cases, had never heard of at all.

Many factories sprang up in the sparsely populated and little explored regions, and for them too reliable sources of mineral supplies were prepared. This was not an easy task. Roads and tracks had to be cut to enable the heavy drilling installations and piping to be hauled to the mountain valleys, into the depths of forests, into the swampy tundras. Often these new roads were nothing more than tracks running for hundreds of kilometres through virgin land.

Other factories were built in places that had long been populated. To avoid the long haulage of raw materials for these plants, it was necessary, at all costs, to "drag them out" of the earth in their vicinity, even where it seemed as though that area had long been explored, prospected and worked out.

But life itself—the surging, full-blooded life of the Soviet Union—backed our Soviet geologists. And this life carried them forward on the crest of a high and powerful wave.

This work was not interrupted by economic crises, such as those which afflict capitalist countries like a fever and every now and again throw them back for many years. Nor was it hampered by competition which wastes the efforts of people. In our country, all branches of economy, including geological survey, are developed according to plan and in the interests of the whole of the working people. The Soviet state has huge funds at its disposal, and this enables it to conduct work on a wide front on an unprecedented scale.

Our Soviet geologists also enjoy the backing of nature herself—who is unyielding to the weak, but responsive to the bold, niggardly towards those who are impassive, but generous towards those who are active and persevering.

No other country is as richly endowed with natural wealth as the Soviet Union. No other country in the world has such a variegated geological structure. The ancient folds of the Russian and Siberian plateaus, the exposed beds of the Urals and Kazakhstan, the gigantic chain of mountains that stretches from the Carpathians, through the Crimea, the Caucasus and Central Asia into Siberia—contain a variety of mineral deposits of the most diverse ages and of every structure. The gigantic forces of nature have not only provided one-sixth of the earth's surface with mountain chains and highlands, high plateaus and low-lying plains, but have also provided them with an abundance of metal and non-metal minerals.

After entering into their historical rights as the masters of their own land, the free Soviet people launched a wide movement to develop and settle their possessions. At the call of the Communist Party thousands of Soviet people—geologists and miners, engineers and road builders—joined in the great labour campaign to discover and conquer the subterranean wealth of their country.

In a hard and stubborn struggle our people achieved victory over the forces of nature. They had to cover colossal distances over swampy, roadless country. They were hampered by technical backwardness and the shortage of trained specialists. Thousands of skilled geological engineers were needed, but there were few of these in old Russia. And—what, perhaps, was the hardest task—it was necessary to shatter the old dogmas, to break down conservatism born of ignorance, inertness and in many cases malice. Many of those who were trying to drag our country backwards, who wanted to prevent the development of the new socialist way of life, had not yet been exposed. These pernicious elements caught up and repeated the conclusions arrived at by the foreign semi-explorer semi-capitalist "experts," spies rather than scientists, who had visited Russia, to the effect that "there cannot be any copper in Turkestan...", "there is no tin anywhere in Russia...", "it is useless searching for oil on the Russian plain...", "no rare metals have been discovered in the young Caucasus Mountains...", "in the old Urals the rare metals have already been washed away...."

The Party of Lenin and Stalin broke the resistance of the enemies and shattered their pernicious theories. It trained large contingents of Soviet prospectors, bold innovators who were undaunted by difficulties and were absolutely loyal to their people.

4*

ST. MARY'S COLLEGE LIBRARY CALIFORNIA

New people grew up. The old schemes were cast aside. A new technique appeared. The ranks of the geologists, the reconnaissance parties of the five-year plan—were steadily augmented, they acquired greater strength and accelerated their progress. The Communist Party trained these forces and showed them the road.

Today, thousands of experienced geological engineers of the Soviet school are in the field. This army of prospectors is headed by a Ministry of Geology, a government institution that exists only in our country.

Soviet geologists are not equipped exclusively with the hammer and mountain compass. Drilling installations bite to a depth of two and three kilometres into the earth's crust. Seismographs detect the slightest deviation of waves along the geological strata when artificial earthquake explosions are effected. Electrical recording instruments indicate the contours of a mineral deposit. Pendulum instruments, utilizing the force of gravity, explore the depths of the earth. Aerial magnetometers peer into the earth from the skies.

The area not yet subjected to a detailed geological survey has been considerably reduced. By the time of the Third Five-Year Plan an area equal to that of the United States of America had been plotted on the geological map. And for completeness and scope this survey far exceeds anything done in this field before the revolution.

The hands of the geologists are no longer tied by the former "theories" of bounds and limits—surveying today is based on different concepts, genuinely scientific and at the same time bold, concepts that do not limit the horizon of the geologist but widen it in all directions.

The subterranean treasures of the Soviet Union are being explored with planned purposefulness on a scale the world has never seen before.

What has been found in the course of the last thirty years?

FINDS

The Leningrad Bolsheviks, headed by the never-to-be-forgotten Sergei Kirov, organized the investigation and development of the Kola Peninsula, beyond the Arctic Circle. It began with a geological survey. Groups of Soviet geologists, under the leadership of Academician Fersman, made great discoveries in this region. In the Khibiny Range they found whole mountains of the greenish, friable apatite with as much as 30 per cent phosphoric oxide content. With the aid of sulphuric acid, this apatite is turned into superphosphate.

Old, pre-revolutionary Russia imported phosphates from North Africa. Russian gold went abroad to enrich foreign capitalists. Only big landowners and kulaks could afford these imported fertilizers.

We did not get our own phosphate easily. The severe climate of the Kola Peninsula, the bare, rocky hills rising over swamps and dense taiga, the short, wet summer, long, cold winters, the dark of the Arctic night with its gales and impassable snowdrifts in the narrow valleys, the absence of roads and inhabited centres and lack of topographical maps—such were the difficulties that had to be overcome.

Soviet people, mustered and organized by the Bolshevik Party, overcame all the obstacles that barred the road to their goal. They pitched their tents, hacked at the rock with their picks, measured the temperature, took photographic surveys of the region, plotted levels on route maps and made test borings. They climbed cliffs, clambered over mountain passes and descended precipices by ropes. During the years they toiled on the Kola Peninsula, the Soviet geologists carried away on their shoulders from the Khibiny Mountains five tons of rock for laboratory analysis.

In addition to the world's largest deposits of apatite, inexhaustible deposits of nepheline were found in the Khibiny Mountains; the nepheline intrudes into the apatite, in grey veins and patches. Nepheline is raw material for the manufacture of aluminium, glass, enamel and paints.

The mineral wealth of the Khibiny Range was a discovery of world importance.

A few years later another phosphorus deposit was discovered at the other end of the country, in the Kara Tau Mounta'ns. There, in Southern Kazakhstan, phosphorite deposits of extraordinary dimensions—a "second Khibiny"—were discovered.

These discoveries firmly established our country at the top of the world's list for phosphorus deposits. Today we have enough phosphorite not only to supply our own needs, but also for export.

The Khibiny apatite, the Kara Tau phosphorite and phosphorous raw materials from other parts of the U.S.S.R. all go to superphosphate plants, most of which have been newly built. The new plants have changed the geography of the superphosphate industry. For example, for the first time in history, phosphate fertilizers are being produced in Central Asia, close to the cotton fields that badly need them.

The U.S.S.R. has also risen to top place for reserves of potassium salts. Potassium, like phosphorus, is needed by plant life. Tsarist Russia imported potassium fertilizers from Germany. But it turned out that our country possesses larger deposits of potassium salts than all the other countries put together. Exceptionally large deposits have been found in the North Urals. The valuable pink-white deposits at Solikamsk are for their dimensions unique in the world. And our potassium mines at Solikamsk are also the biggest in the world.

The Soviet Union now stands second in the world's list of coal-bearing countries. If we estimate the deposits not in tons, but in calories, i.e., their heat-producing properties, our country occupies not second, but first place.

Many new coal deposits have been discovered in all parts of the country. One of the most valuable finds was the Pechora coal field.

Along the tributaries of the River Pechora, in the Arctic Circle, Soviet geologists, headed by Professor Chernov, surveyed gigantic deposits of coal suitable for the manufacture of coke and for ordinary fuel.

Geologists wearing mosquito nets and thigh-high wading boots pushed their way up the rivers into the tundra in frail native boats called "shnyaks," at times punting the boats along with poles, at others hauling them over the shallows with ropes. They travelled not only in the summer by river, but also in the winter through taiga and tundra, when fierce blizzards blind and sweep one off one's feet, when even the reindeer lie down and burrow into the snow.

Hundreds of new, extremely rich deposits of coal and other important minerals have been discovered in the period the Soviet system has been in existence; but the achievements of Soviet geologists are most striking, perhaps, in those places where some work had already been done before.

As everybody knows, our three main coal basins are the Donbas, Kuzbas and Karaganda.

The well-populated, surveyed, and well-worked Donets Basin, our oldest coal-mining centre, with its network of roads and railways, seemed to have been fully investigated. Nevertheless, Soviet geologists, by their surveys, increased the known deposits in this area more than one and a half times. And now they are extending the boundaries of the coal basin to Lozovaya in the Northwest, and to the Don and the Salsk Steppes in the Southeast. They already have visions of pitheads and mines in the wheat fields of the steppes.

The known deposits of the Donets coal basin have been increased one and a half times, but those of the Kuznetsk Basin have been increased thirty-five times! Soviet geologists conducted immense operations in that region under the leadership of Yavorsky, now a Stalin Prize holder. The old figure given for the Kuznetsk deposits was 13,000 million tons, the present figure is 450,000 million tons. It may well be asked: When was our second coal-mining centre discovered? Before the October Revolution. or in our present Soviet times?

Actually, the coal resources of Karaganda too were explored for the first time in our Soviet times.

A hundred years ago, a Kazakh herdsman found in the wormwood-covered steppe some black stones that burned. His master, the bey who owned the herds, sold his land, a hundred square kilometres in area, to an Ekaterinburg merchant for the sum of 220 rubles. Later, this land fell into the hands of some Frenchman, from whom it passed to some Englishman. The coal was mined in tiny pits, most often from open working, to supply the copper-smelting furnaces of the small Spassky refinery. Soviet scientists, foremost amongst whom was Gapeyev, surveyed the vicinity of these pits and discovered one of the country's largest coal deposits. This is Karaganda, our third coal-mining centre.

FOLLOWING OLD TRAILS

In this way our powerful socialist science is laying a broad road where formerly there were only winding bridle paths which had been cut with the utmost difficulty.

Hard was the lot of the Kazakh people under the rule of the tsar and the khans. Like all other peoples, they expressed their dreams of a better life in their songs. The Kazakh epic has brought down to our times an ancient legend: a beloved maiden, the incarnation of happiness, slips away, changes into a gazelle with golden horns, dashes off and disappears among the rocks.... Happiness must be sought and reclaimed from the rocks. The song seemed to say that the future of Kazakhstan lay in its subterranean wealth.

In those parts, long ago, when the earth was still young, powerful subterranean forces rent and crushed the earth's crust. The surface of the earth rose up in gigantic mountain folds, as if the face of the world had wrinkled. The strata that form the earth broke up and, under the terrific pressure of volcanic forces, seething molten masses surged from the depths and either remained embedded in the crust or came out on to the surface. When the molten masses reached the colder outer strata they cooled off, hardened and turned into solid granite. The vapour from these eruptions also cooled off here and there, and was deposited in the form of heavy metals. In the beginning, when the temperature was still very high, tin, tungsten and molybdenum were precipitated, then came copper, lead and zinc, and, lastly, at comparatively low temperatures, antimony and mercury.

Hundreds of millions of years passed. Again and again the territory of Kazakhstan was flooded by the sea; the sea receded and dried up, it left behind rich deposits of salts. More and more new strata of coal and oil were formed. Water and sun, frost and wind gradually wore away the high mountains; smoothed them out until the region became almost a plain. It was not until a much later geological period that the earth was set in motion again and through the cracks and fissures to the southeast of that primordial land arose the steep, rocky fields of the Altai and Tien Shan Mountains.

Chiselling away the earth, time gradually exposed the valuable ores that lay hidden beneath it. It looked as though they had risen to the surface.

In these vast expanses, man began to apply his labour to the unyielding stony soil as early as the Bronze Age. The picks of the barbarians dug out tin and copper; these were smelted in huge bonfires, and the scraps of metal obtained were beaten into knives, arrowheads and ornaments. From here bronze travelled to all parts of the then known world. People came here for bronze even from the remotest countries. This is proved by the Egyptian beads found in Northern Kazakhstan.

All this passed away. The ancient culture of Kazakhstan fell into decline. Under the tyrannical rule of the Russian tsars and of the local feudal rulers, this bounteous land became one of the most backward colonial regions of the Russian Empire. Not a single payable tin deposit was known in pre-revolution- ary Kazakhstan, and copper was mined in infinitesimal quan- tities.

The known copper deposits in tsarist Russia were less than the annual quantity of ore refined in the U.S.A. The tin deposits were estimated at a figure equal to a fortnight's output in Malaya.

Soviet geologists have placed the U.S.S.R. in the front rank of tin- and copper-bearing countries. Tin has been found in Kazakhstan, in the Transbaikal region and also in the far Northeast: the latter deposits were discovered by expeditions that travelled with dog and reindeer sleighs and by aeroplanes. The largest copper deposits, however, were discovered in Kazakhstan.

Nature, for countless centuries, has been wearing down the mountains and making the mineral contents of the earth more accessible to man, but man had scarcely touched them. Soviet people, however, have explored and opened up these riches in less than a third of a century.

In Kounrad, on the desert shores of Lake Balkhash, the geologist Rusakov discovered extremely rich deposits of copper ore. In this small space—less than a square kilometre in area— huge resources of the metal ore are concentrated.

In Jezkazgan, in the very heart of Kazakhstan, near the picturesque Ulu Tau Mountains where, in all probability, the nucleus of the Kazakh nation was formed several centuries ago, the Kazakh scientist, Academician Satpayev, surveyed a big copper deposit very convenient for working. The ore lies near the surface, the ore bed is firm, and the flow of sub- terranean waters is insignificant. This deposit is one of the biggest in the world.

The work of Soviet geologists has been directed by modern ideas of scientific geology. The scientists have been assisted by the latest methods of geophysical surveying. But here and

there, however, the presence of ore was revealed by the remains of ancient mines, collapsed, overgrown with grass and
long forgotten. Sometimes the suffix "kan" or "gan" in the
name of a village, valley or other natural feature served as
a reminder that ore had been mined there some time in the
past. The word "Jezkazgan" for example means "the place
where copper was mined." When working in the steppes
Satpayev never fails to note the local place names. The suffix
"kan" attracted attention to Haidarkan in Kirghizia, where
traces of old workings, walls of caves blackened by the smoke
from primitive crucibles, and deposits of mercury were
found.

In Northern Kazakhstan rich deposits of copper were discovered at Boshchekul. And at Almalyk, in Uzbekistan, near
the southern frontier of Kazakhstan, geologists found concen-
trations of high-grade copper ore.

Under the Soviet system, the Kazakhstan area has become
a world important copper centre, both as regards known resources and output. Thanks to the efforts of the Soviet Government and the Communist Party, a big copper industry has
sprung up in Kazakhstan, equal to the old, greatly-expanded
Urals copper industry.

THE EXPANSION OF BAKU

In the Far North, Soviet geologists have investigated the
Ukhta group of oil deposits. They have prepared for development a vast field of oil and gas deposits which, although it
lies in the Arctic taiga, has been plotted on the map in as
great detail as, say, the environs of Moscow.

Some people think that the oil at Ukhta has only just been
discovered. This is not the case, however. Oil has been known
to exist here for five centuries. As far back as the 15th century
the people of Pechora greased the axles of their carts with
what they called "earth tar." But the true history of the Ukhta

oil is such as gives us every right to call it a Soviet discovery. Ukhta was discovered by the revolution.

A long time ago, when the tsars still ruled, a merchant named Pryadunov made an attempt to work the Ukhta oil deposits, but before he was able to do anything of importance, he was arrested and imprisoned for failing to pay excise duties. Another attempt to survey the oil deposits was made by the trader Sidorov. His attempt also failed: the drill he was using broke and it was impossible to repair it under the conditions obtaining in those days. Guards Captain Voronov was another who tried to do something with Ukhta. He engaged a Danish engineer to do the survey. The Dane, however, had been bribed by Nobel, the oil king. To protect Baku from competition, the engineer falsely announced that there was no payable oil in Ukhta. After this, all oil workings in Ukhta were abandoned.

The search for oil in Ukhta was only resumed after the October Revolution. As we already know, the work has been very successful.

One would think that the owners of the Baku oil fields who opposed the search for oil in other regions, would at least have made a thorough exploration of their own oil fields, but they did not do so. Although the Baku oil fields at one time provided half the world's supply of oil, there was no accurate geological map of the region. In the hands of the oil magnates and speculators the oil fields were merely playing cards.

Today, almost nine-tenths of the oil extracted in Baku comes from strata that have been discovered and investigated by Soviet geologists. Here we have the deepest oil wells in the U.S.S.R., running to a depth of four kilometres. Wells five kilometres deep are now being sunk. Oil has been found far beyond the boundaries of Baku—westward towards Kirovabad where some gushers have been tapped, and southward towards the lower reaches of the River Kura.

Soviet oilmen have learned to sink slanting wells. This

enables them to get at oil that lies under buildings, or under the sea near the shore—the seabed around Baku is
rich in oil. Oil derricks are now built on the sea itself
on metal pylons. There are about two hundred derricks
of this kind off Baku, some of them about seven kilometres from the shore. It is not easy to work these off-shore
wells; it must be remembered that the word Baku means a
"gust of the wind." The sea is calm here only thirty days a
year at most. The forty-metre, latticework derricks, however,
firmly withstand the rough seas; the Baku oilmen are not
afraid of storms. They are out for oil, and they are keen to
get as much from under the sea as is obtained on shore, in
Baku.

Completely reconstructed under the Soviet system, Baku
remains our chief oil region. But we have found a "Second
Baku," whose known deposits are beginning to rival those
of the first.

In the "Second Baku" too, situated between the Urals and
the Volga, the smell of oil was known long ago. It made itself felt as far back as the last century. The boatmen who
hauled their barges up the River Byelaya used to light fires
where they camped for the night. There was a spot where
they threw handfuls of earth on the fire and this would make
it flare up more. This place was beyond Sterlitamak in Bashkiria, near the village of Ishimbayevo. Somebody tried to drill
for oil there on his own account, but soon went bankrupt.

Only under the Soviet government did it become possible
to explore the field thoroughly and to tap it for industrial
purposes.

Academician Gubkin, one of the Soviet Union's greatest
oil experts, compared the structure of the Russian plateau
between the Volga and the Urals with that of other oil fields
in the world and came to the conclusion that there must be
oil there!

In 1929, drilling for potassium was going on in the Upper
Kama Basin, at Verkhne-Chusovskiye Gorodki. Unexpectedly

ST. MARY'S COLLEGE LIBRARY CALIFORNIA

oil was struck. It turned out that this was not payable oil, but its discovery confirmed Gubkin's forecast.

The Carboniferous and Permian strata that contain oil in the Urals, stretch right down to the Volga; these strata gave a promise of oil along their whole length. The survey began. Oil was sought over the vast territory from the Stone Belt to the great river. Drilling installations were carried far into roadless wastes. Test wells were sunk in the Orenburg steppes, in the Vyatka forests, and in the ravines of the Zhiguli Hills. Hundreds of pipes were driven into the ground.

At one time capitalist Baku prevented the development of other oil fields. We have seen how they killed Ukhta. The Baku oil magnates did the same in the area between the Urals and the Volga, where the discovery of oil was to be expected. They paid the village communities in the region to pass decisions prohibiting geological surveys on their lands.

Under the Soviet government, however, Baku helped to develop the new oil fields. Instruments and equipment were taken to the new workings from Apsheron, and also from Grozny, and skilled oil drillers and oil-field managers went there too. The oilmen of Baku and Grozny taught the oil business to the Bashkirs and Tatars.

Comrade Stalin issued the instruction: to find oil in the heart of the country, to find it at whatever cost. This instruction was carried out.

In 1932 a gusher burst out of a well sunk near that very village of Ishimbayevo where the boatmen used to light their fires. The derrick was drenched to the very top with rich black oil. Somewhat later oil was also found at Krasnokamsk, near the Bashkir village of Tuimazy, and also at Buguruslan. And then, in 1937, oil leapt out of the ground along the Volga, first at Syzran, next at Stavropol, and lastly at Saratov.

A new oil country came into being of an area equal to three Italys.

The problem was solved. But the matter did not end there.

The oil that is extracted in Baku is comparatively young—its age is only a few million years. In the "Second Baku" older oil was found, but it was not as old as Academician Gubkin's conclusions had led one to expect. He had hoped to find oil here not only in the Carboniferous and Permian strata, but also much deeper, in the older Devonian strata, whose age is estimated at something like three hundred and fifty million years. He had also predicted the depth of the Devonian stratum—between one and a half to two kilometres.

The oilmen began to dig down to the Devonian stratum. This was the beginning of a new offensive—deep drilling began at many points between the Urals and the Volga.

The Devonian stratum was first reached at Syzran. This was but half the victory: the Devonian rock was found at the depth predicted by Gubkin, who had died in the meantime. Oil, however, was not found in this Devonian stratum.

The battle went on. Explorations were continued even during the war, when the battle front reached the Lower Volga.

In 1944, in the Yablonovy Ravine in the Zhiguli Hills, Devonian oil gushed out of the pipe from a depth of one and a half kilometres! A few weeks later the deep Devonian stratum at Tuimazy also produced a gusher. Very soon these became the leading oil fields in the Soviet East. It was not for nothing that the main street of the new township of Oktyabrsky which sprang up in the Tuimazy oil fields was named "Devonian Street."

Lastly, Devonian oil was reached at Severokamsk and in Tataria.

These oil fields are hundreds of kilometres away from each other. This means that the oil in the Devonian stratum has spread over a vast underground area.

The deep-lying Devonian stratum is much richer in oil than the other strata nearer the surface. During these past years the Devonian stratum has provided the Soviet Union with large quantities of high-grade oil. That was when the

"Second Baku" revealed its real wealth! Its newly-discovered deposits have reserves of oil as rich as the best in Baku. Now we may say that a new "Second Baku" had been found.

But this too was not the end; if anything, it was the beginning. The new oil-bearing region is being constantly enlarged. Oil has already been found on the Siberian side of the Ural Mountains. In the south, the "Second Baku" joins the extensive and promising Emba oil region. Many signs go to show that oil may be found west of the Volga as well. There should be oil in the higher levels of the ancient folds that lie below the Russian plateau. Oil may also be found on the Oka-Tsna divide east of Moscow; another likely spot is the underground ridge that lies buried between Moscow and Leningrad.... Drilling has been started here. Perhaps we are on the eve of new discoveries—Moscow may eventually become the centre of an oil region.

Thus was unravelled the tangled skein, the beginning of which goes back to those bright campfires which the boatmen lit long ago.

In addition to the "Second Baku" more and more new derricks are springing up at Emba, Nebit-Dagh, Ferghana and on Sakhalin. The geography of oil is being completely recast.

As regards oil resources, the U.S.S.R. today firmly occupies first place among the oil-bearing countries of the world.

THE POWER OF THE MAGNET

The U.S.S.R. also holds first place in the world for iron-ore resources.

Long before the revolution it was observed that in the Kursk steppes the compass needle "played pranks." It would not point direct north and south, but would show a deviation varying in magnitude and direction in different places.

By studying the deviations of the magnetic needle the geophysicists drew the outline of a huge magnet spread out

Oil derrick on the sea. Azerbaijan S.S.R.

Kounrad copper mine. Kazakh S.S.R.

A new coal region. Building a by-pass canal on the River
Angren, Uzbek S.S.R.

A coal combine at work in the Kuznetsk Basin

below the earth's surface. This could not be anything but a mass of iron ore of gigantic proportions. In some places the power of magnetic attraction was three or four times greater than that of the North Magnetic Pole!

Before the revolution, however, no iron ore was found there.

The Kursk landowners, on the lookout for profits, provided the money for drilling operations. Drilling began. The deeper the steel drill bit into the earth the more strongly it became magnetized.

But they did not reach the ore. The survey dragged on, profit did not come to hand of its own accord, and the Kursk landlords, accustomed to getting something for nothing, stopped the supplies of money.

The drawings of the magnetic field fell into German hands. During the Civil War a German businessman offered to sell them to the Soviet Government for eight million rubles gold. His offer was rejected.

Lenin sent some Soviet geologists, headed by Gubkin, to search for the Kursk iron. They began their survey under fire: at that time fighting was proceeding in the Kursk steppes.

The Berlin businessmen laughed: "The Russians are looking for iron under Kursk. They may as well sink a shaft in Unter den Linden." They were convinced that the young Soviet government would not be able to accomplish the survey successfully.

The Soviet geologists, not having the drawings, had to remeasure the magnetic deviation over a huge area and draw a new map of the iron-ore mass.

At last the first test shaft was sunk. It passed through strata that were abundant with subterranean water. The steel bits were blunted as they bored their way through a roof of hard rock. By this time the drill had become so magnetized that it could hold a piece of iron weighing seventy-three pounds. A further effort was made, and in April 1923, at a depth of 162 metres, the drillers struck quartzite containing magnetic iron ore.

The amount of iron in the ore and quartzite in the Kursk Magnetic Anomaly is equal to that of all the other iron-ore deposits in the world. The world's iron resources have been doubled!

* * *

This is how Soviet people strove to enrich their socialist country with new mineral resources. They developed the geological map as if they were developing a difficult photographic negative. They made discoveries that changed the world geography of mineral raw materials. In the end, they put our country in front of all other countries as regards mineral resources.

Half of the world's oil resources. Half of the iron ore. Half of the peat. Most of the apatite and potassium. A third of the manganese. Vast resources of non-ferrous and rare metals.

There was much that we did not have—now we have everything: sulphur and boron, nickel and cobalt, helium and radium.... Comrade Stalin said: "As far as natural resources are concerned, we are fully secured...."*

The U.S.A., the richest country in the capitalist world, is far behind us in resources of all the most important minerals, except coal. Before the second world war our known mineral deposits, per capita of the population, were far larger than those of the U.S.A. And the U.S.A. has much less opportunity of increasing her mineral resources than we have. There, prospecting for minerals has been going on for a hundred years, whereas we began in earnest only after the Soviet system was established.

The U.S.S.R. has become rich in valuable minerals, but this does not mean that Soviet geologists have solved all the problems. Much work still lies ahead.

Our mineral deposits are enormous, but not all of them have been prepared for tapping. It is not enough to discov-

---

* J. Stalin, *Problems of Leninism,* Moscow 1947, p. 351.

er a deposit, it has also to be investigated. Engineers must know where shafts have to be sunk, and to what depth. They have to make sure that the veins of ore or coal seams to be tapped are thick enough. The work required to survey a deposit for industrial purposes is often as hard as the search for it.

Excellent raw material in large quantities is not always in the place where it is needed. Big industrial centres often have fuel brought to them from places far away. It is not enough to search for raw materials—they have to be sought, as far as possible, in the places where they are most needed.

The life of our country is constantly presenting our geologists with new tasks, and the geologists are doing their best to keep pace with life.

For the postwar Stalin five-year plan iron ore is needed in the Northwest and in Siberia, new deposits of manganese in the Urals and beyond, new supplies of coking coal in Kuznetsk, oil on both sides of the Volga and deposits of natural gas which we are now using as fuel.

Geologists are also responding to these demands which our country is making: we already have the iron ore of Gimola in the Karelo-Finnish Republic, the iron near Angara in Siberia, the new Tom-Usa coal in the Kuznetsk Basin, gas in Stavropol....

Parallel to the discovery of new deposits of minerals, parallel to the strengthening of the fortifications in the battle for the five-year plan, the general geological survey of the whole country is being continued. During these five years another three million square kilometres will be plotted on the map—an area equal to half of Western Europe.

Now that the geographical map of the U.S.S.R. has been completed, the geological map is being completed. Fifty sheets of the State Geological Survey of the U.S.S.R. on a scale of 1:1,000,000 are already finished. In a few more years the whole country will have been plotted on the map. A great thing is being done—the contents of the earth of a vast country that stretches over two continents are being scientifically documented.

The earth of our country contains vast resources of valuable minerals. The fact that our natural resources are enormous is not the main thing, however. More important is the fact that the socialist system enables us to use them extensively, to employ them in economic production, to place them at the service of our country.

There was an abundance of natural wealth in old Russia too. But the social system that prevailed then prevented it from being tapped and even from being properly explored.

The extensive exploration and industrial utilization of the untold wealth of our country became possible only after the Great October Socialist Revolution. The Bolshevik Party and the Soviet Government promoted the development of this natural wealth and placed it at the service of the people.

Like a powerful magician, our people are calling to life the dead riches of the earth, our people are conquering a wonderful fairyland of subterranean wealth.

Our mineral world is not only being explored and investigated, it is being developed, it is being made available to industry.

The new raw materials serve as supplies for the new factories that are springing up.

Socialist industry is growing stronger year after year.

NEW BASTIONS OF SOCIALIST INDUSTRY

THE MAP OF YEARS GONE BY

THE INDUSTRIAL towns of tsarist Russia were lost amidst an ocean of villages. Russia was an agrarian, an agricultural country.

And the Russian landscape was predominantly rural—fields and villages, fields and villages....

The principal town of the uyezd, or county, consisted of little wooden houses, each with its three windows, paths crossing the grass-grown streets, and the constable at his striped sentry box. The principal town of the gubernia, or province, contained the same wooden houses clustered around the richer dwellings of the landlords and merchants, and countless domed churches. Only in a few regions of the country were there factory buildings and smoking chimney stacks, and besides them the factory settlements—wretched slums in which the workers lived in congestion and poverty.

After the reform of 1861 (the abolition of serfdom), Russian industry began to develop more rapidly than before, but compared with the industries of the western capitalist countries, it was still feeble and backward. In area Russia held first place among the countries of the world, in population she was third, but in industrial output she came fifth.... Ahead of Russia were the United States of America, Germany, Britain and France. The mighty forces of the people were fettered by landlord and bourgeois oppression.

There was a shortage of pig iron and coal. There was no aluminium, nickel, or special steels. Motor cars, tractors, textile and printing machines were not manufactured. Russia built her own locomotives, but they were low-powered. She wove her own cloth, but it was of the cheapest kind. Even scythes were often imported from Austria-Hungary.

There were big industrial enterprises in Russia employing large numbers of workers, but their technical level was low.

The Donets mines had no electric light. At Baku, oil was baled out by hand instead of being pumped. Trees were felled with axes and two-handed saws and dragged to the rivers by horses.

The capitalists paid no attention to conditions of labour. Open-hearth furnaces were in no way protected and exhaled their torrid heat. The flywheels of engines revolved unprotected by screens. In the mines gas explosions were frequent. Forced labour for a master—from dawn to dusk for a miserable pittance—was burdensome and exhausting.

There was a heavy industry in Russia, but it was not the basic industry. Chief place was held by light industry, which produces consumers' goods.

It is easier to build up light industry than it is to build heavy industry, and it was the former that the weak Russian bourgeoisie developed primarily. The preponderance of light industry over heavy was a sign of the country's economic backwardness.

Textiles were Russian, but they were produced on foreign machines, and half the raw material came from abroad.

Foreigners not only sold their goods in Russia, but they owned numerous factories, mills and mines here. They gained control of nearly three-fourths of the Russian iron and steel industry, nearly three-fourths of the Donets mines and over half of the oil industry. Some branches of industry—electrical engineering, for example—were almost entirely in the hands of foreigners.

Hughes, Hartmann, Bromley, Goujon, Thornton, Vogelsang.... Electric lamps bore the mark "Osram," sewing machines carried the trade-mark "Singer," telephones were labelled "Ericsson."

Russia bore the yoke of semi-colonial exploitation. The danger that she would become completely subjected and lose her independence constantly grew.

Far from taking measures to remove this dependence upon foreign countries, Russia's rulers pursued a policy that enhanced it and made it more complete. They proved incapable of overcoming their country's economic backwardness by their own efforts and assumed that they could do this with the aid of foreigners. They opened wide the doors of the country to foreign capital. Instead of making progress, Russia dropped still farther behind and her impotence in the face of the western imperialist powers increased.

The landowners and capitalists of Russia cringed before everything foreign, they fawned on foreigners and aped them. Everything foreign was "fashionable" to them, and they treated everything Russian with disdain. Their children were brought up by a "bonne," hats were bought "chez Lemercier," ties from Alschwang, knickknacks from Daziaro; they went carousing in Paris and "holiday-making" in Nice.

The significance of Russian culture was belittled in every way. Engineers were hired in Germany, books came from France, and vocalists from Italy....

Every effort was made to stifle the creative ideas of Russian people. Foreign specialists were imported into Russia. Pseudo scientists from Berlin were invited to the Academy of Sciences. Western science was lauded to the skies, while talented Russians were given no opportunities. Their discoveries were ignored or pigeonholed, or else foreigners were given opportunities to appropriate the valuable inventions of Russian scientists. Thus, Lomonosov's discoveries were ascribed to Lavoisier; James Watt became famous throughout the world, but the Russian mechanic Polzunov, who built a steam engine six years before Watt built his, died unknown; the electric lamp invented by Lodygin was proclaimed an American invention;

the Russian physicist Popov built the world's first radio transmitter, but the honour of the invention was claimed by Marconi.

"In the sciences, arts, letters and engineering the Russians will always be the pupils of the West," asserted the ruling classes of Russia and their foreign "friends." This raving nonsense served the interests of the imperialists of the West, for it enabled them to sink their roots deeper into Russian soil. And the landowners and capitalists of Russia, fearing and hating their own people, poisoned them with the virus of disbelief in their own creative strength, strove to fortify their own position in anticipation of the revolutionary storm that was rising in the country.

The economic backwardness of tsarist Russia was also reflected on the map.

Industry developed in only a few regions. The factories were crowded together in one corner of the country, while in other parts there were scarcely any.

Look at the old economic map: the central regions stand out like islands in a sea, like mountains in a plain.

A good half of the total industrial output came from the old industrial Centre and from St. Petersburg. Spinning, weaving, chemicals and the construction of the more intricate machines were all concentrated in these places.

A fourth of the total industrial output came from the Ukraine and the Urals, the main support of the Centre. The Ukrainian industries, however, rose no higher than the foundations. They turned out only raw materials and semi-manufactured goods: coal from the Donets Basin and metal from the Donets and Dnieper basins. The processing of metal lagged behind. Iron was smelted in the Urals in old blast furnaces and most of it was shipped away in pigs without being worked up; sheet iron for covering roofs, frying pans and nails were the chief manufactures.

There was one other industrial centre—Baku.

The rest of Russia had but a few crumbs. Industries were

few and far between. The map of many parts of Siberia, Central Asia and the North were just blank spaces marked only with mountain ranges and the courses of rivers, with rare villages or nomad encampments dotted about on them.

The ancient backwardness stifled old Russia: tsarism, the remnants of the feudal system, prevented the development of industry. The home market was restricted, its volume increased slowly.

"Not in depth, but in breadth!" and Russian capitalism moved outwards to the little-known expanses of the East.

Factory owners expanded their market by selling cotton cloth made in Moscow and Ivanovo-Voznesensk to the people of Asia. At the same time they greedily imported raw materials from the East.

This was the cruel path of capitalism.

The articles shipped to the East were of inferior quality and appearance, but they soon ruined the local handicraftsmen. Simple arithmetic decided their fate. Cheap aniline dyes killed the hand carpet-weaving trade, the machine loom eliminated the hand loom.

Factory-made goods invaded the patriarchal life of the outlying regions of the Russian Empire, but these did not include machine tools and motors, reaping machines or automatic hunting rifles. The goods were of a simpler kind—china piyalas (tea bowls), cotton print, overshoes—the mechanized imitations of local handicrafts.

The distant, backward, outlying regions very gradually threw off their archaic habits and took their place in world capitalist economy, but they paid an exorbitant price for the privilege.

The Centre provided the outlying regions with factory-made goods, but compelled them to produce only raw materials—not boots but hides, not cloth but raw cotton.

Manufacture was divorced from the sources of raw materials. Cheap raw materials were brought to the Centre from the distant provinces, turned into manufactured goods and sent back again for sale. In this way the bourgeoisie of Central

Russia strengthened their hold on the country. Labour power was wasted, but the colonies covered the expenses. The Uzbek who grew cotton was underpaid, the Uzbek who bought manufactured goods paid more than their value, and the industrialists of the Centre grew rich....

The outlying regions enriched the capitalists of the Centre, but it did not pay the capitalists to industrialize those regions. The tsarist authorities, directly or indirectly, banned manufacturing industries in those regions. The tsarist government did everything to prevent the building of industrial enterprises outside the Centre. It protected the Russian capitalists from competition. It feared the growth of the non-Russian working class that regarded the revolutionary Russian proletariat as its leader and teacher.

The Centre was the metropolis, the industrial region, whose capitalists subjected the outlying regions to their interests.

The outlying regions were the colonies of tsarism and of the industrialists of the Centre.

The map reflected the intricate pattern of the social systems and social antagonisms characteristic of Russia before the revolution. Luxurious mansions on the prospects of St. Petersburg and working-class huts and hovels in the Donets Basin. The bank premises of the Baku monopolists and the nomad tents in the Apsheron steppe....

The industries that were crowded in the Centre had no coal or oil close at hand. The industrial map was at odds with the map of natural resources.

True, some raw materials were close at hand: combustible shale at Lake Chudskoye (Peipus), lignite in Borovichi and Bobriki, iron ore near Kursk. But these were not the minerals that supplied the industries, and the Centre did not bother about them.

A treasure lay close by, but nobody knew about it. At Kursk the magnetic needle pointed not to the North, but to the ground. But who then could have said that the Kursk Magnetic Anomaly would place Russia at the top of the world's list for iron-ore resources? It was known that coal could be mined in the Moscow region, but the competition of the Donets Basin prevented this.

Fuel for the Centre was hauled over long distances: coal from the Donets Basin, oil from the Caucasus. All raw materials, except flax, also came from a distance. They were brought from the outlying regions or else purchased abroad: pig iron in the Ruhr, cotton on the Mississippi, wool in Australia.

The enriched factory owner grafted new industries on to the old even when there was no technological connection between them. In a place like Rzhev, say, on the upper reaches of the Volga, where flax and hemp were grown, a silk mill appeared—four thousand kilometres from the mulberry groves where silkworms were bred....

Even in the central regions the industries were not evenly and rationally distributed. The factory owners built their factories wherever they thought it profitable without any other consideration, not giving a thought to town planning or public hygiene.

Capitalism also invaded the countryside; the impoverished handicraftsmen provided cheap labour; hundreds of small factories were built in the handicraft centres of the Moscow, Kostroma and Vladimir gubernias.

The industries around Moscow formed a broad, if sparsely dotted, patch on the map, but the St. Petersburg Gubernia owed its "central position" entirely to the city of St. Petersburg—the capital of the country, and the seaport which connected Russia with Western Europe. The only big city in the gubernia, it contained 90 per cent of the textile industry, 90 per cent of the food industry, 99 per cent of the printing industry, 99 per cent of the clothing industry, 99 per cent of the footwear industry, 100 per cent of the tobacco industry and 100 per cent of the electrical goods industry of that gubernia.

A few steps out of the factory villages and small towns reigned the barbaric stagnation of olden days. Old Chukhloma and Poshekhonye, with their dirt tracks and wretched three-field system, lay within the metropolis, within the "Centre."

The outlying regions, which constituted the major part of the area of Russia, remained, practically, without any factories. Those that were built did not usually work up raw materials, they simply reduced their weight. The cotton-ginning mills of Turkestan removed the seeds from the raw cotton to facilitate its transport to the Centre.

The only textile mill in the outlying regions was at Baku, and that worked exclusively for the Iranian market. Textiles sold in the Transcaucasian cotton belt were brought from Central Russia....

Even the mining industries formed isolated points on the map of the outlying regions.

The oil wells of the Caucasus, the lead mines of the Altai, the gold fields of Siberia were all islands in the backwoods of a rural country. Siberia accounted for only two per cent of Russia's manufactures, and Turkestan accounted for even less....

The wealth of the outlying regions was exploited ruthlessly and avariciously. Waste was supreme. Oil was pumped only from the upper strata, those that could be reached most easily. In the forests the best varieties of timber were sought and ruthlessly felled to the last tree.

Water flooded the oil workings, mines were exhausted and abandoned, more than half the gold remained in the waste piles, the taiga was cluttered up with rubbish, the trees along the rivers and roads were destroyed. And all around was an unexplored land, close by lay undiscovered treasures....

Raw material was extracted at isolated spots. The oil fields of Baku were more closely associated with Moscow and London than with the surrounding country of Azerbaijan. Machines, pipes and lime were brought to Baku, and all the oil that was extracted was exported.

The preponderance of foreign capital affected the location of industries. This was also reflected on the map.

The manufacturing industries were concentrated mainly— with the exception of Moscow and St. Petersburg—in the extreme West and in the Baltic ports of Revel and Riga. The most important thing for the foreign capitalists was to get on the Russian side of the customs barrier, and they were only too glad to build factories right on the frontier. Coal, metal and even firebrick were imported from the West. The railways led to the frontiers and to the sea.

The Western imperialists continued to extend their power in Russia. Weak, but no less avaricious, Russian capital lost one titbit after another. Russia stood face to face with foreign capital and learned the full weight of its heavy and oppressive hand.

Shares in the Baku oil industry drifted abroad, Ukrainian iron ore was smelted in France, Americans bought up the furs of Chukotka, Japanese fished in the Sea of Okhotsk, Britishers felled timber in Archangel.

The workings were located so that the raw materials could be easily exported. The lumber camps of the North and the manganese mines of the Transcaucasus lay close to the frontiers. Part of the country became a foreign market for Western Europe and America, but did not become a home market for Russia.

The distant outlying regions with their numerous nationalities! Steppes, forests, mountains stretching for thousands of kilometres! Occasional commercial towns, village huts, nomad tents, forest shacks, miners' dugouts! Far from the Centre lay regions that were still fettered by the patriarchal, feudal ways of life. The culture of the various nationalities was repressed by the oppressive hand of tsarism, by the oppression of the alien and native bourgeoisie, by the oppression of the local princelings and kulaks.

Many a Siberian hunter, splendid marksmen, never wasting a shot, possessed the amazing ability to use only one bullet over and over again. But this was not so much evidence of their skill as of poverty, of the shortage of lead.... In the remote Yakut settlements, in times of famine, which occurred at frequent intervals, a family would eat about three hundred and seventy pounds of larch and pine sapwood in a year.

"To the north from Vologda, to the southeast from Rostov-on-Don and from Saratov, to the south from Orenburg and from Omsk, to the north from Tomsk, there are boundless areas big enough to contain scores of large civilized states. And over all these spaces patriarchalism, semi-savagery and real savagery reign," wrote Lenin. "And what about the out-of-the-way peasant districts of the rest of Russia, wherever scores of versts of country track, or rather of trackless country, separate the villages from the railways, i.e., from material connection with culture, with capitalism, with large-scale industry, with the big cities? Do not patriarchalism, *Oblomovism** and semi-savagery also predominate in those places?" (Lenin, *Selected Works*, Two-Vol. ed., Vol. II, Moscow 1947, p. 717.)

FORWARD LEAP

The First World War completely laid bare the utter backwardness of tsarist Russia: there was a shortage of guns, rifles and machine guns. At times no more than five or six shells per gun per day were supplied. Half the rifle ammunition used was made abroad....

The defeat of the Russian armies and the economic ruin caused by the war, brought Russia to the brink of disaster. The country was in danger of becoming a disfranchised colony of foreign powers.

But our country was saved. It was saved by the Bolsheviks.

At the turn of the twentieth century, the world centre of the revolutionary movement shifted to Russia, which had

---

* *Oblomovism* (Russ. *Oblomovshchina*)—a term derived from Oblomov, the hero of Goncharov's novel of the same name, the personification of inertia, supineness and a passive, vegetating existence.—*Tr.*

become the focus of all the contradictions of imperialism. Steeled in the struggle, the Russian working class created the great Bolshevik Party and rose in revolt against the tsar, the landowners and the capitalists. All the peoples of Russia followed their elder brother, the Russian people, and joined in the battle.

With indomitable will that overcame all obstacles, the working people of Russia advanced along the path indicated by Lenin and Stalin. In October (November) 1917, the workers and the poor peasants, supported by the soldiers and sailors and led by the Bolshevik Party, brought about the Great Socialist Revolution. This marked the beginning of a new era in world history.

The October Revolution overthrew the power of the landowners and capitalists, introduced the new, Soviet system, and opened the way to Socialism and Communism. At the same time it put an end to the semi-colonial state of the country. The chains in which foreign capital had kept old Russia fettered were broken and cast aside. The revolution ensured the independence and sovereignty of our country.

The next task after accomplishing the revolution was to consolidate the Soviet state. The remnants of the exploiting classes had to be eradicated. A socialist economy had to be created. The whole country had to be transformed and socialist society built up.

In this great task the Soviet people were inspired by the Bolshevik Party, by Lenin and Stalin.

Lenin was of the opinion that the "only material basis for Socialism" was large-scale machine industry. It was impossible to build Socialism, to build up a cultured and affluent life for the working people, to make the country technically and economically independent and to ensure the reliable defence of her borders against all enemies without first turning backward, agrarian Russia into a progressive, industrial country.

Therefore, the Soviet people launched their struggle for the industrialization of the country.

The slogan of socialist industrialization of the country was proclaimed by Comrade Stalin, the leader of the Soviet people, at the Fourteenth Congress of the Communist Party. The Communist Party and the Soviet Government roused millions of working people for the task of overcoming Russia's age-old backwardness. With firm determination, our great leader led the country along the road to Socialism.

Old factories were reconstructed and re-equipped with new machinery. Existing shops were enlarged, additional storeys were added, and modern machines were installed that turned out new commodities on an unprecedented scale. By the end of the First Five-Year Plan period, eighty per cent of the installations of the Leningrad electric power stations, for example, had already been replaced by new equipment.

New factories were built. These were easily distinguishable from the old; they were not the old type of red brick buildings with brick ornamentation and tiny, smoke-begrimed windows, but smooth-walled, grey, ferro-concrete buildings with huge windows, glass-vaulted roofs and their own transformer installations. The façades, or the chimney stacks, bore the dates— "1932," "1935," "1938"....

The work of reconstruction began not with what was the easiest, but with what was the most difficult, viz., with heavy industry.

The work of reconstruction was not financed by foreign loans, but by our own Soviet rubles.

The work of reconstruction was accompanied by the training of contingents of industrial workers on the very building sites. The navvies, carpenters and bricklayers became skilled workers, technicians and foremen.

The people were no longer the wage slaves of a master. The factories and machines were their own; they worked for themselves, for the good of their country.

Soviet people learned to master the new machines. Leading industrial workers performed miracles. And the world saw not only new factories, but a new people growing up.

The Stalin Textile Mills, Tashkent. Uzbek S.S.R.

In an Uzbek steel mill

Sumgait pipe works under construction. Azerbaijan S.S.R.

These tractors produced by the Kharkov Tractor
Plant are ready for shipment

It was necessary to make haste. Old Russia lagged from fifty to a hundred years behind the chief capitalist countries in volume of output and in methods of production. The Soviet people had to make up this distance in 10-15 years. No other people in history had been called upon to solve such a problem. And Stalin said: "Either we do it, or they will crush us."

The Soviet people solved this gigantic problem. They overcame unprecedented difficulties and built up a powerful industry in the short space of thirteen years, between the launching of the First Five-Year Plan and the beginning of the Great Patriotic War. Germany achieved a similar growth in industrial output in fifty years, Britain in the course of more than a century.

Before the Great Patriotic War the volume of industrial production in the Soviet Union was equal to that of twelve pre-revolutionary Russias.

An agrarian country had become an industrial country. The new heavy industry helped to raise the level and reconstruct all other branches of the national economy.

Tractors, harvester combines and other farm machines moved into the countryside in an ever-growing stream; the farms received mineral fertilizers. The technical re-equipment of the farms was one of the most important conditions for the victory and consolidation of the collective-farm system, for the implementation of the collectivization policy announced by Stalin. Millions of peasants became convinced of the advantages of collective farming on a scale capable of employing the new machines and joined the collective farms. In the course of a very few years the U.S.S.R. became the land of socialist agriculture, which is mechanized on a scale unequalled anywhere in the world. Socialist society grew and became strong on the solid, material foundation of Soviet industry. The country achieved technical and economic independence, something that old tsarist Russia had never known. Our defence potential reached a higher level than ever before achieved.

The Soviet people had achieved what had seemed impossible; in a very short period they converted a vast and erstwhile backward country into an advanced and powerful industrial state. This leap forward was possible because of the incalculable advantages of the Soviet system, the planned Soviet economy, the tremendous organizational work of the Communist Party and the wisdom and determination of Stalin's leadership.

The Communist Party confronted the people with a gigantic task, led them in the struggle for its achievement, fostered the forces of the people and organized and directed those forces. Fully conscious of their great historical obligation, the people followed the Communist Party and their great leader to victory.

During the period covered by the Stalin five-year plans Soviet industry grew so rapidly that it took first place in the world for rate of growth. For volume of production the U.S.S.R. moved up from fifth place to second, overtaking France, Britain and Germany. The U.S.A. alone is still ahead of us.

The Soviet people developed the industries of their country consciously and in accordance with a plan. They determined with great precision the direction their creative activities were to take; they knew exactly what to build to make their country mighty and prosperous.

But it was not enough to know *what* to build, they also had to know *where* to build.

WHERE TO BUILD?

The Soviet people built up a new industry and at the same time they changed the economic geography of their country, they distributed this industry in a new way.

The problem was posed by Comrade Stalin. At the Sixteenth Congress of the Communist Party, the leader of the people, the inspirer of the plan for socialist industrialization, said:

"First of all the problem of *the proper distribution of industry throughout the U.S.S.R.* However we develop national economy, we cannot avoid the question of how properly to distribute industry, as the leading branch of national economy."

The map not only testifies to the country's transformation from an agricultural to an industrial one; it also testifies to the triumph of socialist ideas of distributing a country's forces of production.

In the Land of Socialism there are no privileged and no neglected provinces. Every region, and every territory, has the right to and the opportunity for all-round economic and cultural development.

We must not, and will not, have backward, purely agrarian regions. Industrialization must embrace the whole country. It must be arranged so that the distribution of industry conforms to the interests of the state as a whole and increases the productivity of social labour. Many years ago Engels wrote that in socialist society industry would be wisely distributed, in accordance with a plan: "Only a society which makes possible the harmonious cooperation of its productive forces on the basis of one single vast plan can allow industry to be distributed over the whole country in a way as is best adapted to its own development and the maintenance or development of the other elements of production."*

To promote the industrial development of the entire country we had to distribute our capital investments not equally for all districts, but in conformity with a certain trend. Natural conditions in the country vary, and all these different natural conditions must be taken into account. And the main thing— the country had a past, and this, too, had to be taken into account.

The geographical design that we inherited from capitalism was uneven and distorted. Industry was congested in some

---

* Friedrich Engels, *Herr Eugene Dühring's Revolution in Science,* Moscow 1947, p. 441.

6*

regions, while in others there was none at all. To even out the industrial geography of the country, the different regions of the Soviet Union had to grow at different rates. The backward outlying regions had to catch up with the advanced Centre.

The formerly agrarian outlying regions—first and foremost the East—became the scene of feverish industrial construction.

On the map the industrial Centre is no longer an island in the midst of a wilderness. At the Seventeenth Congress of the Communist Party, Comrade Stalin said: "Development is tending to the point when all our regions will be more or less industrial; and they will become more and more so as this development proceeds."

By the end of the Second Five-Year Plan industrial production in the Centre had increased eightfold, in the Urals and Western Siberia more than elevenfold, and in Eastern Siberia and the Far East fourteenfold compared with the pre-revolutionary period. The different rates of development of these regions reduced the differences in their levels.

Nevertheless, the Centre is still stronger than the new industrial regions. It is still our leading, most densely populated and most advanced industrial region.

And the Centre is continuing to grow. The new regions are growing more rapidly than the Centre, but the latter does not stand still. More new enterprises are being built. Old ones are brought up to date and provide the country with growing quantities of goods. Having become stronger, the Centre is helping the new regions to grow faster than it is growing itself. That is how we are conducting our systematic and wisely-planned struggle for the new distribution of industry.

From the first day of the Great October Socialist Revolution all the peoples of the U.S.S.R. became equal. From the very outset, the Soviet government proclaimed the legal equality of all nationalities. Then the Communist Party and the socialist state led the peoples of our country on to the path of economic and cultural progress. The cultural backwardness of the non-Russian outlying regions disappeared together with their economic backwardness. Economic progress means cultural progress. At the Twelfth Congress of the Communist Party Comrade Stalin said: "Apart from schools and language, the Russian proletariat must take every necessary measure to establish centres of industry in the border regions, in the republics which are culturally backward—and they are backward not through any fault of their own, but because they were formerly looked upon as sources of raw materials."

During the period of the Stalin five-year plans industrial construction, on the instructions of the Communist Party, was developed in the non-Russian regions. Big, splendidly equipped factories sprang up, which broke up the old, patriarchal way of life. The correct distribution of industry became one of the means of implementing the Lenin-Stalin national policy which makes for the prosperity of all the peoples of the U.S.S.R.

The Bashkirs built a motor plant, the Turkmenians drilled for oil. The Buryats began to build locomotives. The Kazakhs began to smelt copper. Uzbek women discarded their veils and went to work in the new textile mills. The Kirghiz began to produce sugar and cloth. This was a leap from the nomad's saddle to the handling of intricate machines, from the witch doctor's tambourine to the skilled engineer's office. Herdsmen, seal hunters and ploughmen became steel melters, machine installers, electricians and chemists. New people took their places at complicated machine tools in new factories and learned to run them. The non-Russian nationalities acquired their own working-class cadres.

The task of industrializing the non-Russian areas—mostly the Eastern regions—coincided, merged with that of providing a planned and more even distribution of the national economy.

In tsarist Russia there were wide territorial gaps between the mining and manufacturing industries, and between the manufacturing industries and the consumers. This meant tremendous transport expenses. Cotton planted near Tashkent was spun and woven, say, in Orekhovo-Zuyevo, thousands of kilometres away, and sent back to Tashkent in the shape of cloth.

In the Soviet Union the working up of raw materials is organized as near as possible to the source of the raw materials and to the consumers of the finished goods, thus solving a task set by Lenin: to "*distribute* industry in Russia rationally from the standpoint of the proximity of raw materials and the possibility of reducing waste of labour to a minimum in the transition from the processing of raw materials to all subsequent stages of manufacture, up to the production of the finished article."*

For the first time cotton mills were built in the cotton belt itself, in Tashkent, Ferghana and Kirovabad: smaller quantities of cotton goods have now to be transported to those districts from distant places. The last shop of the Nizhni Tagil Steel Mill is also the first shop of the Nizhni Tagil Railway Car Works: the chassis of cars are cast from metal melted there on the spot and not brought from a distance.

Transportation is reduced, labour is saved and made more productive. Long hauls, the uneconomical transportation of goods, are being reduced.

At first, when the distant regions were first brought within the scope of the national economy, the length of railway hauls increased. Since 1939, however, since the effect of the planned distribution of industry began to make itself felt, the length of hauls has been noticeably reduced. They will be still further reduced during the postwar five-year plan period.

As industry advanced into new districts it brought into being new raw materials, new deposits of minerals. A new and more rational geography of raw materials was built up. Regions that had formerly been thought poor, revealed their treasures. In the East, where tremendous construction work was undertaken, huge deposits of mineral fuel and various ores were found—huge treasure stores, like the coal of the

---

* Lenin, *Collected Works*, Vol. XXII, Russ. ed., p. 434.

Kuznetsk Basin and Karaganda, the copper and rare metals of Kazakhstan, the oil of "Second Baku."

In this way the poor lands became rich.

The planned distribution of industry does not mean that every kind of industry must be developed in every region. The industry of each region is specialized, regions are developed in conformity with their natural resources and the requirements of the national economy of the whole country. In the heavily-wooded Archangel Region the felling and sawing of timber is the chief industry. The Crimea has deposits of iron ore and extensive fruit orchards—here the metal and canning industries are the most appropriate. In Turkmenia, rich in sulphates, sulphur and oil, chemicals are produced. On the lower Oka, a region long famous for its handicraftsmen working in metals, all sorts of metal goods are now made.

Socialist planned economy prevents lop-sided development. The industry of the regions that were once compelled to produce and export only some particular forms of raw material has become more complex. Wherever possible, the raw material is worked up on the spot. Byelorussia not only fells and saws timber, but produces pulp, paper, matches, resin and plastics. The Ural towns not only smelt iron, they also produce machines from that iron.

In every region of the U.S.S.R. various branches of industry are developed, each connected with the others, and needed by the others. The Ivanovo Region, for example, produces textile machines and dyes as well as the fabrics themselves. Yaroslavl produces synthetic rubber, fabrics for motor tyres, enamel for automobiles and, lastly, the automobiles themselves. This is a single complex, all parts of which are integrated.

The plan requires the all-round complex development of economy in each of the constituent republics, in each of the economic zones.

The endeavour to integrate mining and manufacture, manufacture and consumption, however, has not developed into a general, rigid and inflexible law. When the interests of the country demand it, when it benefits the national economy as a whole, raw materials, manufactured goods and semi-manufactures are hauled over long distances.

The first tractor, the first blooming mill and the first turbine generator produced in Soviet times were made in Leningrad: this city gets its metal from distant blast furnaces, but it is the home of a large contingent of highly skilled workers employing efficiency methods. Only there could men learn to build intricate machines.

Planned distribution of industry does not mean dispersing industry—building one little factory on every square kilometre of land all over the country.

We are building big plants, which, thanks to their dimensions, can engage in mass production by the most up-to-date methods.

We are also building numerous small and medium-sized factories which work up local raw materials and maintain direct connection with the consumer. This helps to industrialize purely agrarian regions, and factories like these do not take a long time to build.

Industry is penetrating all the pores, so to speak, of the country. Factories for the primary treatment of agricultural raw materials, small electric power stations, machine and tractor stations, repair workshops are all serving to transform the rural districts.

With the help of the socialist towns, the rural districts are rising to an urban cultural level.

The former distinction between town and country in the U.S.S.R. is already being obliterated.

In the first period of industrialization a number of "unique" plants were built: one such plant had to provide the whole country with a certain type of machine tool, or a certain machine part. The output of these plants was transported over vast distances. The development of the given economic zone was not all-sided and complex. The next stage was the building of "doubles" in various regions. The economy of the regions became more self-supporting, and transportation from other districts was considerably reduced. If, for some reason, a plant is unable to produce enough of what is required, there is always a second and a third ready to help. Such a method of distributing industry is also called for by the interests of national defence.

In addition to all the other reasons, the Soviet Government was prompted to accelerate the industrialization of the distant eastern regions by the desire to strengthen the defences of our country. The Government foresaw the possibility of an attack on our country. During the years in which the Stalin five-year plans operated a huge defence base was built in the interior of the country, beyond the Volga and beyond the Ural Mountains.

When the Great Patriotic War against the German fascist invaders broke out, the Soviet Union already possessed a powerful industry and a highly developed socialist agriculture. The wise policy of the Bolshevik Party had prepared our country for active defence.

IN WAR AND IN PEACE

A sudden and treacherous blow of terrific force was struck at the Soviet Union. Nazi Germany hurled a powerful army against us. This army was equipped with weapons that were made not only in Germany, but in the numerous other European countries that the Nazis had conquered.

But it was not the old, backward Russia that rose to meet the Nazis. They were faced by the Soviet Union, which in the period of the Stalin five-year plans had become a mighty industrial power with a first-class army.

The German fascists were met not by a landlord- and capitalist-ridden country with an oppressed and enslaved people, but by a socialist country, in which the people are the masters of their own destiny. The free people rose up to defend their Soviet country with a selflessness and heroism that had never before been witnessed. And in their holy war for their country, the war to safeguard the gains of the October Revolution, the Soviet people were guided by the wise and invincible Bolshevik Party.

In response to the appeal of the great Stalin, the Soviet people threw all their forces into the struggle against the enemy.

The national economy was rapidly placed on a war footing. The Red Army received all the equipment it needed.

In this, the industries that were transferred to the eastern regions played an enormously important role.

The western and central regions with their highly developed industries became the area of hostilities in the very first months of the war. Some of them fell into the hands of the Nazis, others came within range of German bombers.

The Soviet Union had to depend on the eastern regions and develop an intricate war economy in these regions at the height of the greatest war in history. Whole industries had to be transferred from the western and central regions to the East in the shortest possible time. This meant changing the industrial geography of the country in a few months: the distances involved were enormous—a thousand kilometres from the Dnieper to the Volga, and three thousand kilometres from the Volga to the Ob....

Could our people cope with such an unheard-of and seemingly impossible task?

Yes, our people proved that they could cope even with such a task.

The great migration of factories continued throughout the autumn and winter of 1941. These factories had been located in their permanent homes—Moscow and Leningrad, in Kharkov and Dniepropetrovsk, in the Donets Basin and the Baltic Republics—for years, some of them for decades. They had been connected by rail with mines and with goods stations, they had cooperated closely with each other and had

been surrounded by workers' residential districts. A strong
hand, guided by a profound idea, suddenly tore all these plants
out of the fabric into which they were woven. Under enemy
bombs, in pitch darkness, as the electric light had been
switched off, and to the sound of approaching artillery fire,
motors were stopped, bolts were unscrewed, belts were removed
from pulleys and machines were dismantled and packed in
cases. This was prudent destruction: life died out in order to be
reborn in another place.

Hundreds of thousands of workers left their homes, packed
up their belongings, took their wives and children and
moved like a cumbersome avalanche thousands of kilometres
to the East. One of the Bryansk factories filled 30,000 railway
trucks, and the entire evacuation entailed the employment of
over a million.

A constant stream of trains carrying troops and equipment
flowed westward to the front, and on the way they passed a
stream of evacuated factories going eastward. The Soviet railwaymen proved that they were capable of handling this tremendous movement of traffic in opposite directions, although
the strain was terrific. Railway despatchers sometimes did not
sleep for days and nights on end; loaders worked until they
dropped; engine drivers drove extra-long trains at increased
speeds; if fire bars needed repair, mechanics soaked their clothes
in water and crawled into red-hot fireboxes to repair them, for
there was no time to take the engines to the roundhouse to let
them cool.

In the West, work on the railways was hampered by enemy air raids, but people grew accustomed to this too. On the
Kola Peninsula, for example, trains never stopped running for
a single day despite the constant bombing. At stations where
often not a single undamaged building was left and the ground
all around was pitted with bomb craters, burning cars were
quickly uncoupled, the trains were reassembled, and they
continued on their journey according to timetable.

In the East, work on the railways was hampered by the

severe frosts in winter. The water froze in the water towers, the workers themselves were almost frozen stiff with the cold, but even this did not daunt them. The Kuznetsk Basin Railway, for example, fulfilled its 1941 coal-loading plan ahead of time....

In an incredibly short space of time, a vast industry was shifted thousands of kilometres.

But this was lifeless industry. It had to be resurrected in the shortest possible time.

The areas around railway stations in the Urals, in Kazakhstan, and in Siberia were cluttered up with packing cases and machines. Visible amongst piles of metal were the carcases of dynamos, the drums of boilers or the skeletons of milling machines.

People wondered whether this vast encampment of assorted machinery could soon be put into order.

But everything was put in its place with amazing speed and industry was resurrected.

Part of the equipment was erected in premises that were available for them; for the rest, new premises had to be built. The plans were drawn right on the building sites. The foundations were laid before the plans for the whole building were ready—the builders worked to sketches. In spite of piercing winds and the Ural and Siberian frosts, so intense that the hands stuck to the cold metal, the builders kept at their task for twelve and even sixteen hours at a stretch.

In the bare steppe and among mountains, factory buildings rose up, the various parts found each other and became machines, workers moved into newly-built houses and electric power flashed along new lines.

A big engineering works, covering an area of twelve thousand square metres, was erected in a month. Another plant in the Urals, covering an area of ten thousand square metres, was erected in twelve days.

In the new buildings machines were immediately erected and immediately set in motion, sometimes before the buildings were roofed. A huge plant from Zaporozhye started production on its new site within twenty days of its arrival. Another plant, transported beyond the Volga, was started on the fifteenth day and began to turn out more than it had done before.

A huge industry, re-based in the east, was set going. By the middle of 1942, practically the whole industry was in full swing.

This complicated economic operation, unexampled in history, could be carried out only by the Soviet Government, only by the Bolshevik Party. A single, wise leadership relied on the understanding, support and enthusiasm of the whole people.

Nothing like this could have been done in a capitalist country. There, private property and social antagonisms would have proved insurmountable obstacles. It would have been impossible to direct the interests of the individual owners of the various factories and mills into one single channel. The selection of sites on which to re-establish the factories would have been rendered difficult by the private ownership of land. It is doubtful whether capitalists would have been found willing to sacrifice their profits for the sake of the common, national interests of the country. It was no accident that both in Poland in 1939 and in France in 1940, the Nazis captured industries all ready to continue production.

In the Soviet East the people did not limit themselves to re-establishing the evacuated factories. New industries were built up more rapidly than had been done in peacetime. The Soviet people not only fought, they also built.

In tsarist Russia, during the First World War, the output of fuel dropped. In the coal fields of the Soviet East, the output of coal increased during the Great Patriotic War. Big power stations were built to work on coal and peat.

In tsarist Russia, during the First World War, blast furnaces were damped one after another. During the Great Patriotic War in the U.S.S.R. new blast furnaces were blown in.

In tsarist Russia, during the First World War, there was a shortage of munitions from the very outset. In the very first months of the Great Patriotic War, the Soviet Union enlarged old and built new, powerful war industry centres. Guns, tanks, tommy guns, mortars, anti-tank rifles, anti-tank stormovik aircraft and death-dealing "Katyushas" flowed to the front in increasing volume.

Not only were new plants built in the East, but the old ones were reconstructed to meet war needs. A new technology was introduced in the course of the work. The Magnitogorsk and Kuznetsk mills had produced nothing but ordinary metal before the war. The war created the need for high-grade steel for machines, and they produced it. Before the war, steel of this type had been melted in electric furnaces, or in small, open-hearth furnaces. Steel melters did not then know how to melt it in big open-hearth furnaces. The war compelled them to revise the whole technological process, from charging the furnace to pouring the steel. New mechanisms were fitted to the old furnaces, and in a short space of time the huge open-hearth furnaces of Magnitogorsk and Kuznetsk began to turn out the required steel.

Before the war much of the raw material used in the East came from the western parts of the country; the electrical engineers in the Urals, for example, used porcelain made from Donets clays. The war compelled them to find the necessary clay in the Urals. New deposits of manganese, rare metals and building materials were found.

Thus, a new industry grew up in the Soviet East during the Great Patriotic War.

The total industrial output of the Soviet East was doubled during the war; the increase in the output of war supplies was even greater. This gigantic leap forward was the result of tremendous labour enthusiasm, and it called for a tremendous effort.

This was not only a quantitative, but also a qualitative change of great significance. New power generating and metal-

lurgical centres were created, new links between foundry and
forge, fuel and mineral raw materials were formed. The industrial structure of all the eastern republics and regions of
the U.S.S.R. underwent a change—engineering works sprang
up everywhere. In those regions where light industry had been
developed during the years of the five-year plans, heavy industry was now added.

Take Uzbekistan. Until recently, Uzbekistan was an agrarian country. Industry was introduced only in Soviet times.
Big plants were erected that were connected mainly with the
cotton industry—the treatment of the fibre in Tashkent and
Ferghana, the production of farm machinery in Tashkent and
the manufacture of fertilizers in Chirchik. Several years before
the war the republic's economy began to acquire the features
that are characteristic of developed industrial countries. During
the war this process was accelerated. The republic produced its
own coal in Angren, its own rolled steel in Begovat, its own
sugar in Yangi-Yul and Zirabulak, its own "Dnieper Power
Station" on the Syr Darya and, most important of all, its own
intricate machinery, measuring instruments and machine tools.

The factories evacuated from the West were a great help
to Uzbek industry: equipment from the Donets mines went to
Angren, Ukrainian sugar refiners arrived in Yangi-Yul, a new
engineering industry grew up where the factories from the
West settled down.

The soil for the rapid growth of Uzbek industry was prepared during the period of operation of the Stalin five-year
plans.

The foundations of the industrial base in the Soviet East
were laid during the prewar years.

Industries could not have been set up so easily in the Urals
and beyond if there had been no contingents of workers there,
if the necessary power supplies, metal, and the entire system
of allied engineering plants had been lacking.

The way for the rapid and successful development of the
Soviet war industry was prepared by the Lenin-Stalin policy

of industrialization, by the growth and the planned distribution of the productive forces of the country.

It was the result of the mighty power of foresight possessed by the Communist Party, and by the great Stalin.

* * *

The bloody war with German fascism, followed by the war with Germany's accomplice, imperialist Japan, lasted four years.

During the years of peaceful construction, the Soviet Government and the Bolshevik Party had converted our country into a mighty socialist power. Our country withstood a blow that old Russia could not have withstood. Not only did it withstand the blow, but it retaliated with one even more powerful, a blow that was decisive in defeating the fascist invaders.

This time, too, the Bolsheviks saved our country.

The Soviet people defeated the aggressor and were able to return to their peaceful, creative labours. The country began to heal the wounds that had been inflicted upon it by the war. With redoubled energy the people set to work to carry out their historic task of building communist society. Again they set to work to overtake and surpass the leading capitalist countries in output per head of the population.

In the speech he delivered to his electors on February 9, 1946, the great Stalin outlined the path to be followed by the Soviet Union during the ensuing five-year periods. He said that the Communist Party intended to organize a new, tremendous spurt in the national economy that would enable us to raise our country's industrial level about threefold compared with the prewar level. This, he said, would take three new five-year plans, if not more.

Our first postwar five-year plan, the plan for the rehabilitation and development of the national economy of the U.S.S.R. during 1946-1950, was drawn up on the lines indi-

A product of the Kirov Elektrosila Plant, Leningrad

Self-propelled combine harvester. Lenin Harvester Machinery
Plant, Zlatoust, R.S.F.S.R.

Blooming mill at the Novo-Tagil Steel Mills, the Urals

cated by our leader. This magnificent plan set the country the task not only of reaching the prewar economic level in the course of five years, but also of greatly exceeding it. By the end of the five-year plan period, our industry will produce almost fifty per cent more than it produced before the war.

The thirtieth anniversary of the inception of the Soviet government found our people hard at work, and, stinting no effort, they are working now with the greatest enthusiasm to carry out the Stalin plan.

The postwar five-year plan presents a geographic picture all of its own. It possesses distinguishing features which give the map of construction a special character. This is: the necessity of rebuilding the regions devastated by the enemy. Not only are the eastern regions making further progress, but the western regions are being resurrected.

The enemy left a trail of monstrous destruction. He laid waste a territory with a population of 88,000,000—almost half the population of the country.

Byelorussia lost about half of her national wealth. A third of the population of the Ukraine were left homeless. One thousand seven hundred and ten towns were reduced to heaps of ruins; in Sevastopol only three out of every hundred buildings remained standing. . . .

The direct damage to our national wealth caused by Nazi destruction has been estimated at 679,000 million rubles!

The scene that confronted our eyes when the war ended was: new factories, new railways, new industrial centres in the East, and villages wiped off the face of the earth, cities destroyed, in the West. In the East we saw the first open-hearth furnaces in the Kazakh Steppes, a tractor works in the foothills of the Altai Mountains, the Syr Darya harnessed and the Farkhad Power Station rising on its banks, the dams of the first hydroelectric power station on the rivers of the Urals. In the West we saw—the rapids of the Dnieper again laid bare, piles of rubble on Kreshchatik (the main street of

Kiev), the dry reservoirs on the White Sea-Baltic Canal looking like empty eye sockets.

The Soviet people began to restore the economy of the western regions even before the war had ended. As the Soviet Army drove out the enemy, workers followed on the heels of the soldiers. They pumped the water out of the flooded mines, raised blast furnaces that had been dislodged, built bridges and houses, set the factories going again. Labour, persevering labour, was again in full swing.

Gradually the economy of the western regions regained the features it had lost during the occupation. Again the Donets Basin has taken the lead in the country's coal output, Stalingrad is turning out tractors again and flax is planted outside of Pskov again.

The restoration of the western regions got into its full stride when the postwar five-year plan was adopted. Building is in full swing in the places the enemy had occupied. The accomplishment of a great task is under way—the Donets Basin, which the enemy had wrecked and ruined, must not only reach but exceed prewar output in the course of these five years. The industries of Estonia must rise to three times their prewar level.... Our courageous western regions, with the help of the entire Soviet Union, are rising out of the ashes, and this too is reflected on the map—in the conventional signs for rebuilt factories, mines and power stations.

Extensive building is also under way in the eastern regions. The Soviet East is continuing its swift forward drive. In the depths of the country, on the Volga, in the Ural Mountains and beyond, new factories, towns and railways are coming into being.

The capital investments which the postwar five-year plan allots to the national economy of the U.S.S.R. are divided into two almost equal parts—about 115,000 million rubles for the restoration of the war-devastated West, and about 135,000 million rubles for the development of the other regions that did not suffer war damage, especially Siberia and the Far East.

In the course of these five years, about 5,900 large plants will be rebuilt, or newly built; of these, over half have been allocated to the regions that were devastated by the enemy.

Further progress in the East, coupled with the restoration and further development of the West—this is what the economic geography of the postwar five-year plan tells us.

NEW RELATIONS

Our motherland is the Soviet Union. Soviet people are equally at home in the Crimea and in the Urals. The geographical fabric of the country is all one piece, but we divide it into sections, in each of which the threads, historical, economic and natural, are joined together to form a specific pattern. The Crimea is unlike the Urals, and the face of Tatary differs from that of Kirghizia.

The parts of this huge, single piece are linked together, but relations between them are gradually changing. Our new, postwar five-year plan is introducing new features into these inter-regional relations.

One region is rich in one thing, another is rich in another; they help each other, and the country progresses.... Did such mutual assistance exist before the revolution? The Donets coal owners provided Moscow with fuel, but with the aid of artificially lowered railway tariffs they killed all activity in the Moscow Coal Basin. The factory owners of the Centre sold their fabrics in the Transcaucasus and stifled the local industries there. The Volga merchants sold grain in Central Asia and collected tribute from the people there.

Now that capitalism is no more, the relations between the regions have changed. All parts of the country have merged in a single planned movement. Antagonism and competition have given way to friendship and cooperation. The new economic relations are not based on private profit, but on the common good—the interest of the state as a whole, the development

7*

of the forces of the people, the enhancement of the might of our socialist motherland.

During the period of the Stalin five-year plans, the Krasny Putilovets Plant in Leningrad sent tractors to the Volga Basin. Iron and steel workers from the Donets Basin blew in the first furnaces in Siberia. The socialist plan boldly turned the people's energies to the almost undeveloped regions beyond the Volga and beyond the Urals, where they built up a big industrial region, a reliable basis for defence. The Central regions developed themselves and helped the younger regions of the North, East and South to develop.

The Centre is helping other regions today, in the fulfilment of the postwar five-year plan. Moscow and Gorky are helping Novosibirsk to produce automobiles. Chemists from the Centre are helping to organize the production of synthetic liquid fuels in Eastern Siberia, artificial fibres in the Altais, etc.

But there are some new features in this general movement. And their appearance shows how far we have progressed.

The old regions helped the new. Today, the new regions have become so strong that in some cases they can already help the old regions.

Could former "Asiatic" Siberia, say, have helped the industries of "European" St. Petersburg? Of course not! One could not conceive of such a thing. But in our times, the western parts of the country suffered from the war—they were ruined and plundered by the Nazis. And so we see a "reverse motion" in the operation of mutual aid. Children do not forget their parents, and when they grow up they repay them the good they had done them. Magnitogorsk, built in the bare steppes beyond the Urals, now sends a large part of its steel to the West. The new Ural Turbine Plant is producing machinery for the Donets Basin power stations. The fields of the Ukraine became overgrown with weeds under the Germans; their former fertility is now being restored, and fertilizers from the East as well as those produced locally are helping to do this. New factories in the former backwoods—in Biisk and Barnaul—are sending machines to the European parts of the Soviet Union. The iron and steel mills of the East have "adopted" similar mills in the Ukraine that are being reconstructed after the war. Until the West has fully recovered, the now developed East, together with the Centre, will help the West in the way of equipment, materials and contingents of specialists. The general progress in the East has been enriched by ties that were inconceivable in former times.

The "exchange" between regions not only follows new directions, it often also possesses a new quality. Regions that formerly only took, are now able to give. Not very long ago, for example, students were taught: "The Volga Basin has no fuel resources of its own, it obtains fuel from other regions." Today, in the period of the postwar five-year plan, gas, rich in calories, is pumped to Moscow through pipes from Saratov on the Volga. There are oil derricks on the banks of the Volga: by the end of the postwar five-year plan period, the production of oil in the Volga Basin will have increased to eleven times the prewar figure. Not very long ago the Volga served only as a waterway for Caucasian oil, today oil is extracted in the valley of that river. The Volga now plays a new role in the "exchange" between regions.

Before the war some of the rolling mills that turned out special shapes were irrationally located: sometimes steels of a particular shape were shipped from the Urals to the Ukraine, while others were sent from the Ukraine to the Urals. The postwar five-year plan aims at reducing this dependence of one region on another; the growing iron and steel industry of the East and the rebuilt industries of the South are both organizing the production of steel of all possible shapes.

In many cases the "distances" of inter-regional cooperation have been reduced. At one time the Transbaikal region had to wait for equipment from the distant Centre; today there are developed engineering industries one-third of the distance aways—in Western Siberia. During the war, the industries of Novosibirsk increased tenfold. The soils of Central Asia need phosphates; this used to be shipped from distant regions. In the course of the present five-year plan, South Kazakhstan is providing a nearer source of phosphates for Central Asia—the Kara Tau mines.

Under Soviet government regions are being economically "coupled": iron ore goes from the Urals to the Kuznetsk Basin and Kuznetsk coking coal goes to the Urals; cotton goes to Siberia from Central Asia over the Turksib Railway, and the same railway carries coal, timber and grain to Central Asia. New "couples" of this sort are now being organized. Soon, the iron ore of the Kola Peninsula will join up with the coal of Pechora to provide steel for Leningrad and thus take the place of that now brought from afar. Later on, Pechora will stretch out a helping hand to the Urals too.

The map tells us that the various regions of the Soviet Union are beginning to stand on their own feet and at the same time are helping each other in a coordinated way.

In the same way as a chemist in his laboratory makes compounds of constituents of a definite weight, in the same way as a musical chord is built up from a number of proportionate sounds, so the economy of the Soviet Union, and of each of its regions, is being built up by "weight and measure"; a single plan unites electricity and bread, shoes and metal. But the proper correlation does not come about of its own accord—it is created by constructive effort, by struggle, by the labour of the people.

In the period of the Stalin postwar five-year plan the Ural region is not only building machines, but is equipping them with the most intricate measuring instruments that formerly came only from the Centre. Turkmenia is not only pumping oil out of the desert sands, but is also turning it into petrol in its own cracking plants. The Baku oil fields will have pipes and tubing made on the spot, instead of using those produced in other regions. The Ural region will manufacture its own textiles. The Far East will produce its own pig iron.

Industry is continuing its steady approach to the sources of its raw materials and consumption. Every economic zone, every one of the constituent republics of the Union, is undergoing an all-round development.

In the same period the industries of the war-ravaged regions are being restored. But how are they being restored? Before the war the Ukraine obtained its automobiles from other parts of the country: now it will make its own; the buildings of the first Ukrainian automobile plant are already rising up on the banks of the Dnieper. The region on the right bank of the Dnieper was formerly supplied with coal from the Donets Basin; now it will burn its own coal in its boilers, for many new pits are being sunk to the west of the Dnieper. The big city of Lvov did not formerly have any big industries of its own: this five-year plan is providing Lvov with a large number of new factories which will make it an important industrial centre. The industries of the Soviet Baltic Republics are not only being restored, but are changing their structure: an up-to-date heavy industry is growing up in these regions in addition to the old light industries. In rebuilding we are correcting the economic geography of the past.

The historical development of Russia was such that the industrial nucleus of the country developed in a region that had no first-class mineral or power resources. The Centre is now obtaining its own power supplies in the form of local peat, lignite and hydroelectric power. In addition to this, the Centre has to draw on the power resources of the outlying regions. Life-giving rays converge from all directions on the centre of the country, on Moscow, its capital, like the spokes of a wheel centring on the hub. Before the war the Moscow-Donets Railway was built, a broad highway for the transport of coal. Then electric power pylons stretched towards Moscow from the Volga, bringing current from the hydroelectric power stations. Railway lines connect the Centre with the coal in the Far North, at Vorkuta. A gas pipe line connects Moscow with the middle reaches of the Volga. In the North, on the Volga and in the Donets Basin, local industries are growing up; but they share their power resources with the Centre, from which they, in turn, receive considerable help. The number of spokes in the wheel is growing, the wheel is becoming stronger, and it is turning faster and faster....

THE STORY OF THE DONETS BASIN

The black strata that lie underground, the trees of primordial forests processed and compressed by time, contain a vast amount of energy acquired from the sun. Man cut through the various strata of the earth with the steel blades of his tools, raised the coal out of the depths with his machines and flung it into his furnaces so that electric current might run along wires, that metal might be smelted, houses heated and trains moved.

In our country, coal constitutes almost three-fourths of the combustible fuel consumed.

Our country was also rich in coal before the revolution. But year after year Russia was tormented by coal hunger— the "chronic fuel deficit" as it used to be called. Although some of the fine Donets anthracite was sold abroad, a far larger quantity of coal was imported. The St. Petersburg factories used British coal brought by sea from Cardiff and Newcastle. If this connection were broken, if the supply of foreign coal were to cease, Russia's biggest industrial centre would have lost its prop. This is what happened during the First World War, when the Germans closed the Baltic. It was not easy to change over immediately to home-produced coal from the Donets Basin—the railways connecting St. Petersburg with the South were not prepared for such an operation.

And besides, the Donets Basin could not produce very much coal in pre-revolutionary days; it produced no more than 25,000,000 tons a year. The pits were dark, and dust and gas laden—sheer "rattraps." The coal was dug with a pick, human muscle versus the hard coal face, and the coal was brought to the pit mouth by ponies.

Nevertheless, judged by old Russian standards, the Donets Basin was a big industrial centre. It was the chief, in fact, the only coal-producing region of the country. The Donets Basin was a giant on the coal map for the simple reason that the map was almost blank: in 1913 the Donets Basin produced eighty-seven per cent of Russia's coal, the other coal fields providing only thirteen per cent.

Thirteen per cent for the whole remaining part of the country! The Moscow Coal Basin was almost strangled by the competition of the Donets coal field. The coal fields of the East were lifeless, they were simply not known. In a few places —the Kuznetsk Basin, Kizel, Cheremkhovo and Suchan— coal was mined for railway engines and steamships.

Three decades have passed since then. Everything has changed.

The colliery has become a huge plant: a whole township of surface buildings, steel derricks at the pithead, a wide shaft and high galleries. The coal veins are cut by machines whose teeth dig into the "black gold." Pneumatic drills, drumming merrily, bite into the coal face. Electric locomotives pull trainloads of coal along wide galleries. There are pits in the Soviet Union that produce a million tons of coal a year—a ton of coal every twenty seconds.

In the last year of the present five-year plan, the country will produce at the rate of 250,000,000 tons of coal per annum. This is equal to ten pre-revolutionary Donets Basins!

It is difficult to draw a comparison between the Soviet Donets Basin and the coal field of former days. It presents a striking picture of the technical progress we have made and of the tremendous change that has taken place in the life of the workers. No wonder the Donets Basin was the home of the Stakhanov movement.

On the eve of the Great Patriotic War, the Donets Basin was one of the biggest industrial centres in the world. The industrial fabric here was very closely woven. The pits lay close together and the slag heaps rose up like a range of conical hills. Alongside towered the giant blast furnaces with the huge containers of their gas chambers. Here also towered, like a giant palisade, the chimneys of the open-hearth furnaces, backed by whole cities of engineering and chemical plants and workshops. Salt and mercury mines, limestone and sandstone quarries completed the industrial picture. The whole country was dotted with human habitations, sometimes big cities, sometimes small settlements with little white houses enlivened by greenery that has but recently appeared in these parts. In these towns and settlements only the people connected with coal numbered over a million. The Donets Basin was covered with an electric power transmission grid and by a network of rails carrying trains loaded with coal, metal, machines and oil. One heard the rattle of winding gears, the clang of metal, the whistle of steam and the clatter of moving trains.

The fascist barbarians laid their hands on this wealth. The Nazis flooded the mines, blew up the blast furnaces, set fire to the houses. They hoped to put the Donets Basin out of action for decades.

In 1949, our Soviet people will have fully restored the Donets Basin and will have equipped it with still more perfect machinery.

The rehabilitation of the war-ravaged Donets Basin is a battle, it is a feat of heroism, it is a peacetime Stalingrad. The country has struck a special medal in honour of those taking part in this gigantic battle. A great deal depends on victory in the Donets Basin: our growth would be difficult without it.

The rehabilitation of the Donets Basin means pumping out 650,000,000 cubic metres of water, which is the equivalent of pumping dry a lake with a surface area of sixty-five square kilometres and a depth of ten metres.

The rehabilitation of the Donets Basin means rebuilding 2,500 kilometres of collapsed underground workings, which is the equivalent of digging a tunnel across Europe from Moscow to the English Channel.

The battle for coal is at its height. The miner's weapon is not the rifle, but the pneumatic drill. The soldier in this army drives a powerful pump instead of a tank. He does not hurl grenades, he lays bricks. Nevertheless, it is a battle, with all its self-sacrifice and complete devotion to the great common cause.

In the Stalino Region, only twelve pits out of a total of 152 were left intact by the Nazis. In the first period after liberation, September 1943, these pits produced scarcely one-half per cent of the prewar output of the region. Three months later the Stalino Region was producing ten per cent of the prewar coal output; in six months—seventeen per cent; in a year—twenty-five per cent. On the fourth anniversary of its liberation, two-thirds of the Stalino pits had been fully restored.

There is still much left to be done. A long and arduous path has to be traversed to raise the Donets Basin above the prewar level by the end of the five-year plan period.

Not only was the face of the Donets Basin changed during the period of the Stalin five-year plans, the part it played in the country's economy changed also. Its importance was enhanced. It not only supplied coal to the South and the Centre, but also to Leningrad, which no longer imported British coal, and to the new industries of the North Caucasus, the Crimea and the Volga region. And yet, its share in the country's coal output diminished: before the First World War the Donets Basin supplied 87 per cent of Russia's coal; before the Great Patriotic War it supplied only 57 per cent.

These two figures, 87 and 57, briefly sum up the change in the economic geography of the Soviet Union. They tell us that the old region grew rapidly, but the new regions grew still more rapidly. They tell us that a new industry had appeared in the East and had called new coal fields into being.

Stalin said: "Convert the Kuzbas into a second Donbas"
—and it was done.

The entire output of the pre-revolutionary Kuznetsk mines
was carried in the tenders of the Siberian locomotives. The
wealth of the field was only scratched. The ruling classes of
old Russia lacked the strength to breathe life into a coal
field that for size and the quality of its coal is without equal
in the world. Kuznetsk contains two and a half times as
much coal as Great Britain, which was once called the "world's
stokehole." The Kuznetsk coal lies near the surface and can be
cheaply mined. The coal can be used for heating, for smelting,
and for the chemical industry. Some of the veins have a thick-
ness equal to the height of a five-storey building. The problem
to be solved was—how should the galleries be driven through
this mass of coal?

Thirty years ago the Kuznetsk workers asked for an electric power station to be sent them from Moscow. At that
time the only installation that could be supplied them was
a dynamo taken from the Maly Theatre. Today, the Kuznetsk
Basin produces more coal than the whole of tsarist Russia
produced. The technical equipment of the mines is on an even
higher level than that of the Donets mines in the prewar
years; almost all the pits have been sunk in Soviet times, and
they are equipped with the most modern machinery, from
electric drills to tunnelling shields of a type invented there,
in the Kuznetsk Basin itself.

Coke, steel, nitrates, machines.... The greatest importance
of Kuznetsk, however, does not lie in the number of coal-cutting
machines employed, or the number of tons produced. The
Stalin Mine at Prokopievsk has produced four Stalin Prize
winners.

When the Donets Basin was put out of action during the
war, the Kuznetsk mines worked at terrific tension. In those
difficult war years the output of the Kuznetsk mines increased by more than a third.

In Karaganda we inherited two minor pits from pre-revolutionary times; one had been blown up and the other flooded.... During the period of the First Five-Year Plan, trainloads of equipment arrived in Karaganda from the Donets Basin, and Donets technicians arrived with them. At the same time, Kazakhs went to the Donets Basin to learn how to mine coal. In this way a new region was born with the help of an old one. Russians and Ukrainians helped the Kazakhs. Karaganda has become the third largest Soviet coal field.

Kuznetsk and Karaganda dealt the decisive blow to the old, distorted and lopsided coal geography. They provided the industries of the East with a powerful springboard for a new forward leap. They created a firm foundation for the progress of the industries in the East.

Industry, however, did not grow in the East alone—it grew also in the North of the European part of the U.S.S.R. Coal was necessary for the factories and ships of Archangel and Murmansk, for Kotlas and, most important of all, for Leningrad, which, after ceasing to import coal from abroad, was using coal brought all the way from the Donets Basin. The Donets Basin had customers enough without Leningrad. And so, on the instructions of Stalin, a new coal centre was opened up in the North, the Pechora coal field.

This new coal-producing centre was only just being born when the war began. But the war did not hinder its development; on the contrary, the war accelerated it. Remoteness, the wilderness, the cold, the raids by German paratroops on the lines of communication, hampered, but were powerless to prevent it.

With a single mighty drive Soviet people opened up the roadless taiga and the swampy tundra, and straight, like a spear, through the dense forest and across rivers, they drove the steel rails of a road right to the Arctic Circle. The first train arrived at Vorkuta at the end of 1941.

More and more new pits were sunk. A heat and power station was erected, and a whole town was built.

The mines are sunk in permafrost, the permanently frozen soil that is as hard as iron. The entire journey the coal makes from the coal face to the dump at the railway is along heated galleries. When concrete is laid it is heated by electricity.

Compensating for the lost Donets Basin, Vorkuta began to send coal southwards. Leningrad, held tight in the grip of the blockade, was heated by this coal from the frozen north.

The mines to be sunk in the Pechora Basin during the postwar five-year plan period will have a capacity equal to one-fourth of that of all the mines of pre-revolutionary Russia.

The Donets Basin, the Kuznetsk Basin, Karaganda and Pechora send out trainloads of coal for hundreds, even thousands of kilometres. This is a necessity, but it overloads the railways.

Coal must be found and mined in the locality where it is needed. If the local coal cannot serve as a substitute for Donets or Kuznetsk coke for blast furnaces, then let it be used for fuel. Both Lenin and Stalin called for increased production of local coal.

The reduction of the Donets Basin's share of the total coal output of the country from 87 per cent to 57 per cent was due to the growth of the output not only of the other two coal fields of national importance—Kuznetsk Basin and Karaganda—but also of that of the smaller coal fields scattered throughout the country.

Although local coal is not yet being mined to the extent required, there is now scarcely a region where coal mines have not been opened, or new ones added to the old.

The Urals are producing their own coal in ever increasing quantities. Old Kizel, where, according to the latest assumptions, there is both coal and oil, is being rejuvenated and mines are being sunk in the surrounding coal fields of Usva and Gremyachaya. In Chelyabinsk, new surface coal seams are being opened and worked with the aid of powerful excavators. New workings are constantly being opened: yesterday, the Volchanka field in the North was opened; today, the Kuyurgaz mines are being developed in the South.... If we measure this development in terms of pre-revolutionary Donets Basins, then by the end of the present five-year plan period, the Urals will have its own "Donets Basin."

It is the same everywhere. Tashkent has created its own "stokehole" in Angren. Georgia is developing Tkvarcheli and Tkibuli. Bukachacha, Raichikhinsk and Artyom have sprung up along the Great Siberian Railway.... As a result of the operation of the postwar five-year plan the Bureya coal field in the Far East, the Ekibastuz coal field in Kazakhstan, the Uzgen coal field in Kirghizia and the Kugitang coal field in Turkmenia will appear on the coal industry map.

The largest of the local coal fields is the Moscow coal field. This is the "local" coal field for the Centre; but the "locality" it serves is so highly industrialized that the importance of Moscow coal is enormous.

Moscow coal is of a low grade. It has a large ash content and its caloricity is relatively low. But it does not have to be transported far. It has in its vicinity big consumers such as the electric power stations controlled by the Moscow Power Supply Board (Mosenergo) and the industrial plants in Moscow, Tula, Podolsk and Noginsk.

The growth of the Moscow coal field is astonishing. Before the revolution it scarcely produced in a year what the Donets Basin produced in four days. By the end of the postwar five-year plan period it will be the "Moscow Donets Basin."

In this same period the Donets Basin will reach, and even exceed, its prewar level. And yet, its share of the total coal output will be not 87 per cent as it was before the revolution, and not 57 per cent as it was before the war, but less.

This shows that new coal centres—sons of the Donets Basin—are springing up and developing in the country. The geography of coal is continuing to even out.

THE FUEL OF THE CAPITALS

The more evenly the fuel bases are distributed over the country, the less is the expenditure on transportation. But it is not so easy to distribute the fuel industry evenly—there are parts of the country where no coal or lignite can be found, no matter how hard one may search for it. To some extent peat can be used instead of coal, but even peat cannot be found everywhere.

New factories can be built in the vicinity of fuel bases; but whole industrial regions already exist, and these cannot be shifted. There are industrial regions for which the local fuel resources are inadequate, and so, endless trains loaded with fuel go there from distant regions. Foremost amongst these are Moscow, Leningrad and Kiev—which consume huge quantities of coal and wood fuel.

What kind of fuel is most easily transported to these cities?

Coal is bulky. It does not pay to transport low-calory peat over long distances. Wood is the fuel of the past. . . .

To supply big cities situated at long distances from the coal fields, a fuel had to be found that generates considerable heat, is convenient to handle, is cheap and easily transported.

Of all fuels gas has the highest caloricity, it is the most convenient, the cheapest and most easily transportable. And from now on the big cities of Moscow, Leningrad and Kiev will have abundant supplies of natural gas.

The search for gas at Yelshanka, near Saratov, was begun before the war. When the war broke out the drillers went into the army. But the work they had started was not abandoned. It was continued by youths and older men, and also by women. The drills reached the gas deposits and light blue fountains shot up on the banks of the Volga as high as a twenty-storey building. Columns of almost pure methane came hissing and roaring out of the ground, forced upward by a pressure of about

80 atmospheres, hurling boulders into the air and at times tearing out the tubing sunk by the drillers.

During the battle of Stalingrad, when both Donets coal and Caucasian oil were cut off from the Volga, gas from Yelshanka was piped to the factory boilers in Saratov. Then a gas pipe line was laid from Buguruslan to Kuibyshev. In two years these towns saved millions of tons of coal.

At the end of 1944, on Comrade Stalin's proposal, it was decided to build a gas pipe line from Saratov to Moscow. In the night of July 10, 1946, Moscow received its first cubic metre of gas from Saratov.

The metal pipe, welded out of 100,000 sections, runs under the ground for a distance of 843 kilometres. It crosses a hundred rivers, and runs under roads, forests and swamps. Compressor stations pump the gas to Moscow. Freight of this kind needs no cars, flatcars, or cisterns.

The artery divides up into capillaries and the gas reaches boiler rooms and kitchens. During the period of the first postwar five-year plan, 200,000 Moscow flats will be fitted out with gas.

* * *

There is an abundance of natural gas in the foothills of the Carpathians. From there, starting at Dashava, a pipe line is being laid to Kiev, capital of the Ukraine.

Natural gas is already being used for heating purposes in Lvov, Baku, Andizhan. The extraction of gas has also begun in the Urals.

Nature, however, has not provided this cheap and convenient fuel for every city. In places where there is no natural gas we have to find sources from which to make artificial gas.

Leningrad is still farther away from coal than Moscow. It, too, needs gas, but no natural gas has yet been found in its vicinity. Not far from the city, however, there are deposits of combustible shale which will provide Leningrad with gas.

The combustible shale lies along the southern coast of the Gulf of Finland, partly in the Estonian Republic and partly in the Leningrad Region. The postwar five-year plan provides for the building of three big plants at Kohtlajärvi, Ahtma and Slantsy to produce inflammable gas from the shale and to use the residue—shale tar—for the production of petrol, kerosene and bitumen. The gas will be piped over a line about 250 kilometres long to Leningrad, where it will be collected in huge gasometers for distribution to homes.

Gas has never before been produced from shale anywhere in the world.

Better known is the production of gas from coal.

A plant is now being built at Tula to produce gas from the Moscow coal. This gas will supplement the Saratov natural gas for Moscow's gas supply.

But coal can be converted into gas under the ground as well as at gas works. The idea of underground gasification is an old one, and priority in this field belongs to Russia. Underground gasification was first suggested by the great Russian chemist Mendeleyev.

Lenin made note of this idea and expected a lot from it. Not only does this method of producing gas save the expenditure entailed in sinking mines; the most important thing is that people will be relieved of arduous work underground.

Under capitalism, the introduction of this improved method would only serve to increase unemployment and poverty among the working people. Under Socialism, the underground gasification of coal will increase the productivity of social labour for the benefit of the whole people.

The idea was first propounded in our country, and the first steps towards its practical achievement were also taken in our country. But before this wonderful scientific idea could be put into effect, the country had to change. It was only under the Soviet government that the first experiments were made at converting coal into gas under the ground; this experiment is already becoming a branch of industry.

In capitalist countries underground gasification has not been introduced to this day. It does not pay the coal owners to change over to new methods of using the coal—it threatens to depreciate the capital they have invested in the mines. In the capitalist world questions of technical progress are subordinated to the selfish interests of the capitalists.

The underground gasification station in the Moscow coal field already has two generators going. The coal is ignited from the surface by means of a special device and the gas is piped to the Tula factories.

The Soviet people are building up a new economy and in doing so are "discovering" a new nature. They are finding treasures in places where their presence was never before suspected.

Step by step, Soviet power production is becoming technically more perfect.

HIGH VOLTAGE

Gas, convenient and easily transportable over long distances, is helping to change the economic map of our country. Industrial centres located far from the coal basins are beginning to find this remoteness less burdensome.

There is, however, one other form of power which is still more convenient, more portable and more universal, viz., electricity.

It was not the rotor of the electric motor but the piston of the steam engine that provided motive power for the majority of the factories of tsarist Russia. The towns, except the very biggest, were lit by kerosene and not by electricity. Power stations were rare, and of small capacity.

Socialist economy cannot be built up on the energy generated by human muscles or steam engines, the energy of past ages. A growing country needs electric current that is easily transported over long distances, is economical and powerful.

8*

Only large-scale production could serve as the foundation on which the new, socialist society could be built. And only electricity made it possible to convert the economy of backward Russia into the sound technical foundation of large-scale production. Lenin said: "Communism is Soviet government plus the electrification of the whole country."

Kolchak, Denikin and Yudenich had been defeated but the Civil War was not over. The factories were at a standstill. The doors of boiler fireboxes stood open, machines were rusting. Trains scarcely moved; the engines bore huge, barrel-shaped smokestacks that belched showers of sparks. The Moscow streets looked like narrow paths between mountains of snow....

In those days of ruination, and in spite of the opposition of Trotsky and Rykov, the plan for the electrification of Russia was worked out under Lenin's guidance. Our great teacher told his colleagues: "... We must inspire *the masses* of workers and politically conscious peasants by a *great* program for ten-twenty years."

The State Plan for the Electrification of Russia, GOELRO, as it was called, was compiled and adopted; it provided for the construction of thirty big power stations in the course of ten-fifteen years. Concerning this magnificent plan Comrade Stalin said: "It is a masterly draft for a really integral and really *state* economic plan in the *literal* sense of the word."

It was impossible to plan electrification without planning the industrial enterprises that were to use the current. Lenin's electrification plan, therefore, became the country's first extensive national economic plan. And that first plan already expressed the idea of a more rational, planned distribution of productive forces.

Outside observers, like the British writer H. G. Wells, called the authors of this plan "dreamers." Lenin and Stalin, however, were looking many years ahead. They not only saw the ring of battlefronts that had brought factories and trains to a standstill. They saw the future. They knew the strength of the people, the potency of the ideas of Socialism. In the fifteen years allotted, the Soviet people fulfilled the GOELRO Plan almost three times over.

A huge ·cube-shaped building with a battery of stumpy chimneys standing on the outskirts of the town soon became an integral part of every urban landscape. In many cases the stations not only provide power, but also heat for the cities; hot water is piped from the heat and power generating stations to the houses. In some places huge regional power stations have been built. Electric power lines cut across the country in all directions, from the main transmission lines carried on steel pylons posted at regular intervals through forest cuttings, to those carried by chains of wooden poles fitted with glass insulators.

By the end of the postwar five-year plan period the total capacity of all Soviet power stations will reach 22,400,000 kilowatts. This is thirteen times the capacity of what was planned by GOELRO!

Our country is rapidly becoming electrified, and this is possible because it is a Soviet country.

In capitalist countries the production and distribution of electric power are in the hands of private capitalists or capitalist monopolies. There is no thought of public service, the only motive is profit.

In our socialist country all the power stations are the property of one owner, the state, the people, and all stations have been built for one purpose—to promote progress in the national economy.

In our socialist country there is no private ownership of land and of the means of production. Consequently, the socialist state can easily select the most suitable sites for the erection of power stations, and it can make the best use of natural power resources. The choice of sites is determined by the plan, and the plan serves the interests of the people. The people work for themselves and for this reason they work well.

ST. MARY'S COLLEGE LIBRARY CALIFORNIA

This explains why electrification has developed in our country faster than it has in any other.

The economic map of the Soviet Union is dotted with symbols indicating the presence of power stations.

Before the revolution, Russian power stations worked mostly on high-grade fuels—oil and coal. The furnaces ate up this valuable fuel that could have served as raw material for chemicals, or fuel for blast furnaces. The Baku power stations burned oil when they could easily have burned natural gas. Peat, lignite, and combustible shale lay untouched.

The fact that great treasures were committed to the flames was not the only trouble. The huge amount of oil and coal burned in the central regions had to be hauled over long distances: from the Caucasus and from the Donets Basin, places thousands of kilometres away.

Soviet power stations, especially the new ones, use cheap, local fuels. They are built wherever they are needed, in industrial regions, and as far as possible fuel is sought in their vicinity to avoid long-distance transportation. Stalinogorsk and Kashira stations near Moscow burn Moscow low-grade coal. The Chelyabinsk stations also burn locally-mined lignite. The Ivanovo, Balakhna and Shatura stations use peat from the nearby bogs, the Zuyevka and Shterovka stations use anthracite dust, and the Baku and Saratov stations burn gas.

Coking coal is reserved for the iron and steel industry, oil is refined into valuable oil products, and transportation is saved.

These low-grade local fuels, converted into electric power, facilitated the development of industries in regions where it would have been difficult for them to develop on the former technical level owing to the absence of high-grade fuels. Thus, electrification helps the state to distribute industries more rationally, to develop our productive forces more fully.

Electric power can easily be transmitted over scores, even hundreds of kilometres. An electric power station built near deposits of peat or lignite, becomes a power supply centre

ST. MARY'S
COLLEGE LIBRARY

for a large industrial region and not only for a particular plant.

In every large district there are, as a rule, several power stations. All are linked up in a single grid. Even power stations that supply power for a single plant—Magnitogorsk, for example—are linked up with the grid. In the event of a breakdown, or if the station is temporarily closed for repairs, the plant can be switched on to another station and continue to work; the stations hold each other tightly by the hand, like people dancing in a ring.

The grids cover enormous areas—the Moscow, Urals, and Kuznetsk Basin grids. Before the war, the Moscow grid contained twenty big power stations; these were situated in the capital itself and in the surrounding districts. In the capitalist countries, with their anarchy of production, it is difficult to create grids of this kind. In our country, however, not only are the power stations linked up into grids, but the grids themselves are being joined together. The Dnieper Grid has been joined to the Donets Basin Grid, making a system that covers almost half the Ukraine. If power runs down in the Donets Basin, current comes from the Dnieper power station; when the level of the Dnieper sinks in summer and the output of electric power declines, the Donets comes to the rescue.

The plan of the future is to build up a grid that will link up all the power stations in the country; the grids will form a single huge chain, and this chain will direct power resources into industry, no matter where these resources are located. The transportation of fuel will be reduced, the transmission of electric power will take its place. The single nationwide grid will supply abundant power to the whole country and ensure a more equal and rational distribution of the productive forces.

What prevents us from building such a single arterial system right now? There are no social obstacles to this, but technical obstacles do still exist: the distance over which power can be transmitted is still limited.

At the present time, long-distance transmission is effected

by means of alternating current which can travel up to about four hundred kilometres. Direct current could travel a thousand kilometres or more; we therefore have to learn to transmit high-voltage direct current over long distances. This is the task that has been set Soviet electrical engineers by the present five-year plan.

The problem of transmitting direct current has been taken up by the Academy of Sciences, a special research institute having been organized for the purpose. The Mosenergo has started on the construction of the first direct current generating installation.

When the new method of transmitting direct current has been perfected the question of the power grids will take on a new form. New industrial centres will be supplied with abundant power and new deposits of raw materials and fuel will be brought to light.

When the distance over which electricity can be transmitted has been increased, we shall be able still more radically to change the economic geography of our country that we inherited from the past.

HYDROELECTRIC POWER STATIONS

Electric power stations in the Soviet Union are being built to work on the cheapest fuels, materials that formerly were regarded as waste—lignite, peat and coal dust. They are also being built on rivers to use water power, the cheapest of all sources of energy.

It is not an easy matter to build a big hydroelectric power station. A huge dam has to be erected to create a waterhead or a derivation canal: the impounded water accumulates, the river "rises" until it reaches the predetermined height and then hurls itself down into its former bed, now far below.

It costs more to build a hydroelectric power station than a fuel-driven one. The initial cost, however, is soon more than repaid. A kilowatt hour—the equivalent of approximately three working days of one man—at a big hydroelectric power station costs a kopek or even a fraction of a kopek; at fuel-driven stations it costs ten kopeks, or more, owing to the outlay on fuel.

Great rivers flow across the Russian and Siberian plains in an irresistible torrent. Rivers race down from the mountains of the Caucasus and Central Asia with tremendous force, sweeping away rocks and dragging huge boulders along their beds. No country in the world is richer in water-power resources than ours. Old Russia, however, hardly knew what a hydroelectric power station was. The tremendous power of Russia's rivers was used only to turn the tiny water mills of the villages, to carry timber rafts, or to turn the heavy water wheels of the old Ural iron works.

The electrification of Russia was inspired by Lenin, and Lenin was the real creator of the first Soviet hydroelectric power station. The first power station, on the River Volkhov, was built on his instructions. The work was begun during the Civil War, in the period of economic ruin, a hard and hungry period in Soviet history. The whole country helped to build the station. Soviet people have a soft spot in their hearts for the Volkhov Power Station, as the first-born of Soviet electrification and also as a monument to Lenin, the embodiment of the teacher's idea. It has long been officially known as the Volkhov State Power Station, but the people still refer to it as "Volkhovstroi" ("Volkhov Project") as if in memory of its founder, Lenin.

The great significance of those early days was brought to mind with added force during the war, when the Volkhov Station, in the immediate vicinity of the front, never stopped work despite constant enemy air raids and ever-recurring fires. The station sent power, light and life to besieged Leningrad along a cable that was laid on the bed of Lake Ladoga in one night.

Dozens of hydroelectric power stations have been built in all parts of the country since the inception of Soviet government—in the extreme South, on the rivers Kura and

Rion, where it is so warm that the rivers never freeze, and in the extreme North, on the rivers Niva and the Tuloma, where the frozen ground blunted the workers' spades, where frost penetrated the concrete, and ground ice clung to the blades of the turbine rotors. They have been built on the Volga plains, at Ivankovo and Uglich, and in the canyons of the Pamirs at Khorog, where the rivers rush foaming over the rocks. Men have harnessed the Kivach waterfall. A tunnel was bored through a mountain to provide a waterhead for the hydroelectric power station at Kutaisi. A green depression in the mountains has been filled with the waters of the River Khrami; from this reservoir the water will be piped into the turbines from a height of five hundred metres.

All this was crowned by the construction of the Dnieper Power Station.

The course of the River Dnieper was broken by a rocky ridge through which it forced its way over surging rapids which cut the navigable river into two. Only experienced pilots could take these rapids in small, light boats.

During the period of the First Stalin Five-Year Plan the dam of the Lenin Power Station, a ribbed concrete arc, stemmed the waters of the Dnieper: the dam raised the level of the water by thirty-seven metres and formed an extensive lake which stretched as far as Zaporozhye and Dniepropetrovsk, a hundred kilometres up the river. The rapids lay well below the surface of the river. The Dnieper became a navigable river all along its course, intersected by a series of locks, a sort of river staircase. The biggest power station in Europe provided cheap current for the Dnieper Basin, Krivoi Rog and the Donets Basin.

Here, the Hitlerites destroyed everything they could. But in 1943, when the war was still at its height, Comrade Stalin issued instructions for work to be begun on the design for a new Dnieper Power Station. When the Germans were driven from the banks of the Dnieper, building operations were immediately started among the ruins.

The first of the new turbine generators—more powerful than the old—began producing current in the spring of 1947. The Dnieper Power Station is again on the active list—"the creation and the pride of our people," as Stalin called it.

With the reopening of the Dnieper Power Station our country reached its prewar level of electric power output.

When building a hydroelectric station, man encroaches so much upon nature that he transforms the whole surrounding countryside. A concrete or earth wall raises the water level, the river becomes navigable for big ships, and arid fields are irrigated. Power supply, transport, irrigation, fishing and a whole chain of industries connected with each other, grow at a more rapid rate.

Hydroelectric power stations are also built in capitalist countries, of course, and in some there are more than we yet have. But nowhere has the construction of power stations developed with such speed as it has in our country. We began late, but we are rapidly catching up; all the necessary conditions for this exist in the Land of Soviets. In the capitalist countries one riverbank is private property, the other bank is also private property, the shipping companies are private property, the irrigation canals are private property, and so is the fishing industry. It is impossible to combine all these private interests into one single whole.

There were numerous projects for building a power station on the Dnieper even in tsarist times; it was said that there were enough of these projects to fill a freight car. But it did not pay the owners of the land along the river to have their land flooded. Besides, the necessary capital for these schemes could not be found—the prospect of profit was too remote, there were no big customers for the electricity. The projects remained mere paper projects. The idea of building a power station on the Volkhov was also an old one, but the owners of the power stations in St. Petersburg would not allow it to be put into effect, they were afraid of competition.

Being complex enterprises of gigantic proportions, big hydraulic engineering projects have outgrown the framework of capitalist society.

In our socialist country, all branches of the national economy have been coordinated by one single plan. If a hydroelectric power station is being built in one region, the whole country rejoices because the interests of the Soviet people are one.

Hydroelectric power stations are being built at the drops in the level of the Nevinnomyssk Canal. This would seem to threaten heavy loss to the Oil Products Distribution Board (Neftesnab); where kerosene was formerly used, the people will use electric light. But nobody is disturbed by this. Neftesnab is not a private concern chasing after profits, but a state organization that serves the interests of the country and the people.

The dam of the power station on the River Svir raised the level of that rock-bound river and turned it into a deep navigable channel. The Kirov Railway lost some of its customers when freights began to go by water. Nobody even dreams of regretting this. The country, the state stands to gain: river transport is cheaper than railway transport.

The advantages of planned economy multiplied by the enthusiasm of the people who work for themselves and not for a capitalist enable our country to develop the construction of hydroelectric power stations at a speed never before known in the world.

Almost up to the end of the war the Ural region did not have a single hydroelectric power station. The Alapayevsk Station on the River Neyva began to function only in April 1945. By the end of the first postwar five-year plan period there will be six power stations in operation in the Urals.

Hydroelectric power stations are being built on many mountain rivers throughout the Urals. These include the giant Kama Station near the city of Molotov.

During the war six power stations were built in Uzbekistan, and during the present five-year plan period several more will be built with a total capacity of a quarter of a million kilowatts. Among them is the new Farkhad Hydroelectric Power Station on the rapids of the Syr Darya in the Mogol Tau Mountains, one of the biggest power stations in the U.S.S.R. It will provide power to melt the steel of Begovat and the zinc of Kara Mazar, and part of its output will be transmitted to Tashkent. The water used by the station will pass on to irrigate the dry expanses of the Hungry Steppe.

The legendary Princess Shirin, whose castle stood on the cliff overlooking this part of the river, promised her hand in marriage to the hero who would irrigate the desert. While the hero Farkhad was moving mountains and cleaving rocks to allow the water to run through, and to win the hand of his beloved, his crafty rival spread straw mats over the desert. These mats glistened in the sun, and the trickster claimed that it was water that was glistening. Shirin was deceived and gave herself to him, and the rejected Farkhad killed himself by throwing up his mattock and letting it fall on his head.

The evil forces of the past prevented the people from obtaining water, and the people's hero lost his lover and his life. This is the legendary image of a dream unfulfilled. The intuitive genius of the Uzbek people, the builders who are now making this dream come true, indicated the spot that would at some time become the heart of their country's power supply.

THE GREAT RIVER

We Russians love our glorious Mother Volga, but we cannot let her remain as she is.

The great river carries its waters quietly to the sea and in the meantime industries continue to spring up on its banks demanding ever increasing supplies of electric power. The Volga itself must provide this power.

The deep channels in the Volga are ruined by sandbanks and shallows. The snow does not last long in forests that have already grown thin, it thaws quickly and disappears swiftly in the form of extensive floods. In the summer the waters are never overabundant and they carry a very large amount of silt, which sinks to the river bed and, as a consequence, the navigable channel of the river constantly changes. This can be seen, for example, in Saratov: sometimes the Volga water winds far from the Saratov bank and at other times comes back again. The Volga must become a deepwater river.

The Volga cuts across an arid region. Along the banks of the river there are fields of waving corn seemingly trembling with fear lest the hot wind blow like the blast from an open furnace. Down below the water plashes against the banks, but not a single drop reaches the fields. The Volga must be made to irrigate the arid trans-Volga region.

The enormous task of reconstructing the Volga lies ahead. This great Russian river must be compelled to perform three tasks simultaneously: provide electric power, irrigate the arid fields, and remain constant throughout the navigation season. To carry out this triple task we must make a bold, planned and coordinated attack on huge expanses of territory—not merely from Kalinin to Astrakhan, but far beyond, as we shall see.

No other country can undertake such a task. But so colossal is this task that even we, with all the social advantages we possess over the capitalist countries, cannot accomplish it at one stroke.

We are tackling the task in stages, and sometimes we ourselves do not realize how far we have proceeded towards the goal.

A chain of power stations will be built on the Volga and its main tributaries, the Kama and the Oka. These power stations will provide a colossal amount of electric power, which will not only give rise to an industry in the Volga region many times bigger than that which exists at present, will not only pump Volga water into the irrigation canals of the trans-Volga region, but be transmitted over high-voltage lines to other industrial regions, to the Centre and the Urals.

Electric power will be distributed among the most important regions of the country.

In transmitting electric power along parallels of latitude —from the Volga to Moscow and the Urals—instead of along meridians of longitude, the cosmic factor will be taken into consideration. The greatest amount of electric power is required in the evenings. The time in Moscow and the Urals, over 1,500 kilometres apart, shows a difference of two hours. The evening "peak" first appears in the Urals. Two hours later it appears in Moscow. A single switchboard for the whole electric system will send power to the consumers at the times they need it. Extra power will first be transmitted to the Urals, and later to the central regions.

Dams on the river will impound the water and turn the Volga into a long chain of lake-reservoirs of great depth. The water used at one station will go to provide the waterhead for the next. Furthermore, the dams on the upper reaches will impound the spring flood waters and release them at periods of low water in the river. The spring flood waters will be caged and released so that the Volga will remain deep in summer as well.

All this is known as the Volga Reconstruction Project. A chain of hydroelectric power stations, a gigantic centre of electric power, irrigated farming that will never know a crop failure, a deep navigation channel.... On the whole, however, this is work for the future.

But this future may not be so very far away. The offensive has begun, and Bolsheviks advance quickly.

The offensive began on the upper reaches. It began there not only because the Volga is narrower and it is easier to build power stations there, but because the stations in the upper reaches are intended to facilitate the work of the stations in the lower reaches. The stations on the upper reaches will hold back the spring waters and, by releasing them gradually, will regulate the flow of water along the whole course. The upper stations will, as it were, add summer "doses" to the water in the lower reaches and thus keep the lower stations supplied.

During the Second Five-Year Plan period, a comparatively small hydroelectric power station was built at Ivankovo; here the Moscow Canal begins.

Just before the Great Patriotic War, a bigger station was built at Uglich.

In November 1941, the power station at Shcherbakov, formerly Rybinsk, was started. Leaving out the Dnieper Power Station, which has not yet been restored to full capacity, the Shcherbakov Station is the biggest in the U.S.S.R. It uses turbines with rotors nine metres in diameter.

The postwar five-year plan provides for the erection of big hydroelectric power stations to be built at Gorky on the Volga, at Kaluga on the Oka, and at Molotov on the Kama. Later, the campaign to subdue the Volga will be carried lower down the river.

But the water regime of the Volga has already changed, particularly since the Shcherbakov Station was built.

This change manifests itself primarily in formation of the lake known as the "Rybinsk Sea."

The hydro-engineering works at Shcherbakov checked the flow of the Volga and the Sheksna. The low-lying land between the Sheksna and the Mologa rivers was flooded to form a huge lake, so wide that, when sailing down the middle of it, the shores are invisible. Fishermen on the lake use seagoing motorboats. During stormy weather the waves on Rybinsk Sea rise two and a half metres high.

The Rybinsk Sea, a man-made, artificial lake, is half the size of Lake Onega, the second largest in Europe.

Before the land that was to form the bed of the Rybinsk Sea was flooded, all the forests were felled and the valuable buildings were dismantled. Over six hundred villages and six towns, including the town of Mologa, were shifted to other areas. When the gap in the dam was closed, all that was left was covered by water.

Vesiegonsk and Poshekhonye-Volodarsk became "seaports," regular ports of call for shipping. In the North, the water reached as far as Cherepovets on the Leningrad-Vologda Railway, so that Cherepovets has become a sort of Volga outpost for Leningrad.

The whole surrounding country has changed. A clean sandy beach at the foot of the sloping shore, a tree that has fallen into the river, but is still clinging to the land with its roots, a moss-covered pine stands up to its waist in the water.... The hills have become islands from which the local inhabitants have rescued all the elk. Yellow water lilies bloom where formerly daisies used to grow. Sometimes a solid mass of peat breaks away from the bed and moves across the "sea" like a floating island, complete with grass, saplings and tree stumps. Collective farmers plough their fields along the shores of "Rybinsk Sea" but instead of rooks, sea gulls now follow the ploughs.

But the appearance of this "sea" is not the only change. The change is felt far afield. The "doses" of water from the Shcherbakov Power Dam affect the water level as far as mouth of the Kama, and in periods of low water, even farther.

Somewhere near Ulyanovsk waves splash against the sandy bank—they were not there yesterday; a steamer passes over the sand ridge without scraping its bottom—this shows that the sluice gates of the Shcherbakov Dam a thousand kilometres upstream have been raised.

Shcherbakov thinks about Ulyanovsk: this is evidence of the unity of the country, which is living in a single economy, directed by a single, wise will.

CASCADE

A whole chain of power stations can be built on a river. Its course is converted into a sort of staircase by means of dams and locks. The water is harnessed to turn the turbines of the upper station, it pours out to freedom again, gains impetus in its downward rush, is again harnessed, again allowed to run free and still again forced through a turbine. This is called a cascade. Such a cascade will be built on the mighty River Angara. The Angara flows out of Lake Baikal with a constantly maintained swiftness down to the River Yenisei. In the future, a chain of big power stations on the Angara will change the whole of Eastern Siberia.

A cascade is being built on the Vuoksa that runs across the Karelian Isthmus: two "steps" of this cascade have already been built at Rauhiala and Enso. The first of a chain of power stations is being built on the River Terek. The mountain torrent of the Greater Almaatinka roars through a turbine. Several hydroelectric power stations are already functioning on the Chirchik and its arms, in the vicinity of Tashkent; by the end of the present five-year plan period, there will be seventeen stations on this river.

The most interesting of our cascades is that below Lake Sevan, in Armenia.

Lake Sevan lies in a basin formed of petrified lava almost two thousand metres above sea level. It is one of the biggest mountain lakes in the world.

Lake Sevan was formerly a gigantic water tower kept under lock and key. It hung like a huge cup over Armenia, whose fields thirsted for water. But it was very niggardly with its water: of its constant 85,000 million cubic metres, it yielded only fifty million through the River Zanga.

The proposal to release part of the water from Lake Sevan for irrigation purposes was made in tsarist times. But the tsar answered: "There is enough water to fill the flasks of my soldiers in the province of Armenia, why do we need any more?"

The work of releasing the Sevan waters was begun only in our Soviet times. The Soviet people are making efficient use of its age-old water resources.

Like precious liquid from the beak of a pitcher, the lake is "poured" into a hollow that has been dug near the mouth of the River Zanga. Augmented by the water of the Zanga, it rushes downhill to the open mouths of canals which irrigate the fields of the collective and state farms of the Ararat Valley. Every irrigated hectare of vineyard produces five thousand litres of wine, every hectare of irrigated orchard produces eight thousand tins of canned fruit. . . .

But the waters of Lake Sevan not only irrigate fields and orchards. They perform a still more important function—they produce electricity.

The River Zanga is about a hundred kilometres long, but in that distance it drops more than a thousand metres. Thus, the Zanga is a sort of flattened-out waterfall; on its banks several hydroelectric power stations will be built. The water will run from station to station along the open course of the river, through derivation canals and through tunnels. This cascade will produce about as much electric current as the Dnieper Power Station can.

The cheap and abundant power of the Sevan Cascade will transform the whole economy of Armenia. Much has already been done in this respect. Erevan has become a large centre of those industries which consume large quantities of electric power. When the cascade works at full capacity, Armenia's industry will make unprecedented progress.

Of the bigger stations in this cascade, that at Kanaker is already working. Two others are under construction—Gyumush, the biggest of them all, and Ozernaya, the highest of them. Ozernaya Station is being built underground, in the living rock, and Sevan water will be carried away by a tunnel to the River Zanga.

The level of the lake has already sunk by over two metres; a white line shows above the blue surface of the water. Dur-

9*

ing the next fifty years the level of the lake will drop fifty
metres.

And then? After that the level will remain constant.

Will the turbines of the power stations stop running? No,
they will be able to continue running.

Where will they get their water? From Lake Sevan.

The solution lies in the removal of this contradiction.

Lake Sevan is not only a water tower; it is also a steam
boiler. The lake yields fifty million cubic metres of water per
annum to the Zanga and loses as much through filtration into
the soil. From rainfalls and from streams that flow into it,
the lake receives 1,300 million cubic metres per annum. Where
does the difference of 1,200 million cubic metres go? It is
all evaporated by the fierce rays of the Caucasian sun, is seized
and carried away by the winds.

This evaporation must be reduced.

The lake consists of two parts: a large, but shallow part,
and a small, but deep part. It is the large and shallow part
that evaporates most.

One way of cooling hot liquid quickly is to pour it from a
deep, narrow glass into a wide, shallow saucer. In the course
of fifty years the wide, shallow part of Lake Sevan will disappear and the evaporation of the lake as a whole will be reduced. The saucer will go, but the glass will remain.

When the area of the lake has been reduced to one-sixth or
one-seventh, the outgo of water will be about equal to its intake,
which will remain unchanged. The flow of water into the
River Zanga will remain constant, and the hydroelectric power
stations in the cascade will continue to function.

By that time, of course, other, more powerful, sources of
energy may be available for industrial purposes.

If neither electric power nor water for irrigation is needed for the wonderful technique of the future, communist
society, with its abundance of everything man can need, perhaps we will fill this huge mountain bowl to the brim with
blue water again.

THE SMALLEST SQUARES ON THE MAP ARE CHANGING

Big electric power stations change the geography of the country: new lakes appear, others diminish, green orchards grow up in former arid deserts.... But there are also small power stations—village stations. These are scattered over the country in the collective farms and are not distinguished either for size of their water reservoirs, length of waterhead tunnels, or high capacity of generators. Nevertheless, they too are changing the face of the country. Their importance in the struggle for Communism is no less than that of the giant stations; for they have spread over the whole country, have permeated the life of the countryside, and have brought light where darkness had reigned for centuries.

Lenin saw to the building of huge power stations capable of transforming the industries of whole regions. But Lenin also went to the village of Kashino to take part in the peasants' celebration of the opening of the first village power station. Under Soviet government electric light appeared in the log cabins of Russia, where not so long ago rushlights crackled. The peasants called the new electric light "Ilyich's lamp," in honour of Vladimir Ilyich Lenin, who gave it to them.

Village power stations were built in the Soviet Union before 1941, but the real electrification of the countryside began after the war.

In February 1945, Comrade Stalin signed a government order to promote the electrification of the rural districts. The Soviet Government and the Bolshevik Party organized and led a popular movement for the introduction of electricity in the villages. As a result of this movement the entire map of the Soviet Union was dotted with innumerable bright points indicating where rural power stations had been built. During the first year of the movement such power stations were built in thousands of collective farms, hundreds of machine and tractor stations and dozens of state farms.

In that one year, a thousand villages in the Sverdlovsk Region had electricity installed. The campaign assumed immense proportions and impetus, and everybody was drawn into it. Three hundred Ural factories offered their aid. Factories "adopted" villages, helped them with machines, experience and workers, and competed with each other to see who could do the most and do it most quickly.

The Ural Machine-Building Plant in Sverdlovsk electrified a whole district—Manchazh. The workers built modern hydroelectric power stations on the banks of streams where there had formerly been nothing but wooden mills with their slowly-turning millstones; in the villages where there were no streams they used wood-burning locomobiles. The people worked enthusiastically, especially the members of the Young Communist League. Electricity was installed in all the forty collective farms of the district.

The ancient Urals used to be the incarnation of patriarchal, semi-feudal, rural life. But today, electricity burns in every house and every hut. Light shines everywhere. "The flickering lights of mournful villages," wrote Lermontov in his poem "Motherland." But now when you look from the highway or through the woods at night, you can distinguish the villages in the landscape not by dark patches, as was the case before, but by the clusters of lights.

Look at the statistics of a regional public education department—as soon as electricity is laid on in the villages, the results achieved by school children improve. School children no longer go to bed with the sun or sit outside in the dark— they read or do their homework in the evenings.

Some put on the samovar, but others prefer electric kettles. In the old days food had to be warmed up on a brazier, or on a fire between two bricks; today they use an electric stove. Formerly the women smoothed their washing with a rolling pin, now they use an electric iron.

On collective farms cows are milked by electricity. Where there are water sprays, the farmers plug in and water their vegetable gardens. Grain is threshed, winnowed and dried by electricity. Electricity cuts the straw for silage and grinds the corn for flour. Electricity chops cabbage for pickling and pumps water from the well. In the collective-farm workshops electricity turns the lathe, the saw and the plane.

This means not only an increase in the collective farm's income, but also a further step forward in the people's intellectual development. New tradesmen appear in the villages—the village electrician, the village mechanic, etc.

In the Sukhoi Log District of the Urals there was once a village called Tyomnaya (Dark). Electricity was installed, and the peasants gathered at the collective-farm offices and decided to put in a request that their village be renamed Svyetlaya (Light).

The best stations are those run by water power—they are more convenient, and the electricity is cheaper. In our country there are so many small rivers, not exceeding a hundred kilometres in length, that if placed end to end they would go three times round the world. At present, however, we are not using more than one per cent of their energy. There are still many villages in which electricity has not been installed yet.

The postwar five-year plan provides for the construction of small, rural, hydroelectric power stations with a total capacity of a million kilowatts. This is equal to the capacity of two Dnieper Power Stations. Special factories have been opened for the manufacture of micro-turbines. In some places wooden turbines are being made.

Hydroelectric power stations are not only built on hitherto undammed rivers. In some places the waterheads already exist; all that is required is the electric plant. On the Oka, for example, there is the Kuzmin inter-collective-farm hydroelectric power station. It has a capacity of a thousand kilowatts and serves forty-six collective farms. It is run by the water of one of the sluice gates that have long existed on the Moskva and Oka rivers.

Small power stations are being built on the dams of the Vyshny Volochok water system; this is an old, abandoned system that will now be brought into use again.

In Central Asia and the Transcaucasus, the dams of the big power stations raise the water to the fields and give birth to new irrigation systems. On the other hand, new hydroelectric power stations are being built on old irrigation systems.

Every district, every village and every house will have electricity.

In the Soviet Union it is not only the face of regions, territories and towns that is changing—the villages are changing, the smallest squares on the economic map are changing.

MACHINES AND MEN

A country cannot be strong without an abundance of electric power. Nor can it be strong unless it manufactures its own machines.

Without machines you cannot make your own cloth. But it is not enough to weave your own cloth, you have to make automobiles as well. And you have to make the machines to make the automobiles. You must have everything of your own, from beginning to end. The blooming mill provides rolled steel, the steel is converted into machine tools, the machines make automobiles. . . .

Machines are needed in factory and field. Without machines there can be no modern transport, no modern army.

In tsarist Russia, two-thirds of the factory equipment was imported from abroad. Building a factory usually meant erecting the premises and installing foreign-made machinery. Machines were built only in the Centre, in the Northwest, and to some extent in the Ukraine. The East not only lacked an engineering industry, but practically lacked machines.

Comrade Stalin set our people the task of converting our country from a machine-importing into a machine-producing

country and called upon them to work with might and main
to industrialize our country. Under the guidance of our wise
leader, the Soviet people achieved this task in spite of the
enormous difficulties that stood in their way.

From the time of the inception of Soviet government in
our country to the outbreak of the Great Patriotic War the output of Soviet industry as a whole increased almost twelvefold.
Machine building, however, increased fifty-four fold. Thus,
machine building grew much faster than the other industries.

In no other of the most highly developed countries, not
even the United States, does machine building play such an
important part in industry as it does in the Soviet Union.
And this, more than anything else, perhaps, tells us: "Russia
is indeed not what she was—the land of the wooden plough
and springless cart has become a land of machines!"

Our own Soviet-built cars and trucks filled the streets
of our cities, enlivened the highroads and penetrated the countryside. Grey-green trucks and black enamelled cars have
become an integral part of the equipment of our factories,
offices and collective farms. In a matter of ten years the
automobile became part and parcel of our economic life. We
are accustomed to it now, but this was a revolution in the
economic life of the country.

Our own Soviet-built tractors work in the fields. Millions
and millions of hectares are now being cultivated not by horses,
but by machines. With the new collective-farm life in the
Soviet village came the new farming machinery.

Our own Soviet-built aircraft now fly over our country,
reducing distances, bringing the towns closer together and
guarding our frontiers. The U.S.S.R. has become the most
advanced country in the world in the field of aircraft engineering. Our people have produced designers and pilots whose
engineering and flying skill excel those of any other country.
A gigantic technical revolution has taken place in our country
—it cost tremendous effort, painstaking study and persevering
labour.

Our own Soviet-built machines weave our cloth, make our boots and turn out machine parts.

The country has learned not only to use machines, but also to make them—this is a guarantee of its economic independence, of its freedom and sovereignty.

We manufacture electronic microscopes, radar installations and jet-propelled engines. We have our own lines of automatic machines in which 536 different tools bore, cut and measure metal, and assemble the cylinder block of an automobile in two minutes, tended by only two workers.

But this is not all we need. Our growing industry and agriculture still suffer from a shortage of machines.

During the postwar five-year plan period the production of machines must be doubled compared with that of prewar. At the end of this five-year plan period we must have approximately thirty per cent more metal-working machine tools than the U.S.A. possessed in 1940.

Soviet scientists must not only overtake the achievements of science abroad, but in a short space of time surpass them. Soviet engineering must not only equal the engineering of foreign countries, but be much superior to it in all respects.

Our country is advancing rapidly. We shall have machines that are more intricate than those we have today. We shall have at our command the energy of the split atom, and many other things besides.

* * *

The machine-building industry in our country was built up almost entirely in the period covered by the Stalin five-year plans. During all those years it developed rapidly. At the same time the geography of the engineering industry changed.

The development of Soviet machine building began in the Centre. During the period of the First Five-Year Plan this was the only part of the country that had the necessary contingents of skilled workers. At the Krasny Putilovets Works in

Leningrad, the Dynamo Works in Moscow and the Krasnoye Sormovo in Gorky, there were workers who were used to handling metal and machines. Here were factories which, though small compared with present standards, nevertheless, for a beginning, possessed enough machine tools, electric motors and tools.

Here the battle began. Krasny Putilovets began to learn how to build tractors. The AMO Works in Moscow no longer confined itself to repairing foreign automobiles, it began to assemble its own. Sormovo began to build new Diesel engines. The Kolomna Works began to build more powerful locomotives....

Alongside the old factories rose the walls of new ones. In a year the first section of the Moscow Ball-Bearing Plant was built. In Gorky, the Molotov Automobile Plant took shape. The old plants themselves were rebuilt. The little AMO Works in Moscow grew into the gigantic Stalin Automobile Plant. The Dynamo Works was completely reconstructed. The Krasny Putilovets was transformed into the huge Kirov Works.

At the same time we note a big change in the economic geography of the country: the new machine-building plants were erected not only in the Centre, but also in Stalingrad, in Chelyabinsk, Sverdlovsk and Rostov.... The plants in the Centre that had mastered the production of intricate machines, communicated their experience to the new, far distant plants. The country soon made the acquaintance of tractors from Stalingrad and Chelyabinsk, of farm machines from Rostov and Tashkent, of dredgers from Krasnoyarsk and of railway cars from Tagil.

The location of the plants was well planned. Tractor plants were built in the grain-growing regions and within easy reach of the iron and steel mills; railway cars are made where it is easy to get metal and timber; dredgers are built on the fringe of the gold-bearing taiga....

The faces of towns were changed. Old Kharkov, town of tradesmen and artisans, became a city of highly-skilled workers, engineers and scientists. Chelyabinsk was transformed from a provincial backwater into a big industrial centre—there is not a tractor works in the world that can rival that at Chelyabinsk. Rostov-on-Don became an industrial city. The Rostov Farm Machinery Works alone produces more farm machines than were produced in the whole of tsarist Russia....

In the agricultural Volga Basin, in the old Ural Mountains and in distant Siberia, a first-class industry grew up, contingents of workers were trained and a new industrial culture flourished. The tremendous significance of this development was fully demonstrated by the Great Patriotic War.

The Centre was in the war area. The task of opposing the war technique of Germany fell to the lot of the industries of the Soviet East. The efficiency of industrial production in the Soviet East not only equalled the German, but exceeded it. Our army's equipment proved superior, more perfect than that of the Germans. Soviet machine-building plants provided the Soviet army with the splendid machines and other equipment with which it carried out the masterly plans of the Supreme Commander-in-Chief and defeated the powerful enemy.

Naturally, the unparalleled progress made by the industries in the East was greatly assisted by the evacuation of factories and contingents of workers from the Centre. But the relocation of industry could not have been carried out successfully if the East had not previously built up its industries with modern efficiency.

This progress was led by the Urals, the Stalin Urals.

During the war the output of machines and metal goods in the Urals increased almost sixfold. Their share of the total industrial output of the Urals rose from half to almost three-fourths. This shows that first-class industrial technique has been achieved there. There is not only plenty of metal in the Soviet East today, but plenty of skill in using it.

During the war the Urals not only built tanks but equipped them throughout with its locally made products: motors, ball bearings, rubber, electric wiring, radio sets and plastic

fittings. The Urals produced its own machine tools—lathes,
turret lathes, drilling machines, grinding and polishing machines, multiple and automatic machines, and everything else.
Machine building spread to all parts of the Urals. Factories
grew and changed: the Urals Machine-Building Plant increased
its output sevenfold (in value). Towns grew and changed. Until
recently Nizhny Tagil was only an iron mining and steel
industry centre; now, eighty per cent of its industrial output
consists of machines.

In old Russia, if anybody saw a man wrapped up in a fur
coat and loaded down with provisions for a long journey he
would say: "Dressed up to go to Irbit Fair." This trading town
beyond the Urals was the incarnation of everything connected
with the remote backwoods. Today Irbit is an industrial town
famous for its motorcycles.

Here is a picture of the wartime Urals: in Sverdlovsk a
plant was erected to build turbines. The shops were producing
turbines before the building was completed; the country could
not wait—at that time it was the only turbine works we had.
There was a shortage of workers and engineers. There was
a shortage of many things. The plant was working under a
constant strain. Nevertheless, it fulfilled its task. In peacetime,
the best turbine-building plants in the country had been
unable to introduce the production of more than one new type
of turbine in a year. The Sverdlovsk plant started manufacturing four new turbines in one war year.

During the war the industrial Urals introduced many technical improvements: die casting, stamping instead of forging,
high-speed automatic smelting, high-frequency tempering. New
people came to the fore in the Urals, the heroes of labour, the
revolutionaries of production: Agarkov, captain of a team of
welders, Yankin, oil driller, Zavertailo, iron miner, Bosy, milling
machinist. . . .

Today, in the period of the postwar Stalin five-year plan, the
Urals are probably not behind the Centre as regards the scope
of its machine building, or technical level. The Turbine Works

that came into existence such a short time ago now makes steam turbines even for Moscow. Soon the Miass Works will be turning out automobiles.

Machine building has developed in all the republics and regions of the Soviet East. This is the most remarkable change that has taken place in the economic geography of our country; it is evidence of unparalleled progress in the production efficiency of our people. Take the distant Siberian rivers, for example. At Tyumen, on the River Tura, river vessels are built. In Omsk, on the Irtysh, there is a developed farm-machinery and an automobile assembly plant. Novosibirsk, on the Ob, with its production of machine tools and various types of machinery, is one of the biggest industrial centres of the Soviet Union. In Tomsk, on a tributary of the Ob, one of the factories produces electric light bulbs. Krasnoyarsk, on the Yenisei, and Ulan Ude, on the Selenga, build locomotives. On the shores of Angara there is a factory which produces insulators that will stand a load of over thirty thousand volts.

Now look at the other side of the country, at the West, where but a short time ago the ruins were still smoking—there again we see evidences of the growth in production efficiency, of the increase in the industrial might of our country.

Byelorussia was devastated by the Germans. The country is only just being rehabilitated. What is being built there? Many things, and among them automobile, tractor and bicycle works in Minsk, machine-tool works in Orsha, a sewing-machine works near Orsha, a locomobile works in Mogilev.... Some of these factories are already producing.

The Kharkov Turbine Generator Plant, that was razed almost to its foundations, has grown up again and is already producing turbines weighing five hundred tons and containing forty-five thousand parts. In half-gutted Voronezh, excavators are already being produced with steel scoops which pick up well over a cubic metre of earth at a time, and in one minute do as much work as a navvy can do in a day. The Novokramatorsk

Works, in the Donets Basin, has built a blooming mill for the Georgian iron and steel mills. Kiev is turning out motorcycles. Turbines for the rebuilt Dnieper Power Station are again being built in Leningrad. Kaliningrad is producing forty-ton tip wagons. Riga is producing cars for electric railways and radio sets. . . .

Machine building is being widely distributed throughout the Soviet Union. Under the postwar five-year plan new automobile plants are being built in Moscow, Ulyanovsk, Minsk, Dniepropetrovsk, Kutaisi and Novosibirsk. . . .

STEEL SUPPORTS

The Soviet Union cannot live and develop without machines. But to make machines we must have metal.

Old Russia bought metal abroad; not only copper, lead or zinc, but even iron and steel.

Since the Soviet government was instituted, the country has developed its own ferrous and non-ferrous metal industries. We are not dependent on foreign countries for iron and steel, non-ferrous and rare metals.

On the eve of the Great Patriotic War, our country was smelting almost four times as much iron and four and a half times as much steel as on the eve of the First World War.

The old iron and steel mills have been completely reconstructed. New mills have been built, equal to the biggest iron and steel plants in the world.

Mechanically-operated blast furnaces, big open-hearth installations, electric furnaces of new design, giant blooming mills. . . . Blooming and slabbing mills have ceased to be rarities: the Soviet iron and steel industry is as well equipped and as efficient as any in the world.

Our vast country rests upon strong, steel supports. The sites for these steel supports were very carefully chosen; they were indicated by the great architect of the Land of Socialism.

In tsarist times, fifteen iron and steel mills were crowded together in the Donets Basin and along the Dnieper. The metallurgical industry of the South produced three-fourths of the pig iron smelted in Russia. The country was almost entirely dependent on the blast furnaces in the South.

The development of the Urals region, fettered by remnants of the serf system, dropped far behind the capitalist South, whose development had started later. Tucked away among the Ural Mountains were a few score iron and steel mills, but they produced only one-fifth of the country's pig iron. They had small, old furnaces with a cold blast and using charcoal fuel; some were even situated away from any railway. The Urals produced not girders and trusses, but wire, nails and sheet iron for roofing.

The small mills in the Centre, at Tula, Lipetsk and Vyksa produced the remaining five per cent of Russia's pig iron.

The Caucasus, Central Asia and the Far East either used metal brought from great distances, or used no metal at all.

During the period of the Stalin five-year plans the iron and steel mills of the South were reconstructed. The old mills were equipped with new open-hearth furnaces, new batteries of coke ovens, chemical departments and new blast furnaces. Several new iron and steel mills were built in this region, notable amongst them Zaporozhstal and Azovstal.

The iron and steel industry of the South grew as it had never grown before. Iron and steel consumption, however, grew still more rapidly. As far back as the end of June 1930, in his report to the Sixteenth Congress of the Communist Party, Comrade Stalin said, regarding the coal and metallurgical industries of the Ukraine:

"One of the new features in our national economic development is, incidentally, the fact that this basis has already become inadequate for us. The new feature is that while continuing to develop this base in every possible way for the future, we must immediately begin to create a second coal and metallurgical base. This must be the Urals-Kuznetsk

Combine, the combination of Kuznetsk coking coal with the
ores of the Urals."*

And so, in a short space of time, by the will of the
Communist Party, a vast, new industrial region was built up
in the wilderness of the East. Comrade Stalin called this new
region the pride of our country. This second coal and metallurgical centre served as the base for the general industrial
development of the Soviet East.

The transporter belt in this huge system consists of hundreds of capacious hopper-type dump trucks made up into
trains which run to a definite timetable. At enormous speeds,
these trains carry coal from the Kuznetsk Basin to the Urals
and iron ore from the Urals to Kuznetsk. At both ends of
this system there are new steel mills that produce pig iron,
steel and rolled metal from Urals ore and Kuznetsk coal.

Nowhere in the world is iron ore and coal for blast furnaces transported over such huge distances by rail: over two
thousand kilometres. But it pays, for Magnitogorsk ore is very
rich and quite cheap; it is obtained from open workings; and
the Kuznetsk coal provides excellent, clean coke, and is also
cheap; it is extracted from big seams at low depth. Raw
materials of this type justify the expense of transportation.

The wreckers did their utmost to hinder the creation of the
Magnitogorsk-Kuznetsk Combine; they argued that metal obtained in this way would be too expensive. It turned out to be
cheaper than the metal produced in the South.

Only planned socialist production is capable of undertak-
ing such intricate and extensive development. If there were
no Soviet government, there would have been no Urals-
Kuznetsk Combine, and Russia would not have had strong
steel supports.

The Urals end of the combine is Magnitogorsk, Nizhny
Tagil and Chelyabinsk.

Formerly, the ore from Mount Magnitnaya was carried in

---

* J. Stalin, *Leninism*, Vol. II, Moscow 1933, p. 310.

horse carts to a distant, tiny iron mill. Today there is a huge steel mill at the very foot of the mountain.

The reddish-brown ore is dug out with excavators, electric trains rush it to the ore crushers and then to the gigantic blast furnaces which are automatically charged. Through the glass "peepholes" in the blast furnaces the smelters can see the flaming mass bubbling inside. Every four hours the plug is knocked out, and a blinding stream of liquid metal pours into travelling ladles which carry it straight to the open-hearth furnaces to be made into steel before it cools. Then white-hot ingots of steel run over huge rollers to the blooming mills: huge rolling mills then take over and turn the steel into girders or sheets. Nearby stand the batteries of long coke ovens, from which masses of hot coke are extracted; the coke is baked from Kuznetsk and Karaganda coal. Not far from the blast furnaces and the steel shops stands the Magnitogorsk Heat and Power Station whose capacity is equal to two "Volkhovstrois."

Every second or third shell that was fired at the Germans during the war, was cast from steel made at Magnitogorsk.

People of thirty-six nationalities of the Soviet Union toiled side by side, in summer heat and winter frost, to build Magnitogorsk. They dug foundations in the rocky soil and erected the buildings in spite of the icy winds. During the war they, contrary to all the old rules, smelted manganese in blast furnaces, made special steels in ordinary open-hearth furnaces and rolled armour plate on ordinary blooming mills.

Now there are six blast furnaces at Magnitogorsk, the biggest in Europe. At the end of the present five-year plan period there will be eight.

In Nizhny Tagil work was begun on building a mill before the war, and although the plant is not yet completed, it is already producing more pig iron than the whole of the Ural region produced before the revolution.

In Chelyabinsk the construction of an iron and steel mill was begun during the war. It was built according to sketches,

since there was no time to wait for a detailed technical plan.
The work was started in January 1942, and at the beginning
of 1943 the first steel was melted and used for the manufacture of tank parts, crankshafts, and aircraft engines. This was
not ordinary steel, but high-grade steel: the plant uses Bakal
ore which is perhaps the purest in the world.

Special steels will be produced by the Orsk-Khalilovo Mill
now under construction in the South Urals, near the town of
Orsk; nature herself has added to the Khalilovo iron ore that
amount of nickel and chromium that is usually added artificially to make hard, resilient, stainless steel.

The old Urals plants, using charcoal for fuel, stood
amongst forests and on the banks of rivers down which
timber could be floated. They could not be built away from
the forests, although in the woodless South Urals there are deposits of the most valuable ores. The fetters on the Urals
metal industry have now been removed; the coal from Kuznetsk and Karaganda enables us to use iron ore in wooded and
in woodless regions.

The Siberian end of the Urals-Kuznetsk Combine is
Stalinsk, in the Kuznetsk Basin. The first blast furnace at Magnitogorsk was blown in in January 1932; the first Stalinsk
blast furnace was blown in in April of the same year. The
plant there is of the same type as that in Magnitogorsk, but a
smaller one; it may be called its younger brother.

Great is the power of this transformation: Siberia, the
formerly unexplored, Siberian taiga, the place of exile for
revolutionaries, not only began to produce its own metal, but
even melted steel for Moscow—the first girders for the Palace
of Soviets and the rails for the Metro.

The distance from this Siberian steel mill to the theatre
of war was about four thousand kilometres, but the mill was
in the fighting line. And as a unit which fought and won battles,
it was awarded the Order of Kutuzov and other decorations.

The Urals-Kuznetsk Combine produces not only ferrous metals; it includes plants that smelt non-ferrous metals. The metals
10*

go to make machines, and around the skeleton of this heavy industry, light industries and a food industry are growing up.

The whole of this new industrial region is being built according to plan. The lopsidedness that characterized the development of the coal and metallurgical industry of the Ukraine under capitalism, when it had scarcely any machine-building or chemical industries, does not exist here. As in present-day Ukraine, harmoniously organized, complex production is developing at the plants of the Urals-Kuznetsk Combine.

The new Urals-Kuznetsk metallurgical region was built up by the Soviet state at a time when the known deposits of coal in the iron-bearing Urals and the known deposits of iron in the coal-bearing Kuznetsk Basin were relatively small. The coal and iron had to be brought together even though a great distance separated them. And so the shuttlecock had to fly to and fro over a distance of two thousand kilometres—coal was sent one way and iron the other.

This was a great victory for Soviet planned economy: the industrial might of the country grew rapidly, and the long hauls of iron and coal were fully justified.

But time passes—the general configuration of the Urals-Kuznetsk Combine is changing.

Karaganda began to help the Urals, and this coal field is only half the distance away compared with the Kuznetsk Basin. Its coal has been added to that from Kuznetsk and the cost of coal haulage has been reduced. Thorough geological surveys have shown that there is more coal in the Urals than was formerly believed. True, this coal cannot be used for smelting, but it can be used for heating; and some of the coal from Kizel can be used in metallurgy. In addition to this, large deposits of iron ore have been surveyed near the Kuznetsk Basin, in Gornaya Shoriya and in the region of Abakan.

The postwar five-year plan provides for a reduction in the transportation of heating coal from Kuznetsk to the Urals and of iron ore from the Urals to Kuznetsk. More and more new coal mines are beginning to operate in the Urals, and the mining of iron ore in Gornaya Shoriya is growing. The new South Siberian Railway will soon provide a short, direct route to the Kuznetsk Basin for Abakan ore.

The Urals plants will still, of course, have to use a great deal of Kuznetsk coking coal during the next few years. Nevertheless, through the present-day map we can already see the Urals-Kuznetsk Combine in a new light.

There are large deposits of coking coal in the Pechora Coal Basin, only half the distance from the Urals compared with Kuznetsk, but there is no road there—it is separated from the Urals by tundra, swamps, densely wooded valleys and rocky mountains.

In time a railway will be built from Pechora to the Urals. In all probability, somewhere in this railway zone iron ore will be found of which we do not at present know. Meanwhile, the Pechora coking coal has other uses.

Other steel supports are also being built in the U.S.S.R. In the Far East, steel is already being melted in Komsomolsk, from pig iron brought from other regions; during the present five-year plan period, Komsomolsk will build its own blast furnace. Another steel plant is being built at Rustavi, near Tbilisi (Georgia), with blast and open-hearth furnaces and a blooming mill. This plant will supply sufficient metal for the whole of the Transcaucasus. During the war steel began to be melted in Uzbekistan and Kazakhstan. In the future, these republics will also smelt their own iron. The iron and steel industries of the Centre will also become stronger—the region of the Kursk Magnetic Anomaly will come to life. There will also be an iron and steel industry in Eastern Siberia.

Thus, our country has a steel framework resting on steel supports.... These have been created by the joint labour of all the peoples of the Soviet Union. The Ukraine helped to build the Urals-Kuznetsk Combine and the latter stimulated the economic development of the Buryats, the Yakuts and the Kirghiz. Russian builders erected the Chelyabinsk Iron and Steel Mill and then went to Rustavi to help produce metal for the

Georgians, Azerbaijanians and Armenians. The Magnitogorsk, Guriev and Kuznetsk mills provided parts for the open-hearth furnaces at the new Begovat Steel Mill in Uzbekistan. Steel melters from the Donets Basin, side by side with the Kazakhs, operated the first open-hearth furnaces at Temir Tau. The Leningrad Iron and Steel Mill will get its coke from the Komi people and its iron from the Karelians. Komsomolsk, on the distant Amur, was built by young men and women from Moscow and Baku, Minsk and Kiev, Leningrad and Tashkent. The trusses in the steel framework of the country are becoming stronger. They are able to stand any load.

TIMBER

A tossing sea of conifers and leaf trees stretches over boundless expanses, covering a third of the area of our country. It includes the birch woods of the Moscow Region, the broadleafed woods of the Baltic, the tall, mastwood pine forests of the Lake Onega region, the thick fir forests in the basins of the northern rivers, the virgin larch forests of Yakutia, the giant cedars of the Far Eastern Maritime region....

Before the revolution our timber served to enrich speculators in the City of London. They bought Russian timber for next to nothing. Goaded by contractors, Russian lumbermen felled the trees in our forests for a miserable pittance, Russian raftmen floated the timber to the seacoasts, and there foreign vessels loaded up with Russian timber.

Large areas of forest along the rivers of the northern zones of European Russia were denuded by foreign capital. The home market was served by timber that was felled in the forests of the Centre and the West. Trees were felled nearer to the cities to save transport. In the forests on the great divide, the Valdai Hills, Smolensk Region, where the rivers of the Russian Plain have their origin, the ruthless felling of timber dried the sources from which the rivers gained their strength. The timber merchants were not disturbed by the decreasing depth of the rivers, all they were concerned about was profit.

The Soviet Government takes measures to safeguard the natural wealth of the country. Our laws forbid, or strictly limit, the felling of trees in water-conservation zones. Over large areas of the Centre, in districts where the rivers draw their moisture from the forests, the trees are inviolable. Wise management brings order into nature for the benefit of the country. Extra foliage along the upper reaches of the rivers that flow to the arid South means extra ears of corn on the lower reaches.

Whence, then, comes the timber for building purposes in the Centre and for the mines of the Donets Basin? From the North. There we have diverted the flow of timber. Formerly, nearly all of it went abroad, but today it flows in a mighty stream into the interior of the country. Huge rafts on the rivers, long trains on the railways, carry timber for the building of cities, for the scaffolding of new factory buildings, for props in coal and iron mines.

Long strings of log rafts are floated down the northern rivers. Formerly, on reaching the ports at the mouths of the rivers, all this timber was exported. Today, all the ports, with their huge sawmills, divert part of this timber to the home market. Furthermore, much of the timber is "picked up" on the way. Where the northern rivers cross railways, new centres of the timber industry grew up during the period of the Stalin five-year plans; these centres take up the timber from the rivers, saw it up and send it to the South, to Soviet towns and factories. The biggest centre is Kotlas, which turns a huge stream of northern timber into the interior of the country. It gets its timber from two rivers, the Vychegda and the Northern Dvina. The timber is sawn at Kotlas, and then sent southwards by two railways to Vologda and Kirov.

Part of the timber, and no small part at that, still goes for export, but this trade in no way resembles that of old tsarist Russia. In our Soviet Land, the state has a monopoly of foreign trade. No foreign firms boss the show in our forests today. They can now only buy the timber which the Soviet Government sets aside for export, and they have to pay a price which is acceptable to us. The money obtained from the sale of timber does not go into the pockets of private contractors—there are none in our country—but goes into our public treasury. The timber exported today is no longer cheap lumber—raw logs with the branches lopped off; the sawmills at the ports of Archangel, Mezen and Onega, saw and machine the wood, and make it more valuable. Much of the timber that leaves our shores is carried in Soviet ships and not exclusively in foreign vessels as was the case before the revolution; and the Soviet timber carriers are built in Soviet shipyards.

This is the way the geography of the timber industry is changing in the European part of the U.S.S.R. The Centre is being reafforested, and the North is sending timber to the Centre and the South.

At the same time timber from the East is beginning to play a much bigger part in industry.

Lumbering was carried on in the Urals in the past too, but it was carried on wastefully. The iron masters ruthlessly denuded their vast timber lands and thus, not only metaphorically, but literally, lopped off the branch on which they sat. After denuding the forests around their plants they were practically left without cheap charcoal owing to the roadless state of the Urals at that time. As a result, the iron industry in the old Urals fell deeper into stagnation.

Today, when Urals blast furnaces use mostly coke instead of charcoal, the timber felled in the Ural forests goes mainly to the sawmills to be prepared for building purposes.

The timber industry in the Urals has undergone a complete change, but that in Siberia is practically a new industry. The old Siberian towns needed nothing but firewood. The rapidly growing new Siberian towns need beams, planks, window frames, plywood, etc., in addition to firewood. The

Kuznetsk Basin and Karaganda consume trainloads of props. Trainloads of Siberian timber also go to Central Asia.

Wide cuttings have been hewn through the inexhaustible Siberian forests. Steam tugs haul long chains of rafts along the Siberian rivers. Huge sawmills have been set up at points where the rivers are crossed by railways. New towns have grown up that owe their birth to the timber industry—Igarka, for example.

The timber industry of the Far East is growing with equal rapidity; this is a region which in our country is called the "Stalin new construction site." One of the new towns in this region is even called "Lesozavodsk" which means "Lumberville."

Not only has the distribution of the timber industry changed, so also has its technology.

Electric cables from mobile power stations wind like snakes around tree stumps. Electric saws have come to the forest. Automobile engines roar in the forest cuttings—for timber is hauled not only by horses, but also by tractor and truck. The whistle of the steam locomotive is also heard in the forests, where timber is brought out on narrow-gauge railways that drive deep into the primeval forests. On the big rivers rafts are made up not only by hand, but also by special raft-assembling machines.

The timber combines are not mere sawmills any longer—timber provides over four thousand different products, ranging from wood pulp to the ethyl spirit used in the manufacture of synthetic rubber. In the forests of the Karelo-Finnish Republic, of Archangel in the North, of the Urals and of Siberia, huge timber mills have been built. In places where the axe was almost the only known tool there are now machines almost a hundred metres long, and weighing up to two thousand tons.

Life in the Soviet lumber camps has also changed. In the vicinity of the lumber mills, settlements for the workers, and even whole towns, have been built. Comfortable houses are being built for the lumberjacks. In the depth of the forests, where the timber is being felled, there are dining rooms, clubs and stores.

Settlements of this type are built most easily where the lumber industry is mechanized. Mechanization not only increases productivity of labour in the forests, but also makes for a settled and more cultured life.

The general efficiency of the whole lumber industry is being improved. The old method of "selective felling" was ruinous—the best grades of timber were selected for felling and poor trees were left, with the result that the forest as a whole deteriorated and became overgrown with poor trees. Today, under Soviet government, this system is no longer practised; trees of all types are felled.

In addition to "chief utility felling," Soviet lumbermen also practise "forest nursing," which means that the poorer rather than the best trees are felled, with the result that the forest as a whole improves. In this way Soviet people are "training" the forests, are actively controlling nature's processes.

We are concerned not only with the best way to fell trees, but also with the best way to grow them. The forests are the people's property, and the people are interested in seeing their property grow.

Over vast stretches of territory in the central and southern parts of the country, extensive afforestation schemes are in operation. In the West, the forests that were felled by the invaders are being rehabilitated. In the course of the present postwar five-year plan period more trees will be planted in the Soviet Union than are at present growing in the whole of Great Britain.

These artificial plantations are already beginning to change the natural forest geography of our country. In the valleys of the Transcaucasus, groves of fast-growing eucalyptus trees have appeared for the first time. The forest-steppe regions are being improved by the planting of such valuable Far Eastern varieties as the velvet tree and the Manchurian walnut. The pine tree has been introduced into the water conservation zones of the Tien Shan Mountains. The Siberian larch is being planted on the Russian Plain. Houses built with the timber of this tree will stand for centuries.

The scale on which forest conservation and afforestation work is carried on in our country can be judged from the fact that we have a special Ministry of Forestry. There is no such Ministry in any other country.

For all that, our lumber industry is lagging behind requirements; it is not yet producing all the timber and paper that our growing Soviet economy needs.

To produce more timber, the organization of labour in the forests must be improved, more electric saws and timber-hauling tractors must be employed, new roads must be driven into the virgin depths of the vast forests of the northern zones of the European part of the Soviet Union and into the valuable timber lands of Siberia.

NO UPS AND DOWNS

Tremendous changes have taken place in the economic geography of our country during the thirty years the Soviet state has been in existence. Such changes are not, of course, peculiar to our country alone. Changes also take place in the economic geography of capitalist countries. New resources are tapped and developed, new regions are opened up.

But these changes do not take place on the scale they do in our country. Nowhere has the face of a country changed so rapidly as that of our country.

The chief point is, however, that changes in the economic geography of bourgeois countries take place on principles that are entirely different from those that operate in our country.

The capitalist thirsts for profit, and if he thinks it profitable to build a new factory in the capital, he will build it there. If, for some reason, the tundras, or a high mountain plateau, promise greater profit, he goes to those places, provided he has enough money.

The capitalist does not worry about whether or not his factory is situated rationally from the standpoint of the country's interests as a whole, or of its future. Will industry be more evenly distributed over the country? Will yet another agricultural region become an industrial area? Will contingents of local workers and intellectuals be trained? Such questions would appear ridiculous to the profit hunter.

He strives mainly to build factories in centres that are already densely populated, developed and supplied with all the necessary auxiliary services. He is willing to invest his money in a less civilized region if he thinks, for example, that the new place will reduce his transportation costs. He is also willing to select an agricultural region if he thinks that he is likely to meet with less competition there. He will be only too glad to invest money in a remote country if he expects to find there "yellow" or "black" workers whom he can pay lower wages than white workers are paid, as is the case under the capitalist system.

As a consequence, the changes in the economic geography of capitalist countries are sporadic, chaotic, and unplanned. Sometimes the state tries to bring order into this chaos, but it does not succeed; for the bourgeois state serves the interests of these very capitalists and does not wish to go against them. It acts vigorously in this matter only when the distribution of industry is of military, strategical importance. The state prepares for aggression, or to counter the aggression of a neighbour—again at the bidding of the capitalists.

Thus, changes take place in the economic geography of our country and also of capitalist countries. We have new and old districts, the capitalist countries also have new and old districts. But there is a tremendous difference in the fate of these districts.

The textile industry of the United States was once concentrated in the Northeast, in New England. It was born there as an offshoot of the Lancashire textile industry, and there it continued to grow until it reached a very high level. For a time everything went well, Boston produced excellent fabrics.

But in time a competitor region appeared—in the South. Mills were set up between the Appalachians and the Mississippi with the object of employing cheap Negro labour. Many ruined Negroes abandoned their plantations to knock at the factory gates. They could be paid a mere pittance and, being able to produce more cheaply with the semi-slave labour of the Negroes, the capitalists of the South began to capture the market. Massachusetts lost out to Alabama, one state lost to another.

Alabama was on the upgrade; Massachusetts began to decline. Some mills closed down, others cut down production. Things got so bad that in some places mills were dismantled and the machinery was sold as scrap.

In tsarist Russia the textile industry was concentrated in the Centre—Moscow, Ivanovo-Voznesensk, Orekhovo-Zuyevo, Bogorodsk and also in St. Petersburg. Ninety-nine and one half per cent of all the spindles in the country were concentrated in the Centre and St. Petersburg, although neither of these regions produced a single fibre of cotton. At first, yarn was imported from England; later raw cotton was imported from America; before the revolution, half the raw cotton came from the U.S.A. and half from Central Asia.

Today, our textile industry is distributed differently. New textile regions have sprung up in the Soviet Union, mainly in the South, where the cotton is grown.

The building up of a textile industry in the regions where the raw material is produced began with the dismantling of an old textile mill in the Centre and its transportation to the South. The raw material was produced in the non-Russian regions—the Soviet government ensured the industrial and political growth of these regions, and the Russian people rendered their brothers unselfish aid.

Later, during the period of the Stalin five-year plans,

engineers from the Centre helped the South to build big cotton mills in Tashkent, Ferghana, Ashkhabad, Stalinabad, Leninakan, Kirovabad. . . .

The Central Asian and Transcaucasian republics were enabled to manufacture clothing from their own fabrics.

They obtained more than this, however. In regions where there had been no industry before, huge socialist enterprises have sprung up—these were fortresses of culture, strongpoints for the economic and political development of the former colonial outlying regions. For millions of working people in Central Asia and the Transcaucasus, these enterprises are a school of the new way of life, a school of Bolshevik education. Former nomads, Oriental working women who only recently had cast off their veils, have not only acquired new vocational skill amidst the whirling spindles in these large, well-lit sheds; their whole mental outlook has been broadened, they have come to look on the world with different eyes. Collective labour, contact with modern industrial efficiency has transformed the people and, day after day, imbues them with new qualities. Women weavers have developed into real statesmen—members of the Supreme Soviets and members of the Government. Factory workers returned to their villages and helped the peasants build up collective farms.

A textile industry has also been built up in places where there is no locally-grown cotton—in Barnaul and Novosibirsk. The raw cotton is shipped to Western Siberia in the freight cars that on the return journey carry grain and timber to Central Asia. During the war, the cotton industry also began to grow up in Kansk, in Eastern Siberia. Siberia, which once had to purchase every metre of cloth it needed from places thousands of kilometres away, now produces its own ticking, sateen and moleskin. . . .

During the postwar five-year plan period, the textile industry—cotton goods, knitted goods, cloth and silk—will continue to spread over the whole country. Cotton spinning and weaving mills are being built, for example, in Minsk, Gori,

Astrakhan, Chelyabinsk, Ufa.... These are all regions to which the textile industry is a newcomer.

What has happened to the old regions? What has been the fate of the mills in Ivanovo, Shuya, Orekhovo-Zuyevo? Perhaps they, like the mills in Massachusetts, have cut down output, were closed down, or scrapped?

Of course not. They are still running at full capacity.

The mills in the Centre have been enlarged and reconstructed. Where there were not enough weaving sheds, these have been added. Where there were not enough spinning rooms, they have been built.

Everywhere there is growth. The country needs a lot of fabrics, for the whole country is growing.

The rise of new industrial regions in our country does not cause the decline of the old. The relations between the different regions in the Soviet Union are not those of rivalry, but of mutual aid, not of competition, but of socialist emulation.

COOPERATION

There is no competition between regions and no competition between factories. Everything belongs to the people and the people have but one aim—to increase the might of the Soviet state.

If we were to plot the routes of semi-manufactured goods on the map we would find that a number of junctions would be formed: factories obtain many of the parts needed for machines from "allied" plants. Before the war hundreds of components for the production of tractors—starters, dynamos, relays—flowed towards Stalingrad from all directions.... The Moscow ZIS (Stalin Auto Plant) had connections with 257 other factories.

Over a hundred different enterprises are at present taking part in the production of the Moskvich baby car. The Avtopribor (Automobile Instrument) Plant in Vladimir sends petrol indicators, windshield wipers and speedometers; the Moscow Tyre Works provides the covers and inner tubes; the Carbolit Plant makes the steering wheels and other components from plastics; the ATE-1 (Motor and Tractor Electrical Equipment) Plant makes the starters and generators; the ATE-2 Plant makes the klaxons, distributors and coils....

The plan's the thing. It ensures the proper regulation of the work so that distances over which parts are hauled should not be too great.

As far as possible the cooperation between factories is confined to one economic region. That is why the Avtopribor Plant was built in Vladimir and the plant that makes head and tail lights was built in Kirzhach—they are both within the triangle formed by Moscow, Gorky and Yaroslavl. There is an automobile plant at each corner of the triangle.

Each of the plants is specialized, and knows its own job.

All the plants have been linked up together according to plan, they cooperate.

The specialization and cooperation of factories is a well-thought-out system of division of labour; it is easy to do this in the Soviet Union because the means of production are not privately owned, and the national economy is planned socialist economy.

Here is an example of what happened here before, under the conditions of anarchic capitalist production: at the Upper Ufalei Iron Mills, in the Urals, there was a blast furnace and a rolling mill; at the Lower Ufalei Mill, 22 kilometres away, there was an open-hearth furnace and a sheet rolling mill. Pig iron was carted from Upper to Lower Ufalei, steel from Lower to Upper Ufalei; the blooms were also carted from Upper to Lower Ufalei and, finally, the iron sheets that were carted from Lower Ufalei to the railway station passed Upper Ufalei on the way.

The planned specialization and cooperation of factories facilitated the mobilization of Soviet plants for the production of munitions during the war. In the U.S.A. it required a special

Autobus assembly shop at the Stalin Automobile Plant, Moscow

The first high-power turbine built after the war at the Kirov
Plant, Leningrad

Saratov-Moscow gas pipe line. Separator shop of Compressor
Station No. 1

order from the President to prohibit the output of passenger cars and divert the plants to the production of war materials, which the owners regarded as unprofitable. The mobilization of industry in the U.S.S.R. was more rapid and comprehensive than in Great Britain and the U.S.A.

There is, however, a limit to the specialization of factories. Too narrow a specialization gives rise to superfluous transportation and may be harmful. The Eighteenth Congress of the Communist Party of the Soviet Union, in its decisions, uttered a warning against excessive specialization.

There are also enterprises in the Soviet Union that produce a very large variety of goods—these are the combines.

Some of the combines are based on a number of different uses of the same raw material. At the Stalinogorsk Combine, for example, Moscow coal serves as raw material and as fuel; coal is used for the production of synthetic nitrates and electric current. The clay that is dug out together with the coal is made into firebrick.

Other combines exist for the purpose of performing in one place all the operations in the processing of the raw material. At the Tashkent Textile Combine, for example, cotton goes through all the processes of manufacture—spinning, weaving and dyeing.

There are other combines that employ both principles.

The most remarkable of the combines before the war was the Dnieper Combine. The cheap electric power provided by the Dnieper Power Station made it the centre of a family of gigantic plants, all connected technologically and producing aluminium, electrosteel, ferro-alloys, magnesium, chemicals and building materials. . . . The by-products of one form of production served as raw material for another. The work was carried on without waste and without unnecessary duplication. . . . The Hitlerites wrecked the Dnieper Combine. It has now to be built up practically anew. The first blast furnace of Zaporozhstal has been blown in, the turbines of the Dnieper Power Station have begun to churn out current.

11—777

The Dnieper Combine had no parallel anywhere in the world. It would be very difficult for anarchic capitalist production to reach such a high level in the intricate organization of productive forces.

The combines increase labour productivity and open up new ways of utilizing raw materials and power resources.

They accelerate the alteration of our economic map: big industrial centres with a comprehensive production grow up at once in the new regions.

In our narrative of the changes that have occurred in the distribution of Soviet industry we have moved along the roads broken by its various branches: coal, gas, power, machines, steel and textiles.... We now see that there are points on the map where these roads cross.

At the Stalinogorsk Combine the production of power and chemicals is combined with the manufacture of silicate products.

At the Magnitogorsk Combine iron and steel are coupled with chemicals.

At the Dnieper Combine we have steel, aluminium and ferro-alloys combined with chemicals, building materials and electric power.

In fact, all branches of Soviet industry are connected with each other in the same way as all branches of our national economy are linked up together.

Industry obtains raw materials from agriculture and in its turn provides the farms with machinery and fertilizers. The countryside sends food to the towns and itself gets manufactured goods in return. Transport links all branches of economy into a single whole; with the aid of the transport system goods are circulated.

Our national economy has many facets, and socialist industry plays the leading and decisive role in it. The town leads the country. Together with the growth of industry, agriculture is also growing and changing. This too is shown by the map.

VI

NEW FIELDS

CHANGING LANDSCAPE

IN PRE-REVOLUTIONARY times the landscape of the country was predominantly agricultural, rural. Villages surrounded by fields, isolated homesteads. ... More church belfries than factory chimneys rose over the towns.

But the landscape not only revealed that the basis of backward Russia's economy was agriculture, it also showed that agriculture itself was backward.

The fields stretched away endlessly but it could be seen that they were not uniform. One part of the land was divided into large lots, while another would be intersected by numerous weed-grown boundaries, marking off strips of land, a dozen or two furrows wide.

The big patches of land belonged to the landlords, the small strips belonged to the peasants. Very often the landlords' land was also ploughed and sown in strips instead of in a continuous field; this was when the landlords rented out their lands to the peasants at exorbitant rents.

The landlords, kulaks, the monasteries and the tsar's family owned two-thirds of all the arable land. The rest, the worst lands, were split up amongst many millions of poor and middle peasant households.

The fields that stretched across the countryside were not deserted, there were always people at work in them; but this continuous, arduous toil brought them little fruit.

11*

ST. MARY'S
COLLEGE LIBRARY
CALIFORNIA

The little country cart standing with lowered shafts at the boundary, soil freshly upturned by the ploughshare; the crisscross marks of the bast shoes in the furrows; the peasant trudging behind his wooden plough wearily urging on his sorry nag.

Man wore himself out, but the work progressed slowly—the time the ploughman took to reach the end of his strip and come back again seemed endless. And, as a poet remarked, there was a note of despair in his constant repetition of "Gee up, Dobbin...." The peasant put all his weight on to the wooden plough, but still the furrow was no more than three or four inches deep....

His grandfather had used exactly the same sort of wooden plough; he had harrowed with exactly the same sort of wooden harrow; he had sown his seed by hand from the same kind of basket and had threshed with the same kind of flail.

At the beginning of the revolution there was one tractor in Russia, and even that one did not work—but there were eight million wooden ploughs!

The harvest gathered from shallow-ploughed, poorly fertilized land that never saw a proper crop rotation, was not very great. The ears of corn were short, the plants were sparse, and there were bare patches here and there in the fields.... The crops were no better even on the landlord's land: he ran his farm with the same sort of peasant labour and with the same medieval technique. The landlord rarely spent money on improvements; he preferred the labour rent system, or cheap peasant labour. These remnants of the serf system hindered the development of agriculture. Only in a very few places—in the sugar-beet regions of the Southwest, for example—did the landlord farms reach a relatively high level.

In the autumn, after the harvest had been gathered in, the middle peasant thought for a fleeting moment that he could breathe freely. He sold part of his grain, he settled part of his debts, he bought things at the fair, celebrated weddings.... But the sun did not peep out from behind

the clouds for long. By the winter, or at any rate in
spring, his corn bins were empty and he was obliged to buy.
He got into debt again, pulled his belt in tighter. The noose
of the landlord and kulak was drawn tighter until it almost
choked him.

As for the poor peasant, he had nothing to look forward
to even in autumn. Everything that his hard and persevering
toil had produced slipped out of his hand. Part went to pay
the landlord's rent, part went in taxes to the state, part went
to pay for implements and seed hired from the kulak. Poverty
and ruin gripped him as before....

The heavy yoke of the landlords and kulaks, shortage of
land, the backwardness of farming methods, small yields—
all this led to endless poverty, to constant hunger. The bulk
of the population of Russia consisted of the peasants, their
staple crop was grain, but half the peasants never had enough
grain to supply themselves with bread!

Look at this land today.

Our towns have grown, everywhere there are factories—
it is industry and not agriculture that today forms the basis
of our country's economy. But our fields spread far and wide
too—they seem boundless.

They are totally different from the old fields. The ditches
that formerly marked the boundaries of estates have gone,
nor will you find boundary posts marked with the name
of a private owner. The Great October Socialist Revolution
abolished the private ownership of land.

The Soviet state put an end to the landlords as a class and
placed at the peasants' disposal about 165,000,000 hectares
of former landlord, monastery and appanage land, in addition
to the land that the peasants already possessed. The Bolsheviks
released the peasants from bondage to the landlords and from
the land hunger that had tormented them for so long.

The boundary posts denoting ownership disappeared and
after them went the narrow strips of land that were the
characteristic feature of the old Russian landscape. Today we

see extensive, unbroken fields—wide stretches of black or dark-brown fallow, golden seas of wheat, the rough stubble of harvested fields—they are no longer intersected and cut up by innumerable weed-covered boundary lines.

During the first years after the revolution the peasants worked their plots individually. For this reason they were unable to throw off the yoke of the kulaks entirely. The Soviet Government kept a tight rein on the kulaks by means of taxes and by other measures, but for a time grasping kulaks and poor peasants still remained in the villages. The small farms could not make use of tractors and other machines in their tiny fields and could not greatly improve their yields. The shortage of grain and raw materials hindered the growth of industry and of the whole national economy of the Soviet Union.

On the initiative of the great Stalin the Fifteenth Congress of the Communist Party of the Soviet Union, held in December 1927, adopted a decision to develop collective farming on the widest possible scale. The Soviet Government sent tractors, fertilizers and agricultural experts to the rural districts. Twenty-five thousand town workers went into the country to help the poor and middle peasants organize in collective farms. The results achieved by the first collective farms gradually convinced the bulk of the working peasants of the advantage of this system of farming and in response to the call of the Communist Party, millions of them formed collective farms.

Complete collectivization served the Soviet people as a basis for liquidating the kulaks as a class, the last remaining parasitic class in our country. Peasant bondage to the kulaks was abolished.

Our agriculture became socialist agriculture. The collective farms and the big state farms have concentrated in their hands vast areas of cultivated land which constitute the main feature of the Soviet farm landscape.

The new factories that were built during the period of the Stalin five-year plans provided the collective and state farms and the machine and tractor stations with numerous machines. The Soviet state equipped our country's agriculture with an abundance of up-to-date machinery and it became the most highly mechanized agriculture in the world.

Before the war there were over 500,000 tractors in the U.S.S.R. The tractor hauling the many-bottom plough is as firmly established in Soviet agriculture as the wooden one-horse plough was before the revolution.

Many details of the Soviet agricultural landscape changed with the coming of the tractor. The roads no longer show the ruts left by the upturned horse-drawn plough when dragged to and from the field; they bear the deep imprints of the tracks or wide wheels of the tractor; the very rhythmic precision of these imprints of heavy metal upon the ground speaks of something new that was unknown in the old countryside.

Look at our winter crops when they sprout today; their appearance is entirely different from what it was before. Formerly, the seeds would sprout wherever the sweep of the arm, a flick of the fingers or a gust of wind dropped it. Today the emerald green stalks stand in even rows as the tractor-drawn seed drill has planted the seeds. Even the "landscape of sounds" has changed. Formerly the field was silent even when people were at work in it. Silent was the wooden plough as it cut the earth. The despondent cry "Gee up, Dobbin" was lost in space. Today, even when you are at a distance you can hear the regular throb of a motor from somewhere behind a grove. It swells in volume and fades away again. And the heart throbs with joy and excitement in unison with the motor: the fields are abustle with work, with life.

On the eve of the war we had about 200,000 harvester combines in our country. When you see a column of these "landships" sailing across the boundless fields of the Ukrainian or Kuban Steppes you get a vivid demonstration of the fact that agricultural labour has been brought up to the level of industrial labour. In the hands of Borin, a skilled combine operator, one train did the daily work of 950 men, 150 horses,

20 horse-driven threshers and 37 winnowing machines. . . . Yes, these are different fields.

The new collective-farm countryside, freed from bondage, has been given the opportunity to make life more cultured and affluent. The Soviet state has helped the countryside to rear new people, people with broad, national interests and educational attainments, people who work selflessly and have a strong sense of civic duty. There were not and could not be such people in the old, pre-revolutionary countryside. These people have renovated our land, have transformed it, and have raised the labour of the peasant to a level never known before.

The victory of the collective-farm system in the countryside has increased the economic might of our socialist state. Soviet industry has been provided with a sound base in the shape of a highly productive large-scale agriculture.

Soviet collective and state-farm agriculture, operating on new socialist principles and well equipped with modern machinery, is able to employ the most modern methods of scientific farming. Work on the Soviet farms has been placed on a scientific basis and its productivity has greatly increased. Crops have increased all over the country and particularly on the farms operated by the leading men and women in socialist agriculture, the famous Heroes of Socialist Labour.

The following figures show the growth: tsarist Russia harvested between 4,000 and 5,000 million poods* of grain a year. In 1940, the Soviet Union harvested 7,200 million poods. The cotton crop increased three and a half-fold compared with tsarist times.

These successes were not easily achieved. The Soviet people, however, have surmounted all obstacles, including the former technical backwardness and the resistance of enemies who tried to pull them back.

The tremendous task of reorganizing our agriculture was

---

* Pood=16.38 kg., or one-sixtieth of a ton.—Tr.

performed by the Bolshevik Party. The Party drew up the plan for the transformation of the countryside and also guided its implementation.

By its wise and firm leadership, which is based on profoundly scientific principles, the Party of Lenin and Stalin rehabilitated the countryside, effected in it a social revolution of the greatest historical significance.

Profound internal changes have taken place in the Soviet countryside. These changes have even made their imprint upon the outward appearance of the country. They have altered the landscape, and have created new features which, in the aggregate, create the picture of the new, socialist state.

* * *

The further growth of our agriculture was greatly hindered by the war which the German invaders forced upon us.

The Ukraine, the Don and the Kuban—the country's most important granaries—were seized by the enemy. The task of feeding the country and the fighting forces fell to the Eastern Regions—the trans-Volga and Siberia. Men left the villages for the front, the number of tractors and amount of fuel available declined. . . .

The danger arose that the countryside would be ruined and the country faced with famine. The First World War caused a severe decline in Russian agriculture—sown areas were greatly reduced, the crop yields dropped very low, and it took ten years or more to restore them. . . .

Under the Soviet system, which had built up life in the countryside on socialist principles, things turned out differently.

Our Soviet peasantry came through the ordeal of the war successfully. Our agriculture continued to feed the country and the armed forces without serious interruptions.

These successes were due to the collective-farm system, which provided the farms with a new technique and a new culture, united the peasants and merged their interests with those of the state as a whole. These successes were due to the self-sacrificing labours of our Soviet peasantry who honourably fulfilled their duty to their country. These successes were due to the great Party of Lenin and Stalin, which inspired the working people to perform great deeds and guided the entire struggle the Soviet people waged against the fascist invaders.

The war is now over, and we are living in the period of the postwar five-year plan. One of the major purposes of the plan is to effect a further great improvement in agriculture in order to guarantee the material well-being of the people and to create in the country an abundance of the chief articles of consumption.

Like the other branches of our Soviet national economy, agriculture during the postwar five-year plan period will not only be completely restored to the prewar level, but will develop further. The volume of output in 1950 will exceed the prewar output by twenty-seven per cent.

The cultivated area will be enlarged, and what is most important, the crop yield will be increased. Our fields will produce more grain, cotton, sugar beet and sunflowers, and our plantations and orchards more tea, grapes and fruit than have ever been produced in our country before.

To achieve this, the general efficiency of agriculture must be improved still more by the introduction of the most up-to-date scientific methods. In the course of the present five-year plan new, improved machines will go out into the collective-farm fields, amongst them a new type of self-propelled combine harvester. The farms will be provided with no less than 325,000 powerful tractors of the very latest types.

It will not be easy to carry out these enormous tasks, particularly in the districts that were devastated by the enemy. The cultivated area in these districts was greatly reduced during the occupation. The fields became choked with weeds, equipment was destroyed and few cattle remained.

The Soviet state rendered the peasants in the war-ravaged regions generous assistance in the way of loans, machines, cattle and seed. Trainloads of implements, cattle and poultry were sent from the collective farms in the East to those of the West. Thousands of experts in collective-farm organization, agronomists and zootechnicians went to the liberated regions.

Here are the results. Already in 1946, despite all the difficulties, the collective farms and individual peasant lots in the liberated regions had rehabilitated three-quarters of their cultivated area. The livestock of the collective farms and of the farmers themselves had been restored by over fifty per cent.

But there is plenty of work to do in other regions besides those of the West. Although there was no fighting in the eastern parts of the country, the war, nevertheless, caused serious damage to agriculture: the fields were not tilled so thoroughly, many crops were planted on a smaller scale than before. Moreover, in the first postwar summer came a drought such as our country had not known for fifty years....

Today, under the leadership of the Bolshevik Party and with the help of all our people, the Soviet peasantry are liquidating the results of the war and of the drought. The Plenary Session of the Central Committee of the Communist Party of the Soviet Union, held in February 1947, drew up a militant program for the postwar improvement of agriculture in the Soviet Union. This program is being effectively carried out. The spring sowing was carried out with tremendous enthusiasm; the same applies to the summer work on the farms. A bumper harvest was gathered from the socialist fields. Grain deliveries to the state were made ahead of schedule. In the reports which the Soviet peasants send to Comrade Stalin they proudly summarize the results obtained from work done and undertake new and bigger obligations.

The guarantee of further and much greater progress in Soviet agriculture lies in strengthening the collective farms still more. Fully conscious of this, the workers in our socialist fields are now more vigilantly than ever seeing that the Collective-Farm Rules—the Stalin law of collective-farm life—are strictly adhered to. With the help of the Communist Party and of the whole Soviet people, the Soviet countryside is honourably fulfilling the task which faces it—the task of providing an abundance of food for the population and of raw materials for light industry in the shortest possible time, and of helping our socialist state accumulate the necessary reserves of food and raw materials.

THE EARTH'S AWAKENING

The spring breezes blow across the ancient plains of our country. The hot sun rises higher and higher above the horizon, the icy fetters that bind the earth melt in its rays, sturdy young shoots thrust their way upwards to the sky.

The great ploughman makes his way across the open steppes, through forest and swamp, from border to border; his ploughshare bites deep into the virgin soil, and wherever his foot treads the fields are covered with bright green, orchards blossom and fat ears wave over the cornfields. Released from its winter imprisonment, the earth generously rewards the tireless labour of the ploughman, the labour of the people, the creators.

The socialist revolution imbued our people with mighty strength—the magic strength of collective labour that transforms and renovates the surrounding world. The earth in our country is not cultivated by small peasants working alone and without machines, nor by avaricious landlords who reap the fruits of other people's labour; it is cultivated by a strong and united body of free people employing modern machinery. The Soviet people, by their mighty, collective labour, are transforming nature, are consciously changing nature and are bringing to light countless treasures that were formerly hidden. They boldly plough new ground, break down the geographical boundaries to which crops were formerly limited and force their fields to produce increasingly abundant harvests.

Much virgin land has been broken to the plough, much bush land has been cleared, many swamps have been drained and deserts irrigated since Soviet government was established in our country.

The geographical area of Soviet agriculture has expanded considerably. By 1940 the cultivated area had grown almost fifty per cent compared with pre-revolutionary times. This newly-ploughed area is equal to the whole of the Ukraine, the biggest country in Europe with the exception of the R.S.F.S.R.

Look at the North, where the forest belt lies.

Men break up boulders and clear away or bury the rubble. Bulldozers uproot the tree stumps. The territories of burnt-out woodlands, the ground matted with tree roots and littered with boulders left by the ice age, are being cleared.

The hatchet of the woodsman hacks down the young trees. The branches are burned. The forest is no more, its place is taken by extensive fields enriched by the wood ash.

A caterpillar tractor crawls over the bushes, breaking them down and crushing them into the earth. The heavy ploughshare turns up the top layer of soil, splits the stumps and cuts the tree roots to pieces. Twigs and leaves are ploughed in, the virgin soil is turned, and the field is ready for the planting of wheat.

Now look at the extreme South, the desert belt.

Expeditions of soil scientists and irrigation experts move on automobiles and horses across the waterless, sun-scorched plain; they are making plans for the irrigation of the desert.

Excavators are drawn up in line along the track of a future canal. They lift their giant shovels, removing earth to make way for water to flow.

Thousands of people work in unison with their mattocks, building the irrigation system in places where machines have not yet arrived.

And soon the water flows, bringing moisture to the soil—the desert is transformed into a vast cotton field.

New lands are being opened up, old lands are being improved.

In many parts of tsarist Russia the lands were ruined by the old, wasteful farming methods. The peasants had neither the opportunity nor the desire to improve the land they rented on short leases. Correct crop rotation was almost entirely unknown and mineral fertilizers were little used. Even manure was not utilized to the full but was often left to rot behind the cowsheds.

The land became exhausted, "ploughed out."

A start has now been made on the correction of the earth's crust. Poor soils may be enriched. "... Fertility is not as natural a quality as might be thought; it is closely bound up with present social relation."*

The late Academician Williams, a Soviet biologist, worked out a multi-field system of crop rotation which includes fields sown to perennial grasses. Replacing other crops from time to time, they restore the conditions necessary for fertility and improve the structure of the soil by making it friable, cloddy.

The selection of crops for the rotation depends on concrete local conditions. They differ in different regions. The idea, however, is always the same; the correct sequence of crops retains and improves the fertility of the soil. It becomes easier for the fields to "breathe" and to absorb moisture.

The postwar Stalin five-year plan sets a colossal task, one unparalleled in history, viz., to introduce a correct, scientific crop rotation in all the fields of our country—in the fields of one-sixth of the globe.

Such a task can be undertaken only by a socialist country. In the U.S.A., for example, correct crop rotation is employed only on a very small number of farms. And the U.S.A. is

---

* Karl Marx, *The Poverty of Philosophy*, Moscow 1935, p. 137.

considered the most progressive of the capitalist countries in
the field of agriculture.

The entire map of our agriculture will be a sound and
rational one, complying with the requirements of progressive
science.

The fertility of the soil also depends on the depth of the
ploughing. By deep ploughing we "improve" the soil, we give
it a deep nutritive layer. Before the revolution fields were
ploughed about 10 cm. deep, today they are ploughed 20 to
22 cm. Soil improvement is practised over large areas, not
only in the Black-Earth Belt. Deep ploughing is being practised, for example, in the agricultural regions of the Far East.
The demand to put a stop to shallow ploughing that was
practised in some places during the war is contained—amongst
other decisions—in the instructions issued by the February (1947) Plenary Session of the Central Committee of the
Communist Party of the Soviet Union. The Communist Party
shows the people the way to renew and enrich the soil.

Every year sees an increase in the amount of mineral
fertilizers we put into the soil. To produce these fertilizers
the Soviet state has built some first-class factories.

But artificial chemicals are not the only means with which
to improve the soil.

In the Soviet Union, especially outside the Black-Earth
Belt, ever greater use is being made of peat. Peat is rich in
nitrates. Before the war some thirty million tons of peat were
cut annually for use as fertilizer.

Liming reduces acidity in podzol soils; it improves the
physical properties of these soils and helps to produce bigger
crops. Soil is being limed over large areas in the Soviet Union.
By the spring of 1947, for example, about a thousand tons of
lime had been carted from the Sortavala marble quarries to
the Olonets plain in the Karelo-Finnish Republic. And the
workers of the Segezh Pulp and Paper Mills produced 1,500
tons of lime for the collective farmers from the waste products
of their plant. When the snow melted the Olonets collective

farmers began spreading lime over an area of more than two thousand hectares.

For the improvement of the salified soils that occupy huge, previously uncultivated areas in the South and Southeast, the use of gypsum has been introduced. In the Kirghiz Republic, for example, gypsum is used to improve the land planted to sugar beet.

The Eighteenth Congress of the Communist Party passed a resolution stating that it was necessary "to put into extensive practice the liming of podzol soils and the application of gypsum to salified soils."

Much has been done in conformity with this decision, although the job is far from being finished yet. The area over which lime, gypsum and peat are applied is still small compared with the vastness of our country.

* * *

The soils change, and with them change the plants that we grow in them.

The best combination of farm crops has been selected for each geographical zone in the Soviet Union; for every crop a suitable region has been found. Soviet science, however, is revolutionary, it goes farther than seeking a suitable place for a plant.

We must provide everybody, no matter where he lives, with bread, vegetables, fruit and flowers. The boundaries of the areas within which plants will grow, however, are narrower than our endeavours.

Soviet science poses the problem this way: change the nature of plants and by this means recast the geography of plant distribution.

Academician Lysenko has developed a method of turning winter crops into spring crops, and late crops into early crops. This method is vernalization, the bringing of certain physical influences to bear on the seed before it is sown. Vernalization

T. D. Lysenko, Hero of Socialist Labour, Stalin Prize winner, President
of the Lenin Academy of Agricultural Sciences of the U.S.S.R.

M. E. *Ozerny*, Hero of Socialist Labour, team leader at
the Chervony Partizan Collective Farm, Ukrainian S.S.R.

F. A. *Boiko*, Hero of Socialist Labour, Director of
the Gigant State Grain Farm,
Rostov Region, R.S.F.S.R.

A rye field in Vorkuta in the Far North. As a result of the efforts
of Soviet scientists, rye is now grown beyond the Arctic Circle

helps plants to ripen earlier, thus saving the young plants from the hot dry winds. The result is a large increase in the crop. In 1938, a hundred million poods of grain were added to the crop in this way. Furthermore, by shortening the ripening period, vernalization makes it possible to grow crops where they would not grow before because, owing to climatic conditions, they had no time to ripen.

The Soviet scientist has shifted the geographical boundaries of agriculture. Hitherto it was impossible to grow winter barley in the Far North; if it was sown at the end of summer it perished in the winter; if it was sown at the beginning of summer it had no time to ripen and perished in the autumn. Now, the vernalization of barley according to Academician Lysenko's method enables it to grow and ripen in the North. The vernalized grains of the South are penetrating the Arctic.

Under certain circumstances the growth of a plant may be controlled by regulating the amount of light it receives. If kept out of the light for a time, the southern white acacia will grow in the Leningrad climate; formerly, this plant used to die because of too much light—the summer days in the alien North are longer than the southern days to which it is accustomed. . . .

The role played by light, warmth and moisture is now well understood. Artificial combinations of these three factors influence the plant and alter the agricultural map.

Potatoes were deteriorating in the South of the U.S.S.R.; year after year the size of the tubers diminished. It was believed that this was due to the fact that the potato was not a southern crop and that nothing could be done about it.

Then came Lysenko, who developed a new method of planting potatoes in the southern regions. He discovered the nature of the trouble and removed it. Planted in spring, eyes developed during the hottest months, the plant was oppressed by the heat. Lysenko proposed that the tubers be planted later, in the summer, so that the eyes could develop after the heat has passed and then nothing would interfere with the life of the plant.

Lysenko's advice was taken. In the South potatoes are now planted in summer and they grow splendidly. The problem has been solved. A crop that requires considerable moisture has become impervious to drought.... The mind of a Soviet scientist adapted a plant to conditions formerly hostile to it and thus enlarged its geographical boundaries.

To plant crops in new regions science not only changes the nature of these crops, but also creates new varieties.

A chain of state plant-breeding stations stretches over the whole country. In research institutes and on experimental fields Soviet scientists and collective-farm experimenters are developing new varieties by the process of selection and crossing. The Moskovka, a new variety of wheat, is now planted in non-black-earth regions. New varieties of drought-resisting wheat are being introduced in the trans-Volga region. The boundary of the cotton belt has been shifted far to the North with the aid of a new, early-ripening cotton plant.

The scientists determine beforehand what properties the new plants must have: they must be impervious to heat or frost, rains or drought, i.e., surmount the ancient laws of plant geography. Thousands of experiments have been made. Native plants have been crossed with foreign ones, strong with weak, hardy with tender.

We want to take from wild, hardy plants their ability to resist frost and drought, to transmit these qualities to cultivated plants by crossing. Academician Tsitsin is attempting to cross wheat with the wild couch grass, a weed that is so harmful and so difficult to kill that the ancient Greeks called it the "fire of the fields." The idea is to take from the wheat its fertility and the high nutritive properties of its grain and from the weed its perennialness and imperviousness to severe natural conditions. If these experiments turn out successful they will bring about important changes in the geography of grain crops. The new hardy variety will be able to conquer new regions in which wheat does not grow at present on account of cold or drought.

Soviet plant breeding is based first and foremost on the wealth of the vegetable kingdom in our country. When necessary, however, we make use of the vegetation of the entire globe. Expeditions equipped by the Institute of Plant Industry of the U.S.S.R. have travelled the whole world. From the interior of Asia and from South and Central America they brought back valuable wild plants which will serve as material for crossing and developing new varieties. In the Cordilleras, for example, they discovered a wild potato that is impervious to the potato fungus—the phyto-phthora—and will stand up to eight degrees (Centigrade) of frost. Altogether, the expeditions gathered over 200,000 different plants; there were 30,000 samples of wheat alone!

These collections were kept in Leningrad during the siege. Not a single seed, however, was lost. The Soviet scientific workers heroically protected this valuable collection from barbaric enemy bombardment.

Today the Institute's collection is again being used to help plant breeders in their work.

Much has already been done in our country towards the creation of new varieties of plants, but Soviet scientists are still faced with some difficult problems.

The Soviet Government and the Bolshevik Party have created for our agricultural scientists conditions conducive to successful work, and our collective and state farms are expecting from them valuable new plants that will produce high yields and be impervious to disease, frost and drought.

Not only are new varieties of useful plants being created in the U.S.S.R.; new breeds of domestic animals are also being created.

For example, a new breed of cow, the Kostroma, which has a very high milk yield, has been developed. In Kazakhstan a new breed of sheep has been created by crossing Merino with the local breed: the Merino parent gave it a fine

12*

fleece and the local parent gave it the "Kurdiuk," the fat, flat tail. These sheep can travel over long distances from pasture to pasture, are adapted to life under the severe conditions obtaining at high mountain elevations, and provide large quantities of wool and meat.

In Kazakhstan too, the Merino has also been crossed with the Arkhar, the wild mountain ram; the new breed resulting from this crossing is strong and hardy and adapted to life on high mountain pastures. Its wool provides material for excellent cloth. This new, Arkharo-Merino breed has already been passed on to the collective sheep farms in the mountains for breeding. This is the first breed of fine-fleece sheep able to live on the high mountains all the year round.

In this way new breeds of useful animals are being created.

* * *

The Soviet people are waging a successful struggle against nature, against the caprices of the weather. They want to put an end to the conditions in which the size of the crop is dependent upon a shower of rain.

There is a vast zone in the U.S.S.R. that is affected by periodic droughts, where the rainfall is two, three or four hundred millimetres per annum. This zone covers the Middle and Lower Volga, the Lower Don, the South Urals, the Stavropol Region and Northern Kazakhstan.

The earth is dry and so is the air. Rainfall is low, and even then no more than a fourth of the total falls in summer. Hot winds burn up the vegetation. A haze rises which carries myriads of particles of burning hot dust. The sun loses its brilliance. The crops perish.

Drought has been an ancient scourge in Russia. General droughts occurred at intervals of several years. Partial droughts affected some regions of the country every year. In old Russia the droughts caused famine amongst the people and millions of deaths. The livelihood, the very lives of the peasants were in the hands of the capricious and implacable weather.

In the twenty years from 1891 to 1911 there were twelve crop failures. Three of these—1891, 1906 and 1911—were years of widespread famine.

To be able to understand why drought was so ruinous in old Russia, why it assumed the dimensions of an almost irremediable nationwide calamity, we must first take a look at the map. The Black-Earth Belt that stretches from the Pruth in the West to the Ob in the East is the most important agricultural zone, but a large section of this belt passes through areas subject to drought. The droughts attacked the country's granary and for this reason became a nationwide disaster.

But it was not only a matter of geography. Nature possessed great power because man was weak. Working on their separate small holdings, the peasants were unarmed and helpless in face of the droughts. Nor did they receive any help from the landlord government to prevent drought, or to remedy its results.

Drought has not left the Soviet Union in peace.

We may recall the years before the collective farms were formed. The curve on the annual crop chart jumped feverishly up and down. The instability of the crop kept the small peasant farm in constant peril.

To put an end to drought man must join battle with the climate. This was beyond the strength of the small peasant farmers. The struggle against drought cannot be conducted piecemeal, in small areas; it must be conducted according to a single plan covering vast stretches of country. Such a struggle could be undertaken only under the collective-farm system, and when that was established the struggle was launched. To the elemental forces of nature the socialist state and the collective-farm peasantry opposed the might of large-scale, highly mechanized and planned agriculture such as exists nowhere else in the world. The Soviet people boldly joined battle with their ancient foe.

The collective farms and the machine and tractor stations in the drought zone employ the most highly-perfected farming methods—deep ploughing, fertilizers, vernalization, and the ploughing of winter fallow. They accelerate the sowing and the harvesting to get ahead of the hot winds, and in this way save their crops.

The crop rotation system has been scientifically planned. There is a regular change of crops and varieties: crops that stand up best to drought are included in the rotation scheme—sorghum, millet and yellow alfalfa (lucerne). Newly developed drought-resisting varieties of wheat are being planted. Agriculture is rapidly being adapted to the climate over an area of tens of millions of hectares.

But not only is agriculture being adopted to the climate; efforts are being made to create a new microclimate in the fields.

The land is ploughed not only in spring, but also in autumn; autumn-ploughed land holds the moisture better. Screens are put up in the fields, twigs are scattered, ramparts of snow and ice dams are built, thin rows of sunflowers are grown as curtains. In this way the snow and the moisture it contains is retained on millions of hectares of land.

Over the huge territory stretching from the Black Sea to the sphere of the Urals, and from the Volga to the Ob, forest screens are being planted across the path of the winds and across the slopes from which the topsoil is washed away by the spring floods. Special tree-planting machines are employed in this work. Trees—oak, ash and maple—are being planted in the treeless steppes to shelter the fields from the hot, dry winds, to slow down the thawing of the snow and the flow of the spring waters, to keep winter-sown crops warm and to provide an asylum for birds that destroy pests. The velocity of the wind is almost halved on fields that are sheltered by tree belts, which means that evaporation is also almost halved.

At the time the war began about half a million hectares of shelter belts had been planted and thousands of tree nurseries had been organized. The postwar five-year plan provides for the continuation of this work. The decisions adopted by the February Plenum of the Central Committee of the Communist Party called for measures "to ensure the fulfilment of the plans for the planting of shelter belts, proper care of the plantations, and a strict regime in the felling of timber on water divides and at the sources of big rivers, the prohibition of felling of forests, groves and woods in the steppe regions. ..."

In the trans-Volga region, the collective farms, assisted by the state, are damming local streams to hold back the flow of spring flood waters, and they are damming gullies and turning them into ponds in order to use the water for their fields. Every extra cubic metre of water ensures an additional kilogram of grain. Large irrigation systems, such as the Kutuluk in Kuibyshev Region and the Pugachev in Saratov Region, have been built.

It has been observed that the spring floods have almost disappeared in the southern part of the trans-Volga; water that formerly flowed into the streams and then into the Volga is now retained and waters the planted fields. The accumulated water gives humidity to the air as well as to the fields.

In this way geography is being recast, as though the fields were moved hundreds of miles to the North, to a less arid zone.

The effect of all this work is already to be seen. The earth in the arid zones has begun to yield bigger crops. Weather conditions in 1940 were very unfavourable, nevertheless the grain crop in the Volga region in that year amounted to nearly 1,000 million poods, exceeding by almost one-third the crop of 1913, which was the biggest ever obtained in pre-revolutionary Russia.

But drought has not yet been abolished. The enemy has been weakened, but he has not been vanquished. He has still to be reckoned with.

We suffered great loss as a result of the drought of 1946. It began in Moldavia in the early spring and then spread to the Ukraine and the Volga and embraced the entire South.

Our country had not witnessed a drought like this for half a century. Around Voronezh, for example, there was not a single shower of rain from the end of April, when the spring crops were planted, right through May. The rainfall in June was half the normal, and the first real rain that soaked the ground came at the end of June, when the grain was already ripening. In July air humidity dropped still lower. Violent hot winds blew.

The drought reduced the crop and we harvested considerably less than in the previous year.

But here is an important fact: although the area affected by the drought in 1946 was larger than that of the memorable year of 1921 and approximated that of the exceptionally dry year of 1891, the amount of grain harvested in 1946 was immeasurably larger than in 1921. This shows that although drought can still cause our country considerable harm, it can no longer assume the proportions of a nationwide calamity as it did in the past.

Our country is no longer what it was. Agriculture has been revolutionized. The collective-farm system, mechanization, the new scientific farming, planned production—everything that the Party of Lenin and Stalin has brought to the countryside—have raised Soviet agriculture to a level unprecedented in old Russia. A different culture prevails in the countryside and the incentives to work are different. The results of the conflict between man and nature are different too.

The struggle against drought has been particularly successful in the leading collective and state farms where the fullest possible use is made of those advantages that the socialist system has brought to the countryside.

For example: Mark Yevstafyevich Ozerny, Hero of Socialist Labour and team leader on the Chervony Partizan Collective Farm in the Dniepropetrovsk Region, reaped 136 centners of maize per hectare in the dry year of 1946. The Gigant State Grain Farm in the Salsk Steppes, managed by Hero of Socialist Labour Fyodor Antonovich Boiko, gathered over 30.2

centners of wheat per hectare in that same year. Formerly, such results were unattainable in good years, let alone in severe drought years.

Year after year our Soviet people are increasing their power over the elements.

But progressive methods of scientific farming are not being employed everywhere yet. There are still too few dams and reservoirs on the small streams that flow through arid fields. The possibilities of increasing the yields of agricultural crops are far from being fully used.

There are still too few shelter belts in the Soviet Union. Stalin's statement at the Seventeenth Congress of the Communist Party of the Soviet Union (January 1934) still retains its significance: "Afforestation, the planting of protective forest zones in the eastern districts of the trans-Volga is a matter of enormous importance. As you know, this work has been started already, although it cannot be said that it is being carried on with sufficient intensity."*

The Communist Party and the Soviet Government devote considerable attention to the struggle against drought. In their decisions we find attention paid to shelter belts, snow retention and reservoirs. The decisions of the February Plenum of the Central Committee of the Communist Party of the Soviet Union provide Soviet people with a comprehensive program of struggle for bigger crops in the drought-affected lands.

Much work lies ahead. The war complicated the task. Artillery fire thinned out the tree belts that sheltered the fields in the South. They present a picture of uprooted and blasted trees, splintered tree trunks, charred stumps.... Of the former twelve thousand hectares of forest strips in Stalingrad Region a little over two thousand hectares have remained.

In 1935, following a Government order, a special machine and tractor station was set up to create a green belt around Stalingrad, which is situated in the open steppe. Over four

---

* J. Stalin, *Problems of Leninism*, Moscow 1947, p. 487.

thousand hectares of forest, orchards and vineyards were planted. These plantations were almost all destroyed by the Germans
and have to be planted anew.

The experience gained in the struggle against wartime difficulties, however, has not been lost. In those grim years of
war our Soviet people introduced quite a number of new methods in combating the effects of drought. For example, the
collective farms in the Volga Basin began to build up small,
irrigated "insurance" fields. These fields, protected from the
caprices of nature, ensured the collective farmers a minimum
of necessities in the event of a bad harvest. Irrigated fields for
potatoes and other vegetables are being set apart on the collective farms today, in the postwar five-year plan period.

Water, irrigation—this, of course, is the surest method of
combating drought. Fields must be irrigated wherever possible.

The time will come when the cheap electricity of the power
stations on the middle and lower reaches of the Volga will
start huge pumps going to supply Volga water for the fields.
The water will be gradually pumped into huge reservoirs on
the divides and in summer will spread over the fields through
a network of canals. Year after year we shall obtain steady
harvests of wheat over a vast area of our country.

In the irrigated regions the summer temperature will be
lowered and the atmosphere will become more humid. The
climate of an extensive region will change and drought will be
conquered in the trans-Volga region.

But in order that the Volga should have sufficient water
for this purpose, engineers will, in the future, have to draw
on the water resources of the northern rivers, the Vychegda
and the Pechora. The upper reaches of these rivers will be
dammed and part of their waters will flow into the Volga
Basin. In this way we shall reach the point of redistributing
water among the seas.

The task of today, however, is to redistribute the water
among the rivers. At the present time, in the postwar five-year
plan period, a construction job is already nearing completion

that will show that we are able to change the water regime of an extensive area.

In the heart of the North Caucasus, the southern fringe of which borders on the Caucasian Mountains, lies the huge, flat Stavropol Plateau with its fertile soil and hot sun. The plateau is covered with gigantic wheat fields, but there is not enough moisture for the wheat.

The Kuban River races down from the mountains and passes round the western fringe of the plateau. In spring and early summer there is an abundance of water in the river, but it all flows wastefully into the Azov Sea.

At the town of Nevinnomyssk the river is now stemmed by a dam nearly a kilometre long. A canal will convey part of the waters of the Kuban northward across the Stavropol Plateau. The canal will cross the divide, flow through a six-kilometre tunnel, set the turbines of a power station in motion, fill the dried-up streams of the Stavropol region and what is left of the water will fall into the Manych, a tributary of the Don. The waters of the Kuban River will irrigate up to three million hectares of land, will treble the wheat crop and prepare the ground for new orchards and vineyards. Industry will develop on the basis of cheap electricity. The hot, dry winds will die down, the black dust storms will cease, the atmosphere will become more humid and the grey steppes will be covered with a cloak of green.

With shovels and excavators the Stavropol collective farmers are digging out the heavy Maikop clay and bringing into their steppes the waters that flow from the glaciers of Mount Elbrus.

* * *

In the Black-Earth Belt Soviet people are combating soil erosion, a cruel and powerful enemy of farming.

The snow melts in the fields, the spring waters flow away, carrying with them the topsoil, the most fertile layer. When it rains the raindrops beat on the earth, break up the particles of soil and wash them away. The wind blows, sweeps the dust up from the earth and spreads it far around. It is as though nature were grinding down the ploughlands with a huge rasp.

Streams of water flow and the soil becomes impoverished. And they flow swiftly, too—the fields in the Soviet Black-Earth Belt are usually sloping: in the Kursk Region more than half the ploughlands have a slope of over 2°. Sometimes in the spring as much as sixty tons of soil may be washed away from every hectare of land!

The streamlets merge into a big torrent and then resemble a saw rather than a rasp—they "saw" away the slope, and gullies are formed. Gullies grow in size from year to year until they become fixed ravines that sometimes stretch for many kilometres, reducing the area of the fields, cutting across roads and reducing the level of subsoil water. Gullies slash our wooded steppes and rob us of our ploughlands.

Practically nothing was done in old Russia to combat the formation of gullies. The peasants were hampered by shortage of land, they broke up the entire turf covering of the soil and the snow and rain water easily washed it away. Contour ploughing was impossible on the narrow strips of land held by the peasants, and the furrows sometimes ran downhill, facilitating the flow of the water that washed away the soil. The gullies grew, ate up the ploughlands and increased in number, like wrinkles on an old man's face.

In countries where land is private property and economy is not planned, soil erosion is becoming a national calamity. Under capitalist conditions it is impossible to combat soil erosion. In the United States of America, where wasteful capitalist farming is the rule, over half the arable land has been ruined by erosion. Vast areas of fertile land have been turned into desert.

At the end of the last century Dokuchayev, the great Russian soil scientist and geographer, wrote: "Our Black-Earth Belt is undoubtedly undergoing a very slow but persistent process of erosion of growing intensity." He studied the problem and tried to find a solution for it. In some places in the South work was actually begun to fix the soil, but it was soon abandoned, "owing to the lack of credits."

A real, planned battle against the gullies, against soil erosion could be launched only by the collective and state farms. Indeed, such a struggle would be fruitless if it were not conducted according to a single plan over a large territory, if it were not prompted by the endeavour to serve the common good of the whole people instead of by selfish concern for one's own tiny plot of land.

Over large areas of the black-earth regions trees are being planted along the fringes of the gullies where their roots consolidate the soil. Small earthworks are built across the slopes to reduce the destructive action of the water. Winter fallow land is deep-ploughed crosswise to the slopes and this also serves to stem the flow of spring waters. "Curtains" of maize or sunflowers are grown on the slopes....

In the Soviet Union, where socialist agriculture prevails and all the achievements of science are employed, the erosion of the soil can be completely stopped. We can bring our influence to bear on nature on a tremendous and unprecedented scale. We have a whole complex of methods at our disposal—correct crop rotation, the planting of shelter belts, the planting of trees around gullies and the regulation of the local flow of surface water. Everything in nature is connected, and we Soviet people alone are able to bring our influence to bear on the whole of a problem set by nature and not merely on individual aspects of it.

By creating friable soil of sound structure over large areas we check the flow of surface waters and thereby change the water regime of the whole country. By growing trees in the black-earth steppes, by covering the steppes with a dense network of windbreaker shelter belts, we are creating a new climate: the rapid passage of spring is checked, the temperature is lowered and humidity is increased.

Gradually we shall change the face of the steppes. Woods will become an inseparable feature of the landscape. This will be a new geography, a geography created by the people for the benefit of the people.

The new geography of the southern steppes is already in the making.

Take the Kamennaya (Stony) Steppe, one of the outposts that, it is true, are still too few in number.

In 1892 Dokuchayev laid the foundations of a scientific research station in the Kamennaya Steppe in the southern part of the Voronezh Region; but real work could be started there only in Soviet times. Recently, the station was transformed into the Institute of Agriculture of the Central Black-Earth Belt and was named after Dokuchayev.

Droughts used to be frequent in the Kamennaya Steppe. The soil was constantly dried up. Wormwood, the herald of the semi-desert, had already made its appearance. This was the place Dokuchayev chose to launch his offensive against erosion and drought.

Belts of woodland were planted to protect the fields from the hot winds. The slopes were strengthened with turf. Shrubs and trees, including fruit trees, were planted round the gullies. Long ravines and hollows were converted into ponds. The landscape has been completely changed, we now see stretches of fertile farmland surrounded by groves.

But not only the outward appearance of the district has changed. Soil erosion has been stopped. Soil is no longer washed away. The growth of the gullies has been checked. A correct crop rotation has produced a friable, fertile soil. The snow leaves the fields slowly. The atmosphere has become more humid and the reserves of subsoil water have increased.

The economic result of this transformation of nature is that during the past ten years the average grain crop in the Kamennaya Steppe region has doubled.

Assisted by the scientific research station, many of the

collective farms of Talovaya District (where the Kamennaya Steppe is situated) have greatly improved their farming methods; they are now famous throughout Voronezh Region for their bumper harvests. The influence of the scientific research station is spreading throughout the southern steppes.

In 1946—the year in which the centenary of Dokuchayev's birth was celebrated—his favourite child, the Kamennaya Steppe, experienced a severe blow—the drought. Dokuchayev's ideas, however, passed the test.

In May and June 1946 the rainfall in the Kamennaya Steppe was only half that of 1891 and 1921. A drought of unprecedented severity developed.

Nevertheless, the Kamennaya Steppe remained an oasis of fertility. The shelter belts laid out by Dokuchayev, the crop rotation systems introduced by Williams, the whole complex of scientific farming methods that are employed in the Soviet fields, protected it from the ravages of the drought. Leaves quivered, the earth breathed, ears formed on the corn. Autumn-sown wheat produced 16.5 centners per hectare; autumn-sown rye, 15 centners, and spring wheat about 11 centners.

Drought on the fields of the Kamennaya Steppe was vanquished.

This means that it can be vanquished everywhere; the scientific farming methods used in the Kamennaya Steppe can be applied on every collective and state farm. There is nothing to prevent it. Labour effort, serious thought and organization will stop soil erosion, compel drought to retreat, and raise bigger and bigger crops.

* * *

Today we are up against another sort of "erosion" in our Soviet fields that is causing our country very heavy damage. Thousands and thousands of workdays have to be spent in making good this damage. We refer to the "erosion" caused by the war.

The Nazis not only burned down towns and villages and blew up factories. They spoiled the fields over vast areas.

The storm of war swept across the ploughlands of the South, from the Danube to the Volga, leaving them pitted with shell craters and scarred by deep anti-tank ditches.

In the environs of Stalingrad there are five dugouts, sixty-nine foxholes, two group fire trenches, one communication trench, one bomb crater to every half a hectare of field. Over 450 cubic metres of barren subsoil were thrown up from these pits, covering almost all the fertile earth around.... To bring the Stalingrad environs into a state fit for ploughing, over 700,000 cubic metres of earth have to be shifted!

In the Moscow Region the war destroyed over 10,000 hectares of farmland. Wherever fighting took place the land is pitted with shell holes and craters. The clay thrown up on the surface gleams yellow and is overgrown with weeds. The roads wind to pass deep trenches.... About two per cent of the ploughland has been lost—in the Istra District, for example. The damage caused in some of the collective farms in this district is much greater: the Bezbozhnik Farm lost a quarter of its ploughland, and the Dynamo Farm a half.

The traces left by the invaders are gradually being wiped out. The fields are being ploughed over and cultivated. Shell holes are being filled in. Here and there the tank traps are being turned into ponds. Trees are being planted on bare mounds.

In many places the fields have to be "repaired" and these "repairs" entail enormous expense. They form part of the work of renewing the land that our Soviet people are now carrying out.

Improving the fertility of the soil—this is the constant concern of Soviet agriculture, of Soviet science, of the Soviet Government and of the Bolshevik Party. Again and again in the decisions of the February Plenum, the Communist Party called upon our scientists to devise ways of restoring and increasing the fertility of the soil.

Collective farmers deliver raw cotton to the state receiving
base. Uzbek S.S.R.

The Great Ferghana Canal, Uzbek S.S.R., one of the
biggest irrigation systems in the Soviet Union

A flock of fine-fleece sheep belonging to the Stalin
Collective Farm, Daghestan A.S.S.R.

By rehabilitating that which was destroyed by the enemy, by improving, transforming what nature has given us and what we inherited from the old society, we are creating a land of abundance, a land in which labour and intellect are triumphant.

But there are still many problems that have not yet been solved.

The crops we gather in the Soviet Union today are much bigger than those gathered in tsarist Russia, but they are not as big as they should be. Our agriculture is highly mechanized, but it needs more and more new machines. Farm work has been scientifically organized and has achieved a higher level, but much remains to be done to have these progressive scientific methods of farming employed everywhere.

The area under cultivation has been greatly enlarged, but a lot more work will be required to bring to life the vast expanses of the Far East, the cold North and the arid South, regions that are difficult to bring under the plough.

But we Soviet people have everything necessary to accomplish this task.

Bourgeois scientists subscribe to the "law of the diminishing returns," i.e., of the diminishing fertility of the soil. By this they demonstrate their lack of faith in the creative energy of man, lack of faith engendered by the moribund capitalist system. Our scientists have refuted the theory that fertility of the soil constantly tends to diminish owing to the "operation of natural laws." Soviet science has proved that there is no such "natural" and "eternal" law. Our Soviet peasantry have confirmed this deduction by their practical work.

Capitalism exhausted the soil, robbed it of its fertility. Socialism has restored to the soil its lost strength, has breathed new life into it.

In our socialist country the earth will possess the maximum of fertility. We recall here the words of Marx who said that if the earth is tilled properly it constantly improves. Or the

words of Engels who said that the productivity of the earth
may be infinitely increased.

The most progressive social system will create the most
fertile land.

A RATIONAL MAP

Soviet agriculture, like the entire socialist economy, is developing according to a single state plan. Planned distribution of
production is part and parcel of planned production.

The former, spontaneously developing agriculture could not
make rational use of the land, could not specialize the various
parts of the country on a correct, scientific basis. Soviet agriculture develops according to a plan, and this means conscious
specialization of districts, it means altering the old agricultural
map.

The selection of plants for sowing is not determined by
marketing considerations, but by a well-thought-out plan.
"Now that we have passed on to large-scale production and
have ensured for the state reserves of grain, we can and must
set ourselves the task of properly organizing specialization according to crops and branches," said Comrade Stalin at the
Sixteenth Congress of the Communist Party (June 1930).

Specialization in our country does not mean cultivating a
single crop in a district; this would lead to the exhaustion of
the soil. In addition to the main crop, the plan calls for other
crops to be included in the rotation scheme.

In our endeavour to distribute agricultural crops over the
country properly and rationally, we, in particular, have set out
to do away with the division of the country into "producing"
and "consuming" zones.

In tsarist Russia a sharp line was drawn across the map
from Kiev, through Tula and Nizhny Novgorod, to Vyatka, cutting the country into two parts. This line was fixed
on the map and it seemed that it was indisputable and eternal.

To the south of the line was the chernozem (black earth), steppe land with a surplus of grain. This was the "producing" zone.

To the north lay podzol soil, woods, swamps and a shortage of grain. This zone was called the "consuming" zone.

It used to be said: "Vereya Uyezd of Moscow Gubernia has enough of its own rye to last until Easter; Zvenigorod, until Shrovetide; and Bronnitsy and Mozhaisk, until Christmas."

The small peasants of the non-black-earth regions, ruined by the landlords and kulaks, groaning under the yoke of taxation and suffering from land hunger, crop failures and poverty, could not really enlarge their farms. They lacked the means with which to break virgin land or to increase the fertility of the soil. They deserted their villages en masse and went to seek work in the towns. Hundreds of thousands of hectares were left untilled and became overgrown with shrub. And vast regions continued to be called "consuming."

In the period covered by the Stalin five-year plans big industries grew up in the agricultural steppes of the Soviet South. Large towns sprang up where formerly wheat used to grow. The South could no longer supply the same share of its crops it had supplied in the past; the North had to begin growing its own grain. And what could not be done by poor, individual farms was done by the collective farms that worked according to plan, and were supplied with fertilizers and machinery.

At the Seventeenth Congress of the Communist Party (January 1934) Comrade Stalin said:

"Furthermore, we should note the fact that the accepted division of our regions into consuming regions and producing regions is also beginning to lose its hard and fast character. This year [1933] 'consuming' regions, such as the Moscow and Gorky regions, delivered nearly 80,000,000 poods of grain to the state. This, of course, is no small item. In the so-called consuming zone there are about 5,000,000 hectares of virgin soil covered with scrub. It is well known that the climate of

13*

this region is not bad; there is sufficient precipitation, and droughts do not occur. If this land were cleared of scrub and a number of organizational measures were undertaken, it would be possible to obtain a vast area for planting grain, which at the usually high yield in these districts could supply no less grain for the market than is now supplied by the Lower or Middle Volga. This would be a great help to the industrial centres in the North.

"Evidently, the task is to develop large tracts of grainland in the districts of the consuming zone."*

Following the instructions of their leader, our Soviet people cleared vast areas of land in the non-black-earth region of trees and scrub and put this land to the plough.

The "line of dependence" had cut across the map of Russia, dividing the country into "producing" and "consuming" zones. This division existed for decades. Under the Soviet government, however, this line lost its former significance.

The aim of the planned distribution of the various branches of agriculture is, in particular, to ensure that every region will have its own food supply base. The various regions can no longer remain entirely dependent on others for their food. Many agrarian regions have developed into industrial regions during the period of the Stalin five-year plans, their urban population has increased and these regions now consume more grain, vegetables and milk than before. At the Seventeenth Congress of the Communist Party, Comrade Stalin said:

"First of all, we must bear in mind that the old division of our regions into industrial regions and agrarian regions has now become obsolete. We no longer have exclusively agrarian regions to supply grain, meat and vegetables to the industrial regions; nor have we exclusively industrial regions which can count on receiving all the necessary produce from other regions." Comrade Stalin demanded that "every region develop its own agricultural base, so as to have its own supply of

---

* J. Stalin, *Problems of Leninism*, Moscow 1947, p. 487.

vegetables, potatoes, butter and milk, and, to some extent, grain and meat, if it does not want to get into difficulties."[*]

The towns and industrial centres are being surrounded by broad belts of vegetable gardens, greenhouses and dairy farms.

The variety of natural conditions in our country enables us to cultivate many different crops and to breed different kinds of animals. All branches of agriculture must be rationally distributed. The socialist system enables us to do this; the geography of Soviet agriculture is being built up on scientific, rational principles.

Soviet people are creating a new agricultural map which testifies to the increased efficiency in farming in all regions of the country, to the planned agricultural development of places that were formerly barren desert, to the flourishing condition of every region of our country. . . .

But this new, rational map does not come into being of itself. It is being drawn by the labour, the struggle, the great strain of effort of the people.

CHANGES IN CROP DISTRIBUTION

The wheat fields in our country stretch far and wide like a boundless ocean. Their golden waves roll from the Ukraine to the Kuban and from the Kuban to the Altai, and amidst these surging waves tower like rocks tall, grey elevators filled with grain. The grain flows in an inexhaustible stream into railway trucks and is carried to the towns in all parts of the Soviet Union.

Wheat is our principal grain crop.

No other country grows as much wheat as the U.S.S.R. For wheat area, size of crop and quality of grain, the Soviet Union holds first place in the world.

If all our wheat fields could be placed together, they would occupy an area larger than that of the Black Sea.

---

[*] *Ibid.*, pp. 486-87.

And the sea of wheat is constantly expanding.

Our principal wheat region is the black-earth steppe; but in the period the Soviet Government has been in existence, wheat has also conquered non-black-earth regions and has invaded forest lands.

Before the revolution the non-black-earth regions grew almost exclusively the "coarse grains"—barley, oats and rye. Nikitin's *Course of Russian Geography*, printed in 1879, says the following of these regions: "In order of importance rye takes first place amongst crops. It provides the inhabitants with rye bread, kvass, vodka, straw with which to thatch their cottages and feed their cattle and many other less important products. . . ." Hardly any wheat was grown in the North.

Is the soil in the North unsuitable? No. The soil in North Russia is no worse than that of Denmark, and yet Denmark produced rich harvests of wheat. Wheat was grown in Arctic Alaska with seed obtained by the selection and crossing of our Siberian varieties.

Is the climate unsuitable in the North? No. True, there is less warmth here than in the southern regions, but there is enough. Furthermore, the withering breath of drought that often reduces the crop in the South rarely reaches the North. Northern crops are stable.

Is the yield low in the North? No. The wheat yield in the northern regions is usually higher than in the southern regions.

There is every possibility of growing wheat in the non-black-earth regions, but no advantage was taken of these possibilities in old Russia. Wheat could be seen here and there only on lands belonging to landlords and kulaks.

In the Soviet period, after the collective farms were established, the wheat map of our country was altered in conformity with Comrade Stalin's plans. The Central Committee of the Communist Party adopted a decision to extend wheat cultivation to the non-black-earth regions, and year after year wheat was sown in the North as well as in the South in ever increasing areas.

By converting the non-black-earth zone from a "consuming" to a "producing" zone, we converted it from a "coarse grain" to a "wheat" zone.

Soviet science came to the assistance of the collective farms: cold-resisting varieties were developed for the North.

Before the revolution the wheat fields in the non-black-earth regions, north of the Kiev-Tula-Nizhny-Novgorod line, occupied an area of only 250,000 hectares. Before the Great Patriotic War, however, the wheat area in these regions had increased to over 3,000,000 hectares. Although the non-black-earth regions specialize in flax, dairy produce, vegetables and potatoes, they now gather large crops of wheat.

The northern boundary of the wheat belt shifted beyond the 56th parallel into the 60th and then went further north. The Soviet non-black-earth region now produces half as much wheat as is produced by such world grain-exporting countries as Canada or the Argentine.

After the tree stumps were uprooted and the scrub cleared, golden wheat fields covered the virgin non-black-earth regions.

If you pluck a ripe ear in the field somewhere near Pskov or Vologda, grains of wheat and not of rye will trickle into your hand. Plenty of oats and rye are still grown in the North, and their area is still growing. "Coarse grains," however, have ceased to predominate in these fields. Large quantities of wheat and wheat flour are still brought to the North from the South, but the North already has white bread produced from its own wheat.

The importance of the extension of wheat cultivation to the non-black-earth regions was revealed during the war, when nearly the whole of the black-earth steppe as far as the Volga was seized and laid waste by the enemy. The wheat of the North was an important contribution to the country's food supply when it was temporarily deprived of wheat from the Ukraine, Don and Kuban.

But it was not the wheat of the North, of course, that saved us; it was the wheat of the East. Wheat was planted in the trans-Volga, the South Urals, Northern Kazakhstan and Western Siberia also in tsarist times, but the wheat area in these regions has greatly expanded in Soviet times. Siberia has almost doubled its wheat crop.

During the period of the Stalin five-year plans, industries appeared in the East and large towns grew up. This created the need for new agricultural centres. The collective farms and state farms broke new land. In response to the appeal of the Soviet Government, many peasants from the European part of the U.S.S.R. migrated to the regions beyond the Urals. Vast wheat fields sprang up in the formerly empty plains. Tractors, ploughs, seed drills and combines passed over the virgin steppes. Before the war the Urals and Western Siberia were already producing more wheat than the Ukraine and the Crimea. At the Eighteenth Congress of the Communist Party of the Soviet Union (March 1939) Comrade Stalin noted that "the base of market grain has shifted from the Ukraine, which was formerly considered the granary of our country, to the North and the East. . . ."

The fields of the East helped us out greatly in our struggle against the enemy; they were the source of our bread supply. During the war the collective farms and state farms beyond the Urals ploughed up additional land. In 1942 alone Kazakhstan enlarged its cultivated area—mainly wheat—by 800,000 hectares. Many regions that had formerly obtained their grain from other regions were able to supply their needs themselves during the war.

The plan intervened in the grain-growing geography also in the extreme South, in Central Asia. Formerly, wheat was often sown in these regions on irrigated land, and this resulted in a reduction of the cotton area. The cotton growers wanted to get out of the clutches of the grain merchants and so strove to grow their own grain.

In Soviet times the state sees to it that Central Asia is supplied with grain and the irrigated fields are planted to cotton. But this does not mean that cotton has become the sole

master of the fields and that wheat has been driven out of
Central Asia. The irrigated fields are planted in rotation
with a fodder crop, alfalfa, although not yet to the extent that
this should be done. It is the dry lands that are planted to
wheat, the unirrigated fields high up in the foothills of the
mountains where there is insufficient rainfall for cotton, but
enough for wheat.

This is how the map of our principal crop, wheat, has
changed during the thirty years of Soviet government.

This map will undergo still further change in the period
of the present, postwar five-year plan. Wheat is shifting farther to the North and the East. The greatest expansion of wheat
growing is taking place in Kazakhstan and Siberia, where
there is plenty of suitable land that is not yet fully cultivated.
There, in the East, with its continental climate, the best wheat
in the world grows, hard wheat, rich in proteins. Its horny
grain is almost transparent through the cross section.

* * *

Rice fields are kept under water up to a hundred days.
Formerly, the boundaries of the irrigated oases of Central
Asia, Southern Kazakhstan and the Transcaucasus were regarded as the limits of the rice-growing area just as they
were regarded as the limits of the cotton belt. Restricted to
the area of the oases, these two irrigated crops were in constant conflict for water.

In the Soviet period the geographical redistribution of rice
cultivation began. New lands were found further to the north,
beyond the normal rice belt. It was found that this valuable
crop can be grown in many districts among the backwaters of
the River Kuban, on the floodlands of the Lower Dnieper,
in the Volga Delta, and around Lake Khanka in the Far East.

The South still remains the principal rice producer. In a
planned economy, with scientifically organized farming and
proper irrigation, rice is not the enemy of cotton. But while

retained in reasonable quantities in its old southern habitat, rice is also being planted on new lands. A crop that from ancient times has been cultivated on tiny plots of land, with the aid of the buffalo-drawn wooden plough and the sickle, is now being grown on the largest plantations in the world, on which all the farm work, from planting to reaping, is mechanized, and on which aeroplanes and harvester combines are used. Before the war, the new rice fields around Zaporozhye produced record crops.

Where formerly there had been no industry of any kind, rice-hulling mills have been built. In these places industry has entered the rural districts, thanks to rice.

Rice is moving northward. You will find rice plantations— as yet small and experimental—near Kuibyshev, Kursk and Ryazan, and in the swamps of Polesie. This supposedly southern crop will even grow in the environs of Moscow, two thousand kilometres to the north of the old rice belt. A new rice map is in the making.

We have become accustomed to associating rice with hot, far-off Asia, but the efforts of Soviet scientists and the labours of our collective farmers are compelling us to look at the map, to see the world, with different eyes.

In the fertile subtropics of Western Transcaucasia oranges, lemons, tea and bamboo can grow, but at one time maize was the predominant crop there. Today, however, maize is gradually being driven off the most valuable fields; it is shifting to other regions to make room for subtropical crops. The shifting of the conventional signs on the map tells the story of wise husbandry.

Maize was regarded as a southern crop, but experiments have shown that it can grow in the North, in the wooded steppes of the European parts of the U.S.S.R., and in the steppes of Siberia.

In Siberia the cultivation of rye has grown considerably. Millet has found a new home in the Southeast. The sunflower has moved to the East. During the war the cameline (C. sativa)

—the quickest-ripening of all the oil-bearing plants—was widely planted in the Volga Basin and Western Siberia and also found its way to the Transbaikal and the Far East. These are changes not only in geography, but also in previous conceptions.

Cotton grew in Central Asia and in Eastern Transcaucasia. It seemed that the only places in Russia suitable for cotton growing were the sunny, irrigated oases of the Far South. On the map the cotton zone hugged the southern frontiers of the country and so it remained.

Tsarist Russia did not grow enough cotton to supply her needs. Half of the raw cotton required was imported from the U.S.A. and for these imports Russia paid America a hundred million gold rubles a year.

The socialist state could not tolerate dependence on America. Soviet industry had to spin Soviet cotton; thus the need arose for the rapid expansion of the cotton area.

New lands were broken in Central Asia and the Transcaucasus and planted to cotton—and every new hectare provided raw material for about four thousand metres of cotton goods a year. But the expansion of the cotton area on the irrigated lands of Central Asia and the Transcaucasus was not enough. The struggle for cotton independence, now brought to a victorious conclusion, called for the development of new cotton regions. Cotton sought new places to grow in where it would not need irrigation, where it would not be necessary to build expensive and intricate irrigation systems.

Such places exist. From the Lower Danube to the Lower Volga lies a chain of extensive, fertile but arid lands. Rain is rare in these regions. The land needed a drought-resisting crop. This crop was developed—dry-grown cotton.

The Soviet Government redrafted the geographical boundaries of the cotton area, extending them far to the North—from the 43rd to the 47th parallel.

Collective and state cotton-growing farms and machine and tractor stations appeared in the formerly barren steppes around the Black Sea and the Azov Sea. Cotton growing involves considerable labour, but the southern steppes are sparsely populated. Mechanization helped. As there are no irrigation ditches in these fields, the tractor can easily pull big, many-bottom ploughs across them.

The scorching sun blazed in the steppe. In the spring the eyes were dazzled by a multitude of brightly-hued flowers; in the autumn the rustling of wormwood was heard. The steppe was deserted.

The steppe was ploughed up. Furrows stretched far away to the horizon. Roads were built. Cotton-ginning mills were erected. Industry found its way into the rural districts. The Ukraine and the North Caucasus began to grow the raw material they needed for their textiles.

Central Asia and the Transcaucasus are still the chief and decisive cotton regions, but they are not the only ones now. A new cotton region has been created, the most northerly in the world. On the eve of the war over half a million hectares were planted with cotton here, representing one-fourth of the total cotton area of the U.S.S.R.

The first attempt to plant cotton in the European part of Russia was made three hundred years ago, in the reign of Tsar Alexei Mikhailovich. Similar attempts were made later, in the nineteenth century. But it was only under the Soviet government that attempts of this kind proved successful.

The cotton yield in the unirrigated districts around the Black Sea and the Azov Sea is, of course, lower than that in Central Asia or the Transcaucasus; but it is higher than that in India, where cotton has been grown for thousands of years.

During the war the new cotton region fell into the hands of the Germans. They ruined everything, and the cotton area moved south again. Soviet life has now returned to the region, and cotton is coming back too.

The geographical boundaries of the sugar-beet regions were artificially restricted. The cultivation of beet, the root crop that provides sugar, was confined to the Ukraine and Kursk Region. As a consequence, the sugar-refining industry was confined to these regions too. The other regions of the country were deliberately kept dependent on these in the interests of the Tereshchenkos, Bobrinskys and other lords of the sugar market—it increased their profits.

The sugar refineries that were concentrated in the beet-growing regions required large quantities of raw material: this led to the unplanned expansion of the beet plantations in the Ukraine and Kursk Region. Beet was planted even in fields that were unsuitable for this crop. And all around stretched a vast country where no beets were grown at all. The cost of transporting sugar to the East was higher than the cost of producing it.

Socialist construction brings production territorially closer to consumption. The map of the sugar industry is changing—there are sugar refineries all over the country—and this alters the sugar-beet map.

Sugar beet has broken out of the boundaries that kept it confined to the old "natural sugar-beet zone."

In the South, it has for the first time travelled as far as Armenia and Georgia. In these republics there are lands no less suitable for sugar-beet growing than those of the Ukraine. The Transcaucasus now has its own sugar.

Sugar beet is also being planted in the Altai, in the Minusinsk Steppes and in Transbaikal. And Siberia now has its own sugar.

In the East sugar beet has reached the shores of the Pacific. The Maritime Territory also has its own sugar.

Sugar beet is grown in Kirghizia, in South Kazakhstan, in Uzbekistan. In some districts it has already become the main crop. In this way Central Asia also got its own sugar.

Cotton moved from irrigated to unirrigated districts, but sugar beet moved in the opposite direction, from dry lands to irrigated lands. The yield from irrigated lands is two or three times higher than that from dry land.

The Ukraine and Kursk Region are still the main sugar-beet regions, but they are not the only ones today. Before the war almost a tenth of the sugar beet grown in our country was grown in the new regions, and this does not include the sugar beet grown in the Baltic republics and on the Karelian Isthmus.

The eastern sugar-beet regions played an important role during the war when the Ukrainian sugar-beet district—the principal district—was captured by the Germans. Sugar beet penetrated twelve new regions.

Customary landscapes changed. Piles of beetroots lie in the oases in the desert like those to be seen in the wooded steppes of Vinnitsa. Camels carry to the railway stations not only bales of white cotton but also basketloads of yellowish sugar beet. At one time sugar was an expensive urban luxury to the Kazakh, Kirghiz or Uzbek. Today the leading Kazakh, Kirghiz and Uzbek collective farms are growing sugar beet and reaping crops such as had never been heard of in old Russia.

Sugar beet has also penetrated the podzol region. During the war it would have been difficult to find a collective farm in the Moscow, Vologda or Gorky regions that did not have at least a small field under sugar beet. This crop is grown for a different purpose in these regions: it is not treated in refineries, but in the collective farms themselves for making jam and syrup.

Sugar beet has even settled in the Archangel Region. The fields are not surrounded by oak groves and cherry orchards, but by dense conifer forests.

This so-called black-earth crop will conquer more and more regions in the East and the North. Experiments have shown that sugar beet can even be grown beyond the Arctic Circle—on the Solovetskiye Islands, at Naryan-Mar and in the far north of Siberia. Much more work has to be done, however, before it can be acclimatized in these parts.

Long-fibre flax has also moved beyond the bounds of its old habitat. Formerly, flax growing was very unevenly distrib-

uted; it was concentrated almost exclusively in the Northwest corner of the country owing to the demand created by
the Russian spinning mills and by the nearby foreign market. In some places in this region flax occupied three-fourths
of the spring crops area. The frequent planting of one and
the same crop exhausted the soil. Away to the East there
were regions in which practically no flax at all was grown,
and which purchased linen at a high price.

Today, mechanization is helping the collective farms to
grow this crop (which entails a great deal of arduous labour)
in the new, less populated districts of the Urals and Siberia.
Green fields dotted with blue flax flowers are now no longer
a feature of the landscape in the Pskov or Smolensk regions
alone.

This is how the geographical distribution of our crops has
changed during the thirty years of Soviet government. The
old "limits of distribution" have been rejected, antiquated
conceptions have been smashed.

The new geographical distribution of crops is an indication
of the growth and increasing complexity of Soviet economy,
based on deliberate control, on socialist planning.

NEW CROPS

Thousands of years have passed since the first husbandman
ploughed the first furrow on the plains of Russia, but the
character of agriculture changed but little during these many
centuries. The list of farm crops common in Russia was
short and meagre. In a country with a feeble and backward
industry, new industrial crops were hardly ever introduced. It
was always the same rye, barley, oats and flax.... This
limited and spontaneously compiled list of crops bore the
hallmark of centuries long passed away.

Then came the time when the monotony of crops came
into conflict with growing variety in life. The new Soviet in-

dustries created the need for new plants—fibre, rubber and oil-bearing plants. Raw materials for essential and fatty oils, vegetable dyes, acids and plastics were required in unprecedented quantities.

The demand arose for varnish made from the fruit of the tung tree which grows in China, for gutta-percha, which comes from the sap of a tree that grows in Indonesia, for cork, the bark of a particular type of oak tree that grows in Algiers, for the Australian acacia the bark of which is used in the manufacture of tannin, and for the strong, silklike fibre of the ramie, the Chinese nettle.

The immense task arose of revising and extending the list of plants cultivated in our country. This was called for not only by our country's rapidly-growing industry, but also by the fact that agriculture was advancing into former desert areas and suitable crops for these areas had to be chosen. The list of vegetable raw materials had to be radically revised and its enlargement planned.

The acclimatization of foreign plants proved to be no easy task—no two places in the world have exactly the same climate, and natural conditions do not coincide exactly in any two places. Not every plant taken from its native habitat will take root in its new home. A plant may take root and not flower, it may flower but not bear fruit. The nature of the plant has to be remade, it has to be adjusted to its new conditions of life.

During the period of the Stalin five-year plans painstaking and persevering efforts were made to transplant to Soviet soil those grains, vegetables, flowers and fruits from America, Africa, Australia and Asia, that we need.

As a result of these efforts, Soviet agriculture was enriched by the addition of many new crops. Some of them are already being widely cultivated in our collective farms and state farms. Others are still being worked on.

Sorghum has been widely introduced into the arid regions of the country. This plant is so impervious to drought that it

Dynamo Collective Farm, Chuvash A.S.S.R., receives deed of
perpetual lease on its land

On the fields of the Lenin Kolkhoz, Moldavian S.S.R.

I. V. Michurin, transformer of nature, distinguished Soviet
naturalist

is known as "the camel of the vegetable kingdom." The plant was first brought from Palestine and transplanted to Southern Ukraine, the Volga Basin and Kazakhstan.

The soybean is a Manchurian plant that contains proteins as valuable as animal proteins; before the war this crop was sown over large areas in the Ukraine, Moldavia and the Far East, and is already penetrating into the central regions of the U.S.S.R.

The sweet potato, a native of the West Indies that is more prolific and nutritious than the ordinary potato, is now being cultivated in Central Asia. Bread made from wheat flour with sweet potato flour added is more tasty than ordinary bread and does not grow stale so quickly.

The drought-resisting noot, a legume from the shores of the Mediterranean, has been transplanted to the banks of the Volga.

Byzantine oats have become a winter crop in the cotton-growing regions of Azerbaijan.

Indian hemp, a plant whose fibre is a substitute for jute, is grown in Kirghizia and the North Caucasus. It is used for the manufacture of sugar bags which protect the sugar from damage by the absorption of moisture and, moreover, leave no fibres in the sugar.

For the first time in the U.S.S.R., American pecan nuts are being grown in Uzbekistan. These are the most nutritious and oily of the nuts used by man.

The fibres of the Indian mallow are used for insulating cable. This is a new plant to the Soviet Union, and is being grown as far north as Byelorussia.

The ground almond provides flour and oil for the confectionery industry. Peanuts are used in the manufacture of a valuable oil. Southern hemp is necessary for the manufacture of rope. The teazle is used in the textile industry. All these are new plants in the Soviet Union. Grass from the Sudan, American couch grass, Abyssinian ajgon, Dalmatian marguerites and Mexican guayule....

14—777

A lot has been done to adapt these foreign plants to the conditions in our country. For example, we have already developed our own variety of the rubber-bearing guayule. Soviet guayule has a higher rubber content than its Mexican parent. The plant is used differently in the U.S.S.R.—the whole bush, from root to leaf tips, is used in the manufacture of rubber.

This is the way we have enlarged the list of cultivated crops in the Soviet Union.

But the list has been enlarged not only by the addition of plants of foreign origin. During the period of the five-year plans, on Stalin's instructions, a search has been made for valuable wild plants growing in our own country, in the deserts of Central Asia, in the Caucasus Mountains and among the hills of Transbaikal. The whole of the immensely rich flora of our country was re-examined. Expeditions studied countless plants, carried out thousands of experiments to discover the possibility of raising new crops.

We are already reaping the fruits of this work. For example, a plant with strong fibres called "kendyr," that grows wild in Central Asia, is being cultivated in the valley of the River Chu in Kirghizia.

Quite a number of medicinal herbs have been found, and these may now be gathered not only in the hills and forests, but in the fields where they are being cultivated.

A considerable amount of rubber is now obtained from plants that were formerly ignored, or were quite unknown.

In 1931, the rubber-bearing kok-saghyz, a yellow-flowered plant resembling a dandelion, was found in the Tien Shan Mountains, at a height of two thousand metres above sea level. The rubber obtained from the kok-saghyz is as good as that obtained from the foreign tropical hevea tree. Kok-saghyz is now being cultivated in most of the regions of the U.S.S.R. It has moved as far north as the peat beds and drained swamps of Byelorussia.

In 1930 the tau-saghyz, a plant then unknown to botanists, was found in the Kara-Tau Mountains of Southern Kazakhstan; the roots of this plant sometimes contain as much as fifty per cent rubber. The cultivation of this valuable rubber plant has begun.

The bearded spindle tree—one of the wild shrubs that grow in our woods—was found to contain gutta-percha. This plant is also being cultivated.

We are indebted for the cultivation of new useful plants to our Soviet scientists, but not only to them. Collective farmers, hunters, frontier troopers and even school children have taken part in the search for new crops. Kok-saghyz was discovered by a collective farmer named Spivachenko and a Young Communist Leaguer named Bukhanevich. A Kazakh named Dyurbekov showed tau-saghyz to our scientists during one of their expeditions in Kazakhstan. The whole of the Soviet people are imbued with the desire to enrich and strengthen our country.

The rehabilitation of the fields of the U.S.S.R. is a matter for the state as a whole. Soviet scientists conduct their work in accordance with a single plan. And the new crops are introduced into the collective and state farms in accordance with a single plan.

The new crops require a great deal of labour, but this labour is rewarded a hundredfold. Their cultivation serves to increase the incomes of the collective farmers.

The new crops help to renew not only agriculture, but industry as well. To process the new industrial crops new factories are built, very often in places where there was no industry at all. In the remote regions of Highland Karabakh, for example, rubber factories have been built to process the guayule.

New crops mean new raw materials and new branches of industry.

Plants that we have known and cultivated for a long time are now also being used in new ways. In this respect they might well be called "new."

The coarse tobacco plant (makhorka) from which citric acid is now extracted—is this an old crop?

14*

The cotton plant to which the scientist gives a natural colour at will, from beige to brown, from pale blue to dark green—is this an old crop?

The maize that now has over a hundred and fifty uses—is this an old crop?

The ancient bread grain, the patriarch of world agriculture, the wheat plant from whose stalks soap and paper are now made—is this an old crop?

NO WINTER HERE

Soviet scientists bring plants from different countries, but mostly they bring them from southern countries. Amongst the new Soviet crops many are subtropical.

Tsarist Russia spent about 200 million gold rubles a year on imported subtropical raw materials. Russia cultivated hardly any subtropical crops of its own and the Soviet Union had to start practically from scratch in this field.

The Black Sea littoral, from Sochi to Batumi, is hot and moist like a hothouse. The average temperature of the coldest month is above freezing point. In two years, tall trees will spring up in abandoned cornfields, and the stubble that has not yet had time to rot stands in a thick forest. This region is the "moist" subtropics.

In the sheltered mountain valleys of Southern Turkmenia and in the Tajikistan Republic it is dry and hot. There is a low rainfall in summer and scarcely any frost in winter. This is the "dry" subtropics.

On Comrade Stalin's instructions, the former maize fields and reed-grown wastes in Transcaucasia have been converted into fruit plantations, and these are already producing more subtropical fruits than we formerly imported from abroad. And yet most of the trees have not yet started bearing fruit. . . .

The fertility of Western Georgia is something extraordinary. Some tangerine trees produce as much as six thousand fruits a year, and some mature orange trees produce as much as a ton of fruit a year. And yet, even the distinguished geographer of tsarist Russia, P. P. Semyonov Tien Shansky, wrote in 1900: "The choice of plants to be cultivated inWestern Transcaucasia is rendered difficult by the warm and moist climate...."

The fruit of the Chinese tung tree is more than half oil: it is used for the manufacture of a lacquer that protects metal from rust. There were no tung trees in old Russia, but today they are growing in the Transcaucasus over an area of thousands of hectares. And Soviet ships have their keels lacquered with tung varnish.

There were practically no Algerian cork trees in old Russia; cork bark was formerly imported from abroad. Today we have our own cork-tree groves.

The cultivation of plants yielding essential oils was insignificant before the revolution. Today the Soviet Union cultivates about twenty different plants of this kind on plantations covering over 150,000 hectares. The Kazanlyk rose, mint, coriander, aniseed, geranium.... We are producing our own rose, lavender and sage oils. A kilogram of oil obtained from Kazanlyk roses is worth twenty thousand rubles.

The ramie, or Chinese nettle, which produces a valuable fibre used in the manufacture of special fabrics, was not grown in Russia before. Today it is to be found amongst the crops of Western Georgia.

The subtropics provide new raw materials for new factories. Agriculture, which formerly concerned itself mostly with the production of food, is now providing materials for industry on an ever increasing scale.

The higher the living standard of the people the greater is the demand for southern vegetables and subtropical fruits.

Tsarist Russia imported lemons from Sicily, oranges from Palestine, tea from Ceylon and figs from Turkey. Gold was paid for a distant foreign climate.

Citrus fruits cost Russia more than twelve million rubles a year. Today Georgia alone grows about 500 million tangerines, oranges and lemons a year. These brightly coloured spheres containing the concentrated life-giving sunshine of the South are distributed over the entire country.

Before the revolution tea plantations in the Russian Empire occupied an area of about nine hundred hectares. A primitive little factory produced inferior "army" tea. Today, in Georgia alone, tea plantations cover an area of about fifty thousand hectares. During the present five-year plan period this area will be increased to about sixty thousand hectares. Over thirty well-equipped tea factories are operating.

At first tea grew only in Georgia. Then it appeared at Lenkoran, on the Caspian seaboard. In the postwar five-year plan period tea is rapidly penetrating into the Krasnodar Territory. On the northern side of the Caucasus Mountains, near Maikop, tea has stood up to 20° C. of frost on experimental plantations.

Tea cultivation has always been the prerogative of Ceylon, Assam and China. ... Today Russia is among the tea-producing countries.

The Stakhanovites on our tea plantations obtain tea leaf crops bigger than any recorded in the world literature on tea growing. And this is in the extreme northern limit of the tea-growing zone. ...

The Mexican avocado, the miracle tree, the fruit of which contains nine vitamins, has acclimatized itself to the conditions on the Black Sea littoral of the Caucasus. The avocado fruit has a buttery taste and a nutty smell. It produces more calories than beefsteak. It contains less water than any other fruit and about thirty-seven per cent of it is fat. It is like fresh butter in a natural packing. Today we have three hundred avocado trees, while ten years ago we had only two.

Figs and pomegranates grow in the oases of Central Asia. In the Crimea, on the Apsheron Peninsula, and along the Atrek in Southern Turkmenistan, olives are cultivated.

The date palm, from distant, hot Arabia, has already raised its graceful trunk and feathery leaves on the Atrek.

All this has cost tremendous effort.

There are no frosty winters in the subtropics, but on the Black Sea coast of the Caucasus the mercury sometimes drops below zero C. in the winter months. The frost is a menace to tender plants. The cold winter of the first year of the war, for example, caused heavy damage to the orchards and plantations.

To save the plants, their trunks are wrapped up and the heat regime of the soil is regulated by special heaters which are installed in the plantations.... Experiments, invention, labour.

Usually a thousand lemon trees are planted to the hectare. In an experimental plantation in Georgia over three thousand per hectare were planted. When the trees matured, three times as many lemons were gathered of a size equal to those gathered on the usual plantations. Having been planted closer together, the trees withstood the winter better; a favourable microclimate had been created for them.

The most effective method of developing our subtropical regions, however, is to cultivate our own varieties of plants. We have already produced a lemon tree that creeps along the ground and is impervious to frost. Soviet plant breeders have combined the imperviousness to cold possessed by China tea with the flavour and high yield of Indian tea. The perennial cinchona tree, a native of Java, is now cultivated in Western Georgia as an annual plant.

Sensitive plants are susceptible to gusts of cold wind: the plantations are therefore surrounded by belts of trees; the fields are sheltered by green screens.

In some places on the subtropical Caucasian seaboard torrential rains threaten to wash away the mountain soil. To prevent this, the hill slopes are here and there terraced by means of tractors. The plants are set out on these long, narrow terraces which run crosswise to the slope. These fields can be said to have been made: the whole landscape has been altered.

In the Lenkoran lowlands summer is extremely hot. To protect the plantations from the excessive heat artificial shades are erected.

Crops have to be protected from pests. For this purpose pest-annihilating stations have been established equipped with special apparatus.

This is how man is increasing his power over nature in our country.

In the region of Denau, in Southern Uzbekistan, sugar cane has been introduced. The ancients called the sap of sugar cane "honey without bees." This guest from the tropics does not have an easy time so far north: the air is drier, the vegetation period is shorter, the winter is more severe. In its homeland the sugar cane gets 5,000 mm. of rain a year, in Denau there is not a drop of rain all the summer and the plantations have to be artificially irrigated. The persevering labours of our Soviet people have been rewarded. The difference in climate has been overcome by the selection of early-ripening varieties, by feeding the growing plants and by crossing the wild Central Asian sugar cane with cultivated American varieties. During the present five-year plan period a rum distillery is to be built in Uzbekistan. The raw material will be the sugar canes which have never before been grown in our country, and which it was believed never could be grown.

Our Soviet subtropics are not very big in area. They lie right on the very edge of the map of the U.S.S.R. We have very few places that are protected by mountains from the cold breath of the North and have no frosty winter.

But the socialist plan enables us to utilize the gifts of nature in our country in a systematic and rational way. There is nothing to prevent us from taking from nature everything she has to give. No obstacles in the shape of private property, anarchy of production, a disunited peasantry or technical backwardness stand in our way.

If all this is taken into account, our subtropical region will turn out to be not so very small. Natural deficiencies are compensated by the advantages of the Soviet social system. Every year sees an increase in our subtropical plantations and larger numbers of oranges and lemons are sent to Archangel, Igarka and Khabarovsk.

Neither the fertility of the red soil nor the potency of the southern sun will be wasted in our country.

ORCHARDS

When we wish to describe something that is bright and beautiful we often compare it with a flourishing orchard. Orchards beautify the country with their vivid blossoms and the fragrance of their fruits. Furthermore, fruits and berries are an important item in the people's diet.

Fruit growing is a big and important branch of the national economy.

There are numerous orchards in the Soviet Union, but we need many more, not only in the fertile regions of the South, but also in the Centre, in the East and in the North. We want fruit growing to spread all over our country, all the way to its northern limits.

Nature placed obstacles to the spread of fruit growing to the northern regions; but the creative minds of our scientists, supported by the Communist Party and the whole people, have broken down these obstacles. By dint of untiring effort, Ivan Vladimirovich Michurin, the great Russian scientific horticulturist, opened the road for the advance of fruit trees to the North. He changed the very nature of the plants, he grew many new varieties that had never been heard of before.

Michurin began by growing southern fruit trees in Kozlov, in the Tambov Gubernia, where he lived. But these trees could not acclimatize themselves to the strange conditions and perished. Then Michurin began to employ the crossing method and produced new varieties; but these varieties failed to combine the fertility of the southern trees with the hardiness of the Central

Russian—the local characters predominated in the new trees; apple trees were impervious to frost, but the fruit was sour.

The deduction Michurin drew from this revealed his genius. The deduction was that the local characters predominated in the environment to which they were accustomed; therefore, both parents of the hybrid must be selected from varieties alien to Kozlov. The two varieties crossed must be placed in equal conditions. Michurin began to select couples in conformity with his theory; he began to cross southern fruits with those of the Far East instead of with local Kozlov varieties.

In this way he developed the Michurin Beurré Zimnaya pear. Michurin transferred the pollen of the French Beurré Royal pear on to the stamen of the wild Ussurian pear. The new variety proved to be both fertile and frost-resisting. From the French parent it inherited its large size and excellent flavour, and from the Ussurian its ability to withstand frost of 30° C. and more. The pear was developed in Kozlov, where the fruit from France and that from the banks of the Ussuri River were equally foreign. The North had been conquered by combining plants from the southern orchards with sturdy plants from the East Asian taiga. The great transformer of nature removed geographical boundaries that had been regarded as "natural."

By crossing plants and subsequently adapting them Michurin developed over three hundred new varieties in the course of his lifetime. Applying a whole complex of measures that he devised, he crossed plants that were not only far removed from each other geographically, but even belonged to different species; garden cherry with bird cherry, pear with rowan, apple with currant, peach with almond. It was easier for him this way to shatter the heredity of the plants and give them new qualities, that is, to control nature.

In tsarist Russia this great scientific feat remained almost unknown and unappreciated. Few people knew of it outside of Kozlov. Michurin was left to his own devices.

It was the Soviet Government that recognized the national importance of Michurin's work. The dreams of the great Russian scientist came true, and his work began to be of service to the whole people.

The Soviet Government and the Communist Party did everything to ensure that the work of the scientist bore fruit. After the revolution Michurin no longer worked alone. He directed the work of a whole staff of scientific workers who conducted their researches in splendidly equipped laboratories and studies. After Michurin's death the work he had begun continued and expanded. Many of Michurin's pupils have themselves become leading scientists.

Michurinsk—the present name of Kozlov—has become the scientific centre for the "northernizing" of fruit trees. Not only is research conducted here; people are taught here to employ Michurin's methods. In the town there is now the Michurin Horticultural College and a Michurin horticultural school.

Michurinsk, of course, cannot grow fruit trees for the whole country because the nature of the regions differ. Each locality must develop its own local varieties. Michurinsk provides not only saplings for planting, but also sound advice. Work in the localities is conducted by Michurin stations, experimental fruit growers, collective-farm laboratories and Michurin circles in the collective and state farms, all of which put Michurin's ideas into practice.

This is the decisive feature of the Michurin movement. The horticultural map of our country can be corrected only by the creative efforts of the masses, by the hard work of the large body of men and women who have set out to develop new varieties adapted to local natural conditions. Only the people can create the new horticultural geography. Here lies the source of success.

The Michurin movement could become a mass movement only in our Soviet country, in the land of collective farms and progressive science, the land in which the creative forces of the whole people are unfolding on a scale hitherto unwitnessed. Michurin's great words—"We cannot wait for favours from

Nature; we must wrest them from her"—could find a powerful response only in our country.

During the period of the Stalin five-year plans the orchards in our country more than doubled in area. Big orchards were laid out in many of the collective and state farms. Formerly the orchard was only an adjunct to the farmer's vegetable garden. Today orchards occupy whole fields—row after row of apple trees planted in straight lines. The biggest orchards in the world have been created.

Fruit growing has begun to spread over the country and to conquer new territory.

The frosty winters prevented the apple and pear from spreading to the Urals or Siberia. We Soviet people, however, decided that wherever there were factories, where there were towns and settlements, orchards can and must be laid out. And the orchards were planted. In the Urals and Siberia, twenty thousand hectares of orchard have been planted since the Soviet government was established.

The Siberian climate is one of extremes: hot in summer and heavy frost in winter. But the heat can be utilized, and shelter from the frost can be created. Professor Kizyurin of Omsk introduced into Siberia what is called in Russian the "creeper orchard": the tree trunks grow horizontally, along the ground, instead of vertically.

In winter the apple-tree branches are pegged down to the ground and they lie under the snow; it is warmer there than above the snow, and the Siberian frost no longer has any terrors for the apple tree.

The Siberian summer is one of dry atmosphere and brilliant sunshine. In the European part of the Soviet Union with its mild, damp climate, it takes longer for the trees to change from the sapling to the wood and they are less equipped to meet the winter. In Siberia, the saplings that have matured well during the hot, dry summer, fear the frost less. In the European part of the Soviet Union fruit trees begin to bear fruit at a comparatively late period in life. In Siberia, however, the apple tree bears fruit in the second or third year after planting. An eight-year-old orchard may produce as much as fifty tons of apples per hectare.

Right close to the earth apples weighing a pound each ripen. The weight of the fruit pulls the low branches down to the ground and they gradually adopt the form of creeping plants; there is no need to peg them down.

This is how European varieties of fruit are penetrating beyond the Urals.

The creeper orchards that were planted on the banks of the Irtysh just before the war produced their second crop of fruit by the end of the war. Thousands of apple trees, all bearing fruit, are growing in the place about which we used to sing: "On the wild banks of the Irtysh...."

The Central Russian varieties of apples known as Byely Naliv, Grushovka Moskovskaya, Korichnoye and Anis grow on horizontal trees in the regions of the Ob, Yenisei and the Lena.

Apple, pear, plum and cherry trees bear fruit throughout the Urals, from Magnitogorsk in the South to Verkhoturye in the North.

In the Far East excellent pears, cultivated grapes and cold-resisting plums have been developed.

New orchards in new regions.... And new ways of conducting them. The Ural Machine-Building Plant in Sverdlovsk was the first to plant a collective orchard for its workers. Not only are the people there growing apples where they never grew before, they are growing something else as well, viz., an active, creative attitude towards nature. They are developing new, collective methods of labour.

Soviet people do not concern themselves only with their individual interests; they work to promote the public welfare. School children in Chobotovskaya, near Moscow, planted an orchard on a vacant lot. But this is not all: they sent out a call to the Young Pioneers and school children of the whole country —"Let us beautify our country with orchards!" In this way the all-Union competition for the best young fruit grower was initiated. This mighty movement of the people is spreading far and wide—it is rejuvenating and enriching our country.

Fruit growing has made exceptional progress in the East and in the North during the past few years. The war did not put a stop to this admirable cultural effort to create fruit gardens all over the country.

Work in the localities continued: new orchards have been planted on the Northern Dvina, on the Ob and in the Urals, and in the Far East.

Nor did the work in Michurinsk come to a standstill. During the war many new varieties of fruits and berries were produced and over 300,000 saplings were sent out to the collective and state farms.

Fruit growing suffered terribly in the districts occupied by the Hitlerites. The enemy cut down fruit trees for firewood, ruined the apple orchards of Byelorussia and trampled down the vineyards of Moldavia. The present five-year plan provides not only for the planting of new orchards, but also for the rehabilitation and improvement of the old.

BEYOND THE ARCTIC CIRCLE

World agriculture gravitates towards the temperate and subtropical zones. The nearer we get to the Arctic Circle the less the amount of ploughland. This is the non-agricultural zone.

In old Russia it was only the Black-Earth Belt that came extensively under the plough. Only 1.5 per cent of the country's cultivated area lay to the north of the St. Petersburg parallel. An ocean of coniferous forests hid tiny islands of cultivated land—rare glades, scratched with the wooden plough and planted to "coarse grains"—barley, oats and rye.

In the Far North, on the shores of the Arctic Ocean, there was no agriculture at all.

Tundra. Moss-covered swamps on top of permafrost—the

eternally frozen subsoil. No towns nor villages. The occasional encampments of dying tribes. For the reindeer breeders and fishermen agriculture was an unattainable level of civilization.

On the map of Russia there was a line that marked the "agriculture borderline" to the north of which lay a good third of the country's total area. For centuries this boundary was considered immovable.

The economic development of the Far North would have been impossible without agriculture to supply food for the inhabitants, if not fully, then at least to some degree.

Swamps and stones. In June ice still lies under the mossy clumps. The lowlands are boggy. The summers are short, damp and cold. The Arctic winter lasts nine months. . . .

It seemed to be a superhuman task. An entirely new branch of production had to be created in a new region. And this was done by the workers of the Soviet North, led by the Communist Party.

Sergei Kirov, who had charge of the settlement of the Kola Peninsula, said that under Soviet government there is no land that cannot be turned to the good of man if it is in able hands. Soviet people showed how true these words were.

Agricultural stations were organized in the Far North, among them the Khibiny Station, where Eichfeld, the pioneer of agriculture in the Far North, worked.

The Khibiny Station was established on the Kola Peninsula in 1923; it was situated in the midst of swamps and boulder and pebble ridges. It was a wild spot that looked as though a glacier had only just passed over it.

Before the revolution the Russian inhabitants of Murmansk had tried to grow potatoes, but the plants either perished or produced tubers no bigger than marbles.

Agricultural science considered that root crops require a total average daily temperature for the period of development and growth amounting to $1,500°$ Centigrade, barley, $1,600°$, oats, $1,940°$, peas $2,100°$. The total average daily temperature during the short summer at Khibiny amounts to only $1,135°$. Consequently it seemed as though it was no use trying.

A patch of ground was cleared of stones for an experimental field. The swampy ground was drained and broken. The earth was treated with lye. The temperature regime of the soil was regulated. The necessary bacteria were implanted and fertilizers were added. This, already, is not adaptation to local conditions, but the changing of those conditions.

Year after year seed brought from all ends of the earth was sown at Khibiny—from the more southerly parts of the Soviet Union, from Canada, Alaska and South America. The necessary varieties were selected and crossed. The seed was vernalized. The plants were cultivated carefully, perseveringly, persistently.

A hard struggle, endless experiment, bold discarding of customary conceptions. The experimenters crossed the ice of frozen lakes on skis to reach their fields. . . .

And their efforts were not in vain.

The deficiency in heat was compensated by the abundance of light—in summer, in Khibiny, the sun shines continuously for six weeks. Many of the southern grains, if properly cultivated, are able to form ears and ripen in the long days of the Far North.

It turned out that the barley, wheat and potatoes brought from the mountain regions of Tunis, Algeria and Abyssinia grew better in the Far North than those cultivated in more northerly climes: those plants were accustomed to cold nights and this is what told. It also turned out that the drained swamps of the Far North differed from those of the Central regions in that they required not only potash and phosphates, but also nitrates. Old measures and ideas had to be cast aside

The territories beyond the Arctic Circle responded to the efforts and courage of the Soviet investigators by producing crops that seemed fantastic for these latitudes.

Potatoes yield thirty, forty and even fifty tons per hectare; moreover, they are free from disease. Barley ripens in three months. Oats grow to the height of a man. Fodder grasses may be cut twice in one summer. Other crops now grown beyond the Arctic Circle are cabbage, carrots, onions, mangelwurzels, swedes, turnips, kohl-rabi, peas, beans, radishes, pumpkins and cucumbers. . . .

And so the northern outpost of Soviet agriculture sprang up on the Kola Peninsula. This is not an oasis in the desert. With the help of the scientific station, the local inhabitants have begun tilling the soil. State farms have been established. At Apatite Station a big state farm named "Industria" has been set up. The northernmost machine and tractor station in our country has been set up on Kola.

The new, Arctic industrial zone is now producing its own vegetables and milk. And this is a region that was formerly called "nature's coffin."

At Kirovsk the world's only Arctic Botanical Garden has been laid out. In a town that gets a little warmth from the Gulf Stream but is nevertheless on the same latitude as the cold pole, dahlias, chrysanthemums, and roses bloom.

The agricultural front is slowly but surely, with difficulty but victoriously, advancing northward.

The new town of Igarka, a hundred kilometres north of the Arctic Circle, has its own vegetable and dairy farms; a new variety of potato has been developed here for the northern regions. In Naryan-Mar seven hundred centners of cabbage per hectare have been gathered. The state farm at Norilsk cultivates over two hundred hectares of open ground in the wooded tundra.

Vegetables hold first place, grain comes second. In no other country in the world does grain ripen at such high latitudes. Still, it is easier to transport grain, and so vegetables remain the chief crop in Arctic agriculture.

The nomad population of the Far North, the Nentsi, Saami, Evenki and other northern peoples, knew nothing of agriculture or of vegetable food. Living in flimsy, portable reindeer tents, they constantly roamed in search of pasture for their reindeer or for new fishing grounds. . . . The peoples of the North now plant fodder crops and vegetables. For the first time in history reindeer are fed on hay, and in addition to reindeer, cows are now bred.

The growing of hay and vegetables to supplement hunting, fishing and reindeer breeding links the nomads with the settled population and promotes their cultural development.

Agriculture is approaching the shores of the Arctic Ocean. Not only can hothouses be seen in these parts, but also vegetables growing in the open. Part of the crop that is planted perishes, but part lives and grows.

Lit by electricity during the polar night, the hothouses produce vegetables and mushrooms, and lilac blooms.

Not under glass, but in the open, on the diabasic rocks in the midst of the icy sea, are green patches of Chinese cabbage.

Flowers grow in the open.

Arctic agriculture is not easy to conduct. The expenditure of labour is enormous, the cost price of the produce is high. For this reason we still have to send hundreds of thousands of tons of potatoes and vegetables to the North.

A lot of work still remains to carry out the task set by the Soviet Government and the Communist Party, viz., to establish a large, stable food-supply base in the Far North.

But year after year the number of fields, vegetable gardens and hothouses in the Soviet Arctic increases.

The geographical boundary of agriculture in our country has been expanded to an unprecedented degree.

IN THE MOUNTAINS

The people who live at the highest altitudes in the Soviet Union are those of the Pamirs—the Tajiks in the narrow gorges, and the Kirghiz in the flat valleys.

There are human habitations on the "Roof of the World" that are almost four thousand metres above sea level. At such heights the atmosphere is rarefied. If you walk quickly you find it difficult to breathe. The sun is hot, and when there is no sun it is cold. The moon is so bright that it hurts the eyes to look at it. . . .

In the Tajik gorges there was a little farming—tiny patches of Pamir rye as high as 3,300 metres above sea level. In the high, bowl-like valleys of the Kirghiz there was no farming at all: the Kirghiz nomads bred only yaks and sheep. Nothing but clots of dry, dusty grass grew on the gravelly earth.

Under the Soviet government the collective-farm system has become widespread in the Pamirs. Science found its way to the mountains and with it came agriculture.

In order to push agriculture up into the gorges of the Western Pamirs a botanical garden was laid out at Khorog at a height of 2,320 metres above sea level; this is one of the highest botanical gardens in the world. It is the height of the Krestovy Pass, the highest point on the Georgian Military Highway.

Here there are hardly any smooth, level spaces. The stony earth was broken with picks and crowbars and levelled out. Plants that are new to the Pamirs have been grown, and the surrounding collective farmers have been helped to cultivate these crops.

At the altitude of Khorog, frost-resisting grapevines produce over ten kilograms of fruit to the bush. We find fruit trees clinging to the steep slopes, where grain does not grow. The apple tree is now to be found as high as 2,800 metres. Apricot and walnut trees are growing at a height of 3,000 metres. The Western Pamirs have made their first acquaintance with potatoes, strawberries and flowers.

In the valleys of the Eastern Pamirs, lying above the clouds, the work was still harder; here everything had to be started from the beginning.

Soviet scientists headed by Professor Baranov founded the Pamirs Biological Station in Chechekty, near the Chinese frontier, at an altitude of 3,860 metres, only three hundred metres lower than the peak of the Jungfrau, in the Swiss Alps.

15*

The valleys of the Eastern Pamirs get only 60 mm. of rainfall a year, less than any other part of the Soviet Union. There are only twenty days a year when water does not freeze at night. The land is bestrewn with boulders. The wind is so strong that it carries away pebbles. The atmosphere contains only half the normal amount of carbonic acid gas. The radiation of the sun is greater than anywhere else.

Soviet botanists and agronomists have made use of these natural peculiarities.

In the daytime heat and strong sunlight, sugar forms rapidly in the cells of the plants collected by the botanists. During the cold nights this sugar has no time to be converted into starch, so it accumulates in the tissues of the plants and binds the water in them, thus considerably lowering its freezing point. In the Pamirs sugar greatly increases the frost-resistance of plant life.

This region of climatic extremes is also surprising in its botanical extremes; the sugar content of the stems of barley or oats is as high as thirty-five to forty per cent of their dry weight—it is real "sugar-hay." With such an unusually high sugar content the plants easily withstand the cold autumn. The severe climate hardens the plant so that it can withstand the climate. Man becomes cognizant of these processes and controls them to suit his own purposes.

The potato, whose tops usually freeze at 1° below zero (Centigrade) has withstood an 8° frost at the end of summer in the Pamirs. The record is held by the Chinese cabbage—it withstood a frost of 15° and not even the leaf tips were frost-bitten!

Another change in conceptions. In the Pamirs plants do not grow at night but during the day.... In the struggle for height, it was not the tested northern and mountain crops but the quick-ripening and drought-resisting plants of the tropical countries—Indian barley, Arabian wheat, Abyssinian peas—that won the day.

On the hard, bare earth isolated clusters of teresken used to grow amongst the stones. Here and there lay the twisted horns of the arkhar ram. On this territory today there are irrigated fields. Some crops grow as high as 3,600 metres above sea level, others at 3,800 metres and others again at 3,900 metres. At the Pamirs Station the Japanese radish produces a root weighing almost a kilogram. This seems like a miracle to whoever has travelled in the Eastern Pamirs.

The Kirghiz of the Eastern Pamirs have started farming for the first time in their history. At first this was unusual work for the herdsmen; they did not plough or plant properly. A few years passed and the former nomads, with the help of agronomists from the scientific station, acquired all the necessary farming skill.

WATER FROM THE FIELDS

Fields need water in proper measure. In the U.S.S.R., however, there are regions where there is a superfluity of water and others where there is a shortage. Near Batumi the annual rainfall is about 2,500 mm., in Byelorussia it is 600 mm., in the trans-Volga it is 300 mm., in the lower reaches of the Amu Darya it is 80 mm. and in the Pamirs it is only 60 mm. In the warm South, the moisture evaporates rapidly, in the cold North it evaporates slowly. There are places where evaporation is slow and rainfall high; there are other places where the rainfall is low and the evaporation is rapid.

The proverb: "Where water is plenty, trouble is plenty," arose in the North. In the South they said that "to dream of water means good luck."

The fields need water in proper measure. In the Soviet Union man changes the water regime of districts: in some places he drains swamps, in others he irrigates the desert.

In the North there is a zone of swamps. They stretch from Byelorussia to the Far East. Water is stagnant on the divides and in the lowlands and is choked with sedge and moss. These lands are unsuitable for farming. Even in places where grain will grow it is often swamped, is affected by disease and perishes. Wheeled tractors stick in the mud.

If the level of the subsoil water is artificially lowered it is possible for air to enter the ground and fertile ploughlands may be broken on the reclaimed soil. Man regulates the water, air and nutrition regime of the plants and gathers big crops where formerly the water squelched and gurgled underfoot.

Gigantic reclamation works have been launched in our country in Soviet times. During the period of the First Five-Year Plan alone more swamps were drained in the U.S.S.R. than were drained in tsarist Russia during the whole of the nineteenth century. But this was only the beginning of the great transformation of the earth's crust in our country.

Excavators and shovels straighten out rivers and increase the speed of their flow. Ditching machines rumble across the earth, leaving a yard-deep trench behind them. "Mole" machines burrow under the surface of the earth. The network of ditches and canals drains the swamp like a sponge. Machines break up and roll earth that was formerly under water.

This is how the intensive draining of swamps is carried out—not only the surface water but the subsoil water as well is removed. In tsarist Russia there was no intensive draining of marshland.

Drainage works are of a complex nature: they not only create new ploughlands and meadows but also new waterways and roads, new fisheries and peat workings. Reclamation experts, hydrologists, forestry experts, agronomists and ichthyologists all work together. Their work can only be correlated and made rational in all its details in a country that works according to a single plan.

Before the revolution drained land was used for pasture and meadows. Today, the collective and state farms more and more frequently plant them to flax, hemp, vegetables and wheat.

The hemp, grass and vegetable crops on the marshlands are very big, much bigger than on ordinary soils that are not so rich in decayed vegetable matter.

Byelorussia is the chief region in which swamps are being drained.

Before the revolution a reclamation expedition worked in the Polesie marshlands in Byelorussia. In those days the work was confined to the draining of some of the land owned by the landlords and the digging of a few main canals along which contractors floated their timber. The peasants got none of the drained land.

During thirty years of Soviet government the appearance of many parts of Polesie has changed. It was formerly a boggy, unpopulated tangle of forest, with mists, clouds of mosquitoes and fever-laden air. Today the air is healthy, the land is firm and dry and is sown to fodder crops and hemp. State farms tens of thousands of hectares in area have been established; these are the biggest farms ever established on drained marshland.

Collective farms, power stations, hemp mills, hospitals, schools, roads—where there were formerly impassable bogs....

The Soviet state spends huge sums on draining collective-farm lands. Machine and tractor stations have special reclamation divisions. Factories produce special machinery for the swamps.

And in response to this help from the state a mighty, popular land reclamation movement of collective farmers arose.

On the eve of the war huge areas of Polesie had been drained by the people themselves. On the initiative of the collective farms of Lyuban District, thousands of Byelorussian collective farmers turned out to drain the swamps and uproot stumps and scrub. The plan for the work was discussed at general meetings. Collective farms, their brigades and teams competed with each other to obtain the biggest results.

In Lyuban District alone about six thousand hectares were drained in fourteen days—as much as had been drained during the whole period of the Second Five-Year Plan.

Similar work was undertaken in the Kirov Region. Hundreds of collective farms, thousands of collective farmers, singing songs and carrying flags, marched out to storm the marshes. They did as much work in a day as was normally done in a month. In a fortnight they drained over three thousand hectares, laid drainage pipes and built bridges.

It began to rain and the ground became soggy, but the people continued working. When the clay stuck to the shovels they heated them over bonfires.

Yezelnitsky Canal was dug in four days. Such a job would formerly have taken four weeks. The canal was not dug from the mouth up, in the usual way. The collective farmers did not wait for the water to run off of its own accord. They lined up along the course of the future canal and dug the whole length of the canal at one go, bailing out the water with buckets.

Drained fields and pasture land, here in small islands, and there in large stretches, lie across the whole country, from Byelorussia and the Karelo-Finnish Republic, through the Moscow Region, the Ural region, the Barabinskaya Steppe and Birobijan to Kolyma. Almost all the agriculture in the Far North is conducted on drained marshland.

During the German occupation 300,000 hectares of drained land in Byelorussia were swamped again. These lands will be drained once again during the postwar five-year plan period. And then a gigantic land reclamation scheme covering an area of four million hectares will be undertaken in the republic that will completely transform the old Polesie region.

The plan provides for the draining of 615,000 hectares of land in the U.S.S.R. in the course of five years.

In particular, the floodlands flanking the River Yakhroma in the Moscow Canal area will be drained. Land-reclamation units from the local machine and tractor stations and collective-farm teams have already regulated the flow of the river and have lowered the level of the water; they are now digging the minor network of drainage canals, clearing scrub and ploughing the new lands.

The Yakhroma floodlands are the bed of a dried-up lake on to which many of the nutritive substances that feed plant life have been washed down from the soil of the surrounding hills. The fertility of the soil here is almost as high as that of the best black-earth lands in the South.

These lands, before draining, produced a crop of poor hay from sedge. After draining they will produce rich crops of planted grasses, cabbage, beets and onions. The grass will feed large herds of milchcows, and the vegetables will be sent to Moscow along the canal. The cattle will provide manure and the crops in the whole region will be increased.

The backwaters of the River Kuban—the low, swampy floodlands of the river are being drained. Dykes are being built along the riverbanks. Thousands of hectares of unfertile land that were formerly hotbeds of malaria have already been made healthy and planted to rice.

In the Transcaucasus, on the Black Sea littoral, lies hot, humid Colchis. Banks of silt carried down from the mountains raise the level of the river beds. A tidal sand ridge prevents the overflowing water from reaching the sea. The water remains stagnant, and the decaying vegetation befouls the already stifling atmosphere. Wild growths of reeds cover the ruins of ancient villages, the populations of which died out from malaria.

In this way 250,000 hectares of fertile land were lost, land on which a young bamboo will grow half a metre a day, land that will produce three or four crops a year.

On instructions from Stalin the draining of the lands of Colchis has been begun.

More than ten thousand hectares have already been drained. The malaria-infested jungle has been turned into health resorts and subtropical plantations. New roads have been built. New bridges have been erected. New collective-farm settlements have sprung up, inhabited by people who have come down from the hills. The low-built hovels, toppling over with age, have gone; their place has been taken by well-built, two-storey houses with red-tiled roofs. Collective-farm power stations provide these new settlements with electric light.

The town of Poti was often flooded by the waters of the River Rion. The river has now been dyked and its course has been changed. A new path has been found for it, away from the town.

Millions of Australian eucalyptus saplings have been planted along the roads and around the fields of Colchis. This tree dries the ground, and from it railway sleepers, telegraph poles, paving blocks, acetic acid and essential oils are made. The odour of the eucalyptus drives away the malaria-bearing mosquitoes. In Colchis a eucalyptus tree grows nearly twenty metres high in ten years.

After the interruption caused by the war, reclamation work in Colchis has been renewed. The postwar five-year plan says: "The work of draining the Colchis lowlands shall be resumed and twenty thousand hectares of farmland shall be brought under cultivation."

With the aid of excavators and suction machines man is creating a new, healthy and flourishing region.

The region is still in the course of creation, but it already has a precise map. The Florida drainage project that was at one time drawn up by American magnates, pales into insignificance before the colossal Colchis Project.

This project will be carried out to the full, for it is so decreed in the socialist plan, and the Soviet people want to and are determined to carry it out.

WATER TO THE FIELDS

One-seventh of the area of the Soviet Union is enclosed with a ring marked "250 mm. of rain per annum." These are the vast dry plains beyond the Caspian.

Within this region there are places where the rainfall is only one-half or one-third of this. There is no rain in summer. This is the desert and semi-desert zone.

The rare and scanty rivers do not flow to the open sea and ocean, but to the bottom of a gigantic flat bowl. They by-pass

the hot, thirsty land and, falling into the closed basins of the
Caspian, Aral or Balkhash, are evaporated by the merciless
sun.

Amongst the sands and salt marshes there are many places
with fertile grey soil. A cloudless sky, dry air and an abundance
of sun—a poplar tree grows to maturity in something like five
or six years in this grey earth. The soil produces huge crops
of cotton, and seven crops of alfalfa grass can be mown in a
year. Fruits grown in this region are just full of sugar. Here
plants like Indian hemp, kendyr, southern hemp, castor-oil
plants, grapes, peaches, apricots, cantaloupes, walnuts and figs
will grow.

The region possesses unbelievable fertility, but it can be
released only by means of artificial irrigation.

Since ancient times, settled life here has been confined
to occasional oases covered with a network of irrigation canals.

The canals take their water from the rivers that flow from
the mountains. Ten million people live on the plains of Central
Asia thanks to the fact that snow melts or rain falls in the
Tien Shan and the Pamir Mountains. The road these waters
take is a long one, but they get there: snowfall in the mountains, the thawing of a glacier, a turbid stream, a network of
canals and, at last, a stream of water flowing around the stem
of the cotton plant.

Irrigation methods remained unchanged for thousands of
years. The dams were built without cement, the rivers would
break them down and carry away the results of millions of
hours of hard human toil. The water was lifted from the canals
to the fields by Persian wheels—huge wooden wheels with
endless chains of earthenware pots on them. The water was
distributed amongst the fields along tiny narrow canals dug
by hand with mattocks. The map recorded irrigation systems
inherited from the distant past: a fanlike design, with winding canals.

Irrigation gave life to the peasants, but at the same time it placed them in bondage to the beys and the mullahs, for they, and not the peasants, owned the water.

Large areas were left unirrigated. In pre-revolutionary times Lenin wrote: "This area is largely useless at the present time not so much because of the natural qualities of the soil in this or that outlying region, as of the social qualities of the national economy in Russia proper, which doom technique to stagnation, and the population to oppression, wretchedness, ignorance and helplessness."*

The Soviet Government effected a land and water reform. Water ceased to be a means of exploitation. It became the property of the people, it began to serve the cause of Socialism.

The building of huge irrigation systems began. More water on the fields meant more cotton.

This was not only an attack on the desert—it was an offen-sive against the old way of life. In 1921 Lenin wrote about the Transcaucasus. "Irrigation is needed most of all, and it most of all will transform the region, will regenerate it, will bury the past and ensure the transition to Socialism."**

In the thirty years the Soviet government has existed the irrigated area of our country has increased by more than three million hectares. On the map of Central Asia, the Trans-caucasus and Kazakhstan are marked new canals, reconstruct-ed rivers, villages inhabited by settled nomads, land that has become habitable and fertile.

The pre-revolutionary laws gave the land irrigated by the tsarist authorities in the Hungry Steppe near Tashkent only to "Russian subjects professing the Christian faith and owning certified property to the value of at least a thousand rubles." Soviet irrigated land is the property of the whole people. It is tilled by the sons and daughters of fraternal peoples who have abolished exploitation and poverty, oppression and national inequality for all time.

---

* V. Lenin, *Collected Works*, Russ. ed., Vol. XI, p. 359.
** *Ibid.*, Vol. XXVI, p. 192.

Irrigation work in the Soviet Union is carried out on a complex system; the aim is not only to create new ploughlands, but also to improve waterways and to build hydroelectric power stations at the points where the water level changes. This system can be employed because all branches of our national economy are subordinated to a general plan.

Approximately 7,500,000 hectares of land are irrigated in the Soviet Union. A large part of our farm produce is gathered from these lands.

The most extensive irrigated areas are in Central Asia. Here there are many irrigation systems—on the Syr Darya, the Amu Darya, the River Chu, the River Murghab, on all the big rivers that come tumbling down into the desert from the mountains. Canals are scores of kilometres long and irrigate tremendous areas.

The new irrigation system in Tajikistan, for example, has already rendered thousands of hectares of land fertile in the valley of the River Vakhsh: the best, long-staple cotton is now planted in this valley. These places were formerly desert—cracked, sun-baked land and growths of wild reeds on the riverbanks that grew to three times a man's height. Powerful excavators dug canals. The river was diverted to a new channel, many parts of which had been hewn through solid rock. The River Vakhsh, formed from the melting ice on the tops of the Pamirs, runs along a ferroconcrete bed, passes through the ironclad "windows" of the sluices and is distributed by a network of tiny canals. The desert is no more—the valley has already been settled by thousands of collective farmers who have come down to the fertile level ground from the slopes of the stern Pamirs. Not only nature and the whole economy of the regions, but life itself has changed.

New villages have been built. Arterial roads and a narrow-gauge railway have been laid. The town of Kurghan-Tyube, with the biggest cotton-ginning mill in Central Asia, has grown immensely.

The "new" Valley of the Vakhsh contains a fourth of all Tajikistan's cotton fields.

Many irrigation systems have been built by the collective farmers themselves with the aid of the Soviet state.

Two years before the Great Patriotic War, some 160,000 Uzbek and Tajik collective farmers, in fulfilment of a promise given to Stalin, dug the Great Ferghana Canal, the biggest piece of irrigation engineering in the Soviet Union. Working according to former standards, a job like this would have taken several years; but thanks to the patriotic enthusiasm of the masses it was performed in six weeks. Such is the potency of free collective labour.

The labour of the collective farmers has changed the geography of the Ferghana Valley, the chief cotton-growing oasis in the U.S.S.R. The plenteous waters of the Syr Darya used to run through the bottom of the valley, but they did not irrigate the valley; that was done by a number of tiny streams flowing from the surrounding hills. Large areas of unproductive land were left without water. Today, the new canal takes its water from the Syr Darya (or rather from the Naryn and the Kara Darya, the confluence of which forms the Syr Darya) and distributes it generously over the valley, gathering water on the way and regulating the flow of the minor irrigation systems. The hands of man built the canal and raised, as it were, the Syr Darya to water the fields of Ferghana.

Many canals have been built in Soviet Transcaucasia. Extensive lands of the former arid wilderness of the Caspian Steppes are now covered with cotton fields. Before the war the collective farmers of Azerbaijan, for example, built the Stalin Canal at Samur-Divichi, to the north of Baku.

In 1940 alone, the last prewar year in the U.S.S.R., the irrigated lands were increased by 250,000 hectares. In one year! Before the revolution it took thirty years to irrigate an area of that size.

The offensive against the barren deserts in the U.S.S.R. is only just developing. Vast projects are to be carried out. Many of them will be carried out in the first postwar five-year plan period.

In Azerbaijan, on the lower reaches of the Kura and the Arax, there is a vast, flat sun-baked lowland—the Mil, Mughan and Shirvan steppes. The summer climate here resembles that of Egypt. Hundreds of thousands of hectares can be turned into fields and orchards. Canals have been built in the Kura lowlands under the Soviet government, but so far no more than a tenth of the region has been brought under the plough: there is not enough moisture. In winter the ground serves as pasture; in summer it is a desert. In the hollows there are malarial swamps and saltmarshes.

The River Kura has an abundance of water in the spring, but it does more harm than good. The name of the river—Kür, in Azerbaijanian, means capricious. Its bed being higher than the surrounding lowlands, it breaks through the dykes that line the banks, overflows into the surrounding fields and carries whole villages away.

At the village of Mingechaur, the point where the River Kura has cut its way through a narrow gorge in the small Boz Dagh mountain range, a huge engineering work has been begun. A dam 76 metres high—almost as tall as a thirty-storey building—is being erected. The dam will be the biggest in Europe and Asia. Two million carloads of earth will be required to build it.

A new lake—the "Mingechaur Sea"—with an area of about 750 square kilometres will appear on the map of the U.S.S.R. Canals will cut across the lifeless semi-desert, and, when the work has been completed, will irrigate about a million hectares of land on which will be planted cotton and wheat, orchards and vineyards, plantations of essential oil-bearing plants and tung trees, melons and vegetables. Over 100,000 hectares will be cultivated during the present five-year plan period. The new lands will provide grain for the whole of Transcaucasia. Pastures for the sheep and cattle will be found in other regions. Locks will raise the level of the River Kura and make it nav-

ST. MARY'S COLLEGE LIBRARY CALIFORNIA

igable. There will be no more floods. A fishing industry will develop. Swamps and stagnant water will be drained. Malaria will disappear. At the point where the level of the river bed changes, the Mingechaur Power Station will be built: this will be one of the biggest in the U.S.S.R. Its current will be transmitted to Baku, Kirovabad and other districts. The face of a vast area will be completely changed.

In Central Asia the "Uzbek Sea" is being built by the labour of the collective farmers. It will be formed in the valley of the River Zeravshan, not far from Samarkand.

In summer the Zeravshan does not carry enough water to irrigate the fields. The valley of the Zeravshan provides a fourth of all the cotton grown in Uzbekistan, but the yield is lower here than in the Ferghana Valley. A dam is now impounding water to form the Katta-Kurghan Reservoir, which will have a capacity of 600,000,000 cubic metres. The "Uzbek Sea" will collect and hold the spring water and supply it to the fields in summer.

In 1940 work was begun on the Katta-Kurghan Reservoir, but the war stopped the work. It has now been resumed. Part of the reservoir has already been built and a flat mirror of blue water lies in a yellow frame.

The Chumysh Dam, on the River Chu in Kirghizia, was built during the period of the Stalin five-year plans. The irrigated fields have been planted with southern hemp which grows so tall that a man on horseback can hide in it. In order to extend the irrigated area, the Great Chu Canal was begun in 1941 and the work was continued in spite of the war. Townspeople from Frunze turned out to help the collective farmers who were digging the canal. During the war ten thousand hectares were irrigated and two power stations were built. Now the building of the gigantic Orto-Tokoi Reservoir has begun—this will be the most important link in the Chu Canal system.

Near Lake Issyk-Kul the River Chu will be impounded by a huge dam at a height of three thousand metres above sea level. The Orto-Tokoi gorge will be flooded. A new lake will appear high up in the mountains which will supplement the waters of the River Chu and the canal during the hot weather, when water is scarce. The land irrigated by the Great Chu Canal will provide bumper crops of wheat, sugar beet and rice.

On the Chu, as on the Zeravshan, the Kura and other southern rivers, Soviet people are regulating the flow of water: the winter and spring flow is held back, the summer flow is increased. Man is beginning to regulate the exchange of moisture between mountains and desert. . . .

During the period of the postwar five-year plan a big dam will be built on the lower reaches of the Syr Darya, near Kzyl Orda. This is a part that is famous for its rice. The dam will enable farmers to treble the rice area and also to increase the yield. Reedy swamps will give way to fields. The whole district will get electric power. This droughty district will be regenerated, brought back to life. And yet irrigation engineers in tsarist times called the Syr Darya a "river of the past"!

The postwar five-year plan provides for the proper irrigation of the Volga-Akhtuba floodlands. These lands form a narrow strip in barren semi-desert from Stalingrad to Astrakhan. Countless arms of the Volga run through this rich valley, which is covered with layers of fertile silt and bathed in the rays of the warm sun. Without the help of man, however, the floodlands remain a wilderness: they are covered with flood water almost to the middle of summer, but as soon as the water subsides they become an arid desert. The fertile land must be protected from flooding by the construction of dykes, and from drought by means of artificial irrigation. Then it will provide three crops of vegetables every summer, and cotton, rice and grapes will grow there.

So far only a seventh part of the floodlands has been dyked, and only a fifth part of this area is irrigated. The reclamation, irrigation and cultivation of this Soviet "Nile Valley" is one of the tasks of the postwar five-year plan.

16—777

Great changes are drawing near in the Turkmenian Republic. Today the waters of the Amu Darya pour into the Aral Sea in a mighty flood and all around there is nothing but hot, dry, sun-baked desert. Tomorrow, the Amu Darya will turn towards the Caspian Sea, towards the thirsty, waterless lands.

An experiment in turning the waters of the Amu Darya into the Kara Kum Desert was made some fifteen years ago and proved successful. Year after year, at the thirtieth kilometre on the Bassagha-Kerki Canal in the southeastern corner of Turkmenistan, water from the Amu Darya was diverted into the desert. The flow of water has won kilometre after kilometre of land from the desert. Spades helped the water wash away the hills that stood in its road. Slowly the water advanced. It penetrated into the Kara Kum Desert for scores of kilometres.

At first the sand soaks up all the water. Then it gradually becomes covered with a layer of fertile silt about half a metre thick. Reeds grow. Birds settle in the oasis. The jeiran, the desert gazelle, comes down to the water to drink. Fields of wheat, alfalfa and cotton appear....

During the postwar five-year plan the work will be continued on an immense scale. The construction of the Great Kara Kum Canal will begin. The old, dry river bed of the Kelif-Uzboi will carry part of the water of the Amu Darya westwards across the Kara Kum Desert.

The canal will begin near the town of Kerki. No special dams will be built on the Amu Darya. The entrance to the new canal will coincide with that of the Bassagha-Kerki Canal and will then form an extensive reservoir-lake, continue into the desert, cut across it like a blue ribbon and then, near the town of Mari, will flow into the Murghab. This will be the first section of the canal, nearly four hundred kilometres long. The Murghab Oasis, the chief oasis in the Turkmenian Republic, will receive an abundance of water from the Amu Darya. In the future the canal will go farther westwards and supply water to the Tejen Oasis as well.

After that it is proposed to carry the waters of the Amu Darya as far as Ashkhabad.

Along the canal there will be irrigated lands. Where there are now shifting sands there will be green fields and pastures. A navigable waterway will stretch across the desert. The whole of the southern part of Turkmenistan will be rejuvenated.

Thus, the waters of the Amu Darya will be given to the lands lying on its left bank, but this mighty river has enough water to irrigate large areas on its right bank as well.

It is planned to build a huge canal that will carry Amu Darya water northwards from the Kelif district to the lower reaches of the Zeravshan, to Bukhara. At one time the Zeravshan flowed into the Amu Darya, but now water from the Amu Darya will flow into the valley of the Zeravshan.... The canal will run for more than five hundred kilometres across the Karshi Steppes and provide them with water and electric power, thus transforming the whole western part of the Uzbek Republic. The geography of the Central Asian oases will have to be written anew.

The time will come when we shall also turn the underground rivers against the desert.

When the water flows down from the mountains it does not all remain in the river beds; part of it soaks into the subsoil and forms subterranean streams, sometimes bigger than those that flow on the surface. In some places in the Kara Kum this water is reached by deep wells. In the Muyun Kum Desert the water from the distant mountains comes to the surface of its own accord and forms abundant cold springs in the midst of the hot sands. Part of the desert may be watered with these underground streams.... This, however, is a matter for the future.

The first postwar five-year plan provides for an increase in the irrigated area of the U.S.S.R. of 656,000 hectares. New canals will irrigate the desert. And at the same time those lands that were abandoned during the war will be put under cultivation again.

16*

To enlarge the cultivated area, Soviet people, in conformity with far-reaching scientific projects, are sending batteries of excavators, suction and hydraulic diggers and tractor-drawn digging machines into the desert. Water is washing from the map one section of desert after another.

VICTORY OVER THE DESERT

The irrigated area of the U.S.S.R. can be trebled at least. The desert expanses, however, are enormous—they cannot be brought to life by melting glaciers and mountain torrents alone. Sooner or later the river water will prove insufficient. Already many of the rivers in Central Asia are becoming not fuller, but shallower the farther they flow. Their waters are taken for irrigation, they disappear into the desert and never reach anywhere. In addition to this, many of the regions lie in the uplands where it is difficult to take water to them.

Sandy, clayey, saline, stony deserts occupy an area of the U.S.S.R. equal to that of half of Western Europe. Are these, then, always to remain deserts? A dead patch on the map of a flourishing country? A symbol of man's impotence?

The scorched ground burns the feet through the bootsoles. The wind licks you like a flame. Sand grits in the teeth. It is a day's journey from well to well....

The sandy deserts represent the extreme of barrenness. No wonder! Plant tissue dies at a temperature of 54° C.; the sand reaches a temperature of 80° C. Sandy deserts, however, are easier to cultivate than any others, and in the South of the U.S.S.R. this type of desert is the commonest.

On the left bank of the Amu Darya lies the huge sandy waste of the Kara Kum, and to the right the sandy-wilderness of the Kyzyl Kum. Vast expanses of sand-covered territory lie to the north of the Aral Sea and around Lake Balkhash. There are patches of sandy desert around the lower reaches of the Volga, the Don and the Dnieper.

These barren wastes can and must be cultivated.

It is not only a matter of providing protection against the sands, which in some places creep over the fields, villages and railways. Shifting sands of this kind may be combated by planting sand-binding plants.

It is not only a matter of checking the shifting sand—we must take from the sand all the wealth it contains.

Is the desert dead?

The sand of the desert absorbs and filters the winter and spring moisture, but owing to poor capillarity it does not evaporate it. There is always a stratum of fresh water under the sand, and plants may drink from it if their roots are long enough. The Turkmenians and Kazakhs, desert dwellers, know that wherever there is sand they may look for water.

A sandy desert that is covered not with vegetation but with shifting dunes is an exception, not the rule. Shifting sand is not only the work of nature but also of man who, under the old social system, was unable to conduct his economy in a wise and thrifty manner. Pressed into the desert, the herdsman cut down the growths of saksaul trees, fought with his neighbours for pastureland, grazed his herds without any plan, and the hoofs of his animals broke up the sand.

The maps show that shifting sands lie mostly round villages and wells.

Where the sand was not broken up, the desert is covered with a growth of vegetation. Camels and sheep graze on it. Amongst the grasses of the Kara Kum there are some that are very nutritious, like the sand sedge known as "ilek." It contains more proteins and fats than alfalfa.

Sandy deserts are suitable for the breeding of the karakul sheep, a very valuable breed. The desert is immense, and its pastures can feed millions of valuable animals.

The development of socialist stockbreeding will be the principal way of utilizing those desert areas that will not be converted into agricultural land by irrigation.

The planned grazing of collective-farm and state-farm

herds, the scientific selection and rational rotation of pasture-lands and correct composition of herds will prevent the pastures from being turned into shifting sands.

Soviet people work according to plan on a scientific basis. This has helped them achieve important successes. But not everything has yet been achieved, not all possibilities have been utilized.

The desert can provide more than we have ever taken from it. In Kazakhstan, for example, only one-third of the pasturelands is being utilized.

The time will come when the very vegetation of the desert will change. Plants of low nutritive value, or totally unsuited for fodder, may be replaced by those of greater nutritive value. In collective farms and at scientific stations tests have been made with such plants as the erkek, a perennial grain whose nutritive value is about the same as that of bran; it is very unexacting, sturdy and drought-resisting. Cultivated grasses provide crops twice as big as the wild grasses, and their nutritive value is four times as great.

Desert plants sometimes display unexpected qualities. The seeds of the desert wormwood are used in the manufacture of a vermifuge—santonin. The desert dactylis provides raw material for anabasin sulphate, an insecticide used in orchards.

There are quite a number of dyes in the desert: kermes gives a black dye; harmel, red; spurge, yellow; wild buckwheat, green.... The desert is not an empty wilderness. These valuable plants are being regularly gathered.

The saksaul, the desert tree, provides excellent fuel and at the same time binds the sand. The supply of firewood in the black saksaul growths amounts to forty tons per hectare, which is quite a lot. The planting of saksaul is now replenishing the badly-thinned woods of the desert.

If the land will not be used for irrigated farming it will be used for stockbreeding, for gathering valuable plants, forestry.... Nothing will be wasted, everything will be brought within the scope of economic life.

But agriculture must be developed even where there is no irrigation.

The nomad in the roadless and poorly vegetated desert formerly ate very little bread. He never saw vegetables or fruit at all—with the exception of the heat-resisting, thick-skinned watermelons with their low sugar content and whitish flesh that he grew near the desert pools, scraping up the argillaceous sand with his fingers: these melon patches sometimes lay a hundred or so kilometres from his winter habitation.

Times are different now. Real settlements are now springing up in the deserts. The requirements of yesterday's nomad are increasing. Industries using the minerals that have been discovered in the desert are growing up: these include the mirabilite (Glauber salt) workings at Kara Boghaz Gol, the oil fields on the Emba and at Nebit Dagh, the sulphur refineries in the Kara Kum, the copper mines of Jezkazghan. People live and work in the desert: they need vegetables, they need vitamins.

Soviet agriculture has set itself a task that was inconceivable in old Russia, that of planting fields and orchards in the desert.

Some of the methods that have been applied are crossing plants, chemical treatment of the soil, shading, binding the sand with a film of oil.

Persevering work on the experimental fields around the industrial centres showed that under certain conditions farming is possible in the unirrigated desert.

In the sands near the Aral Sea there is a scientific station working for the conquest of the desert. The rainfall here is only a fourth of that of Moscow. In summer there is tropical heat, in winter Siberian frost.

To compel the unfertile land to bear fruit, the most up-to-date methods of scientific farming have been applied in the distant desert: the soil was carefully tilled, the proper crop rotation was found, experimental selections of plants were made. As a result, despite the heat and the absence of water, the experimenters reaped five centners of barley and millet to the hectare without irrigation. The seeds of the plants that had conquered the desert went from here to the surrounding collective farms. Stockbreeders have called agriculture to their aid and have thereby changed the age-old, local economic system. Not only has agriculture become an adjunct of stockbreeding; it has also eased the task of the stockbreeders.

Agriculture has appeared in places where it had not existed before. And so farming methods that never existed before were bound to appear.

At the Aral Scientific Station the trench method of growing potatoes, vegetables and melons was tried. The vegetables are planted at the bottom of trenches over a metre deep; this brings them nearer to the subsoil water.

Thus, the plant is able to obtain the moisture it needs and the walls of the trench protect it from the hot winds.

Trenches of this sort have now been dug at Kara Boghaz Gol, at Repetek and on the collective farms. Bright green vegetation amongst the burning sands. The trenches require a considerable expenditure of labour and do not work out at all cheap. But these are only the first steps. . . .

At Jezkazghan, in the heart of Kazakhstan, copper ore is mined. Gravel, aridity, wormwood. . . . Windless days are rare. Uspanov, a Kazakh scientist, started growing vegetables here. His vegetable patches are irrigated with the brackish water from the River Kengir. In the orchards black beech and poplars protect currant bushes and apple trees from the wind. What is more, he even obtains grain crops in this region without any sort of irrigation: he has gathered crops of three, five and seven centners of barley and wheat to the hectare.

The Emba Oil Fields are being planted with trees. The earth has to be broken up with picks before a tree can be planted. The Botanical Gardens and vegetable gardens near the Balkhash Copper Refineries are laid out on deposits of sharp-pointed reddish gravel, sand and clay dust. In Kara Boghaz Gol grapes grow in sands formed from sea shells. Wheat ripens without irrigation at Tas-Kuduk in the heart of the Kyzyl Kum

Desert. At Iolatan, in the southern Kara Kum, a barley crop
has been reaped on unirrigated soil.

The struggle against the desert is, of course, not an easy
one. Still, even in its driest and hottest parts the desert has
provided man with bread.

It is not the cultivation of grain crops in the desert that is
the important thing—grain can be brought in. The main problem to be solved by unirrigated agriculture in the desert is the
planting of vegetable gardens and melon patches around the
inhabited centres. In this respect the Far South and the Far
North have a task in common.

HERDS IN THE DESERT

The deserts of Central Asia cover an immense territory. The
natural conditions are not the same all over. The best pastures
are in one place in one part of the year and in another place
in another part of the year.

By summer the thick spring carpet of vegetation—brome
and bluegrasses, tulips and poppies—is burnt up and withered;
in winter, however, the wind blows the snow down from the
steep slopes into the hollows and the full-blown, rain-washed
wormwood and salt-wort, touched by the frost, become nutritious fodder for the sheep.

In winter the mountain pastures are covered with deep
snow, but in summer, when the plains are scorched and dried
up by the hot sun, rich, succulent grass grows there.

The herds are driven from place to place. In winter they
are kept on the sandy pastures and grasslands along the rivers
where there is little snow; in summer they either go to the
North into the feather grass steppes, or to the mountain pastures in the South.

Turkmenians, Kazakhs and Kirghiz had been nomads for
centuries. Some of the Kazakh clans travelled as much as a
thousand kilometres a year with their herds. Millions of peo-

ple spent their whole lives wandering from place to place in search of untrampled and unnibbled grass.

The wisdom of the people, based on long experience, worked out the best system of changing pastures from season to season. For the working people who were tormented by the oppression of the beys, the long drives were a heavy burden. They spent their whole lives in their portable felt tents, and their herds were dependent on what fodder they could get on the hoof. When the steppe was covered with a sheet of ice the sheep could see the blades of grass below it; they stamped upon the ice until their hoofs bled, but they could not reach the grass.

In times of such ice formations the animals died from hunger. And when the animals died, the people who fed on them died too.

This was the situation in many regions of Russia. The Buryats, Oirots, and the peoples of the North were also nomads. Instead of towns they had their summer and winter encampments. They did not live in houses, but in all sorts of tents or wigwams—kibitka, kosh, vezha, yurta. They were ignorant of concrete, bricks and even of timber: felt, turves, bark and reeds were their building materials.... And everywhere cattle perished and hunger, disease and ruin reigned....

The tsarist government was in no hurry to put an end to the nomad way of existence. On the contrary, it forced the settled native populations to become nomads. The tsarist authorities drove them from the fertile lands into the deserts and mountains.

The Soviet Government, the government of the people, however, could not remain indifferent to the sufferings of the nomad peoples; it helped them to adopt the settled way of life, and this was facilitated by collectivization. A problem that mankind had never faced before was solved—collective farms of former nomad herdsmen were established on vast, unlimited expanses of land.

The nomads retained their accustomed form of economy—cattle breeding, but they began to conduct it on entirely new lines. The herds are still driven from pasture to pasture, but only the men who herd the cattle go out with them; the rest of the population remains at home. Moreover, the routes are properly planned and scientifically chosen.

Formerly the cattle had to find their own fodder in the winter months, tearing it from under the snow with their hoofs and horns. When ice formed, or if there was a heavy snowfall, the herds were left without food. Today there are machine-mowing stations and machine and tractor stations which help the collective farms to grow emergency stocks of fodder—hay, silage and root crops—in case of winter shortage.

Formerly the lasso and the dog were the nomad herdsman's only help. Today, at the winter settlements and in places where there are villages, warm cattle sheds and corrals are built to protect the cattle from the wind, wells are sunk and veterinary stations are opened.

Formerly the nomads were ignorant and went to their medicine men to be treated for sickness. Today there are schools and medical dispensaries in the settlements. Culture and literacy are making rapid progress.

In heat or frost, in drought or rain, the nomads formerly lived in their felt, bark or rag tents. Today real houses are built at the settlements. Around the settlements vegetables and grain are planted.

New inhabited centres have been recorded on the map of the deserts—collective-farm settlements, centres of settled cattle breeding that have grown up in the wilderness.

One of the biggest desert settlements is Tamdy-Bulak in the Kyzyl Kum. Formerly, a dozen or so wretched yurtas were huddled together here, near a spring between the stony, bare sides of the Ak-Tau Mountains and the sandy wastes of the Jaman Kum. Today it is a little township composed of white, European-type houses, a club and a cinema, a medical dispensary, a school, shops and a post office. Automobiles run there from the Kermine railway station. Aircraft fly there from Tashkent.

HUNTING GROUNDS

In pre-revolutionary Russia valuable breeds of animals that provide man with fur, horn or meat were ruthlessly exterminated.

The noble European deer was killed off. The wild boar was greatly reduced in numbers. The wild goats that lived near Moscow were destroyed. Little remained of the beaver, sable, seal, and Siberian muskrat. Wild deer became difficult to find.

Only in Soviet times was hunting and trapping organized on sound, economic lines. The wasteful slaughter of animals useful to man has been stopped. Not a few scientist-enthusiasts, but the whole collective body of Soviet people are concerned with the preservation of useful wild animals.

Formerly the rich factors reaped the fruits of the hard labour of the hunters in the taiga. The hunter went out after "soft gold" not for himself, but for others; "he killed sables and slept on a straw mat." The Evenk or Yakut hunters, perfect marksmen, killed squirrels by shooting them in the eye so as not to spoil the skins, and then handed them over to the factors in payment for the spirits or matches they had acquired on credit. The fur trader and not the hunter or trapper was the master of this forest wealth; and this wealth dwindled, the forests were plundered greedily and thoughtlessly.

Today, under the Soviet government, the people themselves have become masters of the forests. The hunters of the taiga hand over their furs to their own socialist state and in return receive manufactured goods, hunting equipment, tobacco and food. The hunter now looks upon his work differently; he protects valuable breeds of animals which the people, the country, need.

The rapacious trading hunter no longer roams our forests. The kulak has been abolished. The tireless toilers of the taiga, the Evenki, Yakuts and other inhabitants of the Siberian forests, are organized in artels, or cooperative associations. The fur receiving stations, run by the state, help the artels, provide them with everything they need and bring literacy, education and culture into the taiga.

The hunting industry in the U.S.S.R. is developing within the framework of the national economic plan. For the first time hunting is combined with science. The hunting regulations forbid indiscriminate killing. The state looks after the rational reproduction of animals useful to man. Wolves are killed all the year round, but the squirrel is not touched in the close season, the elk, spotted deer and white heron may not be killed at all.

The strong and handsome elk was living out its last days in European Russia. But even in the difficult years of the Civil War the Soviet Government found time to provide for the protection of this useful animal. At that time a decree was issued forbidding the hunting of elk. Years passed and the elk multiplied. It appeared in places where it had not been seen for a long time, near Ulyanovsk on the Volga, for example. Today there are about two thousand elk in the Moscow Region alone. They have not heard a shot fired for many years and have already ceased to fear man. They are to be met in the forests around Moscow, beyond Sokolniki. In December 1946 an elk came through Ostankino Park to Moscow, stood there and looked round, and went back again....

Valuable wild animals are not only being protected but bred. More and more forest regions are being populated with animals useful to the country. They are bred in places where they formerly lived—the beaver has again appeared in the northern parts of the country where it had been completely exterminated. The animals are also bred in new regions where they have never been before.

An investigation of the Far Eastern forests showed that Kolonok were breeding in the floodlands and otter in the big rivers, while the smaller streams with their small fish, crayfish and frogs were free of such animals. There was room in the forests for a new animal that could be useful. And so the

American mink was introduced into the Far East. It has become part of the fauna of the Ussurian taiga; it has found its place there and provides us with fur.

In many parts of Northern Kazakhstan there are islands of pine forest in the steppes. They could be inhabited by rodents that live on pine cones. A few years ago a hundred squirrels were let loose there. Today they number tens of thousands. Man helped the squirrels cross the open steppes and they soon settled down in their new home.

Before the war squirrels from the Altai were transferred to the mountains of the Crimea. They find plenty of food in the forests and do not touch the vineyards or the orchards. Today there are several thousand squirrels in the Crimea. The squirrel has also been let loose in the Caucasian Mountains.

The suslik (marmot) was transferred to the desert island of Barsa-Kelmes, in the Aral Sea. Hunting them began five years later, and in three years thirty times more animals were killed than had been originally let loose on the island.

The Ural Mountains prevented the hare from reaching Siberia. During recent years the hare got round the Urals in the South and to the joy of Siberian sportsmen it gradually spread across the trans-Ural steppes. In order to speed up the transfer, hares trapped in the Ural foothills were transported across the mountains. Today the hare is to be found in many parts of Southern Siberia, from the Ob to the Transbaikal.

The valuable spotted deer, from the antlers of which a valuable medicine is made, is not only firmly established in the Far East; it is being resettled in the Ukraine, in the Volga Basin and in the Urals. The Ussurian racoon breeds on the Russian plain. The Altai woodchuck has become acclimatized in Daghestan, at Ghunib. The muskrat has been transferred to the Dnieper region for the first time in history. The Siberian roe deer now lives in the forests near Moscow. At the Zavidovo Hunting Preserve, north of Klin, seven wild pigs from the Caucasus were let loose ten years ago. Today there are four hundred of them.

Some animals have been transferred from district to district within the country, others have been brought from abroad.

There are endless reserves of sedge grass and other marsh grasses in our vast country. These supplies of grass may be turned into fur and meat with the aid of the North American muskrat. It is a small, yellowish animal with a long tail and webbed hind paws. The skin of the muskrat is handsome, strong and warm, and is usually used as a substitute for seal-skin. The flesh of the muskrat is edible.

The acclimatization of the muskrat began in the U.S.S.R. twenty years ago. Something like fifty thousand of the animals were let loose in five hundred different places; the first two and a half thousand of them were brought to the Soviet Union from abroad.

The muskrat multiplies rapidly. It has settled down splendidly in its new home.

At first the muskrat was let loose in the northern forests, but later it was transferred to the valleys of our southern rivers where it began to multiply even more rapidly. Today the delta of the River Ili, in Kazakhstan, provides more than a half of all the pelts obtained from this new fur-bearing animal.

The war stopped the breeding of muskrat for a time, but the work has now been resumed. Muskrats are being introduced in the valleys of many of the rivers of the European part of the U.S.S.R.—Dnieper, Don and others.

The muskrat is now to be found in a third of the territory of the Soviet Union. Since trapping the animal was first begun, several million skins have been obtained. In many places the muskrat already holds first place amongst animals trapped. Here and there it already competes with the squirrel, which is the chief commercial fur-bearing animal in our country.

Another animal, the nutria or coypu, was brought to this country from the Argentine: it is a big rodent that lives in swamps, has a long tail which is covered with scales and scanty, short hair. This "swamp beaver" has valuable fur which we call "monkey fur."

The nutria feeds on reeds and it was let loose in the valleys of the rivers of the Caucasus, Kazakhstan and Central Asia. A winter sheet of ice on the rivers, however, means death to the nutria and it became acclimatized only in the warm regions: it is bred in the Rion, the Kura and to some extent in the Kuban. In these places it is already being trapped.

In the postwar period the acclimatization of the muskrat, the nutria, and many other animals, will be practised on a much larger scale.

Everything in nature is interconnected. It is like a complicated train of gear wheels: one of them moves a little and all the others move in unison, tooth by tooth. Sometimes people do not know and do not appreciate these interconnections: by breaking the couplings of the train in one place they involuntarily disturb it in another. Carelessness in fighting field pests led to the destruction of insects and thus the birds were deprived of their food and flew away: without the birds caterpillars mutiplied and ate up all the foliage in the oak groves— this is what happened sometimes.

To make fewer mistakes one must understand the interdependence of natural phenomena. Knowledge comes from science and practical experience.

Some years ago valuable subtropical plants were brought to Georgia from abroad. Hidden amongst the leaves was an insect unknown in our climes—the icerya. The icerya is death to the tangerine tree. It multiplied rapidly on the Black Sea coast—no chemical could save the tangerine groves from the insect. In countries where the tangerine is a native there is another insect that lives on the icerya and does not allow it to gain mastery of the tangerine plantations. There were no such insects in Georgia, where the tangerine is a foreign tree. This was realized, and the rhodolia beetle was brought from Cairo to Georgia. When the beetle multiplied, the icerya began to die out and the tangerine groves were saved.

The apple orchards of the South suffered from the ravages of the aphis. Its enemy, the aphelinus, was brought from afar.

The aphelinus lays its eggs inside the body of the aphis, the eggs mature and the aphis dies. The aphelinus was brought to the Crimea, the Ukraine and the Caucasus and the apple trees were cleared of the aphis. Only the blackened, dried skins of the aphis were left hanging from the branches, each of them with a hole out of which the aphelinus had flown. . . .

There are useful insects as well as useful animals. We transfer them to the places in which we need them.

We also transfer fish to new waters.

Grey mullet from the Black Sea were taken by air to the Caspian. They multiplied and in a few years were regularly caught off the Apsheron Peninsula and off the shores of Turkmenistan.

Millions of young Caspian herring were placed in the Aral Sea: today they fill the nets of the Aral fishermen. Sea and lakes have exchanged their wealth.

The number of fish in the Caspian increased. The enclosed Caspian Sea, however, possesses very few of the sea-bed animals on which the fish live. The mullet was followed by deliveries of molluscs and annelida to the Caspian. Very soon fishermen discovered them both in the stomachs of the fish.

The viviparous fish gambusia devours the larvae of the malaria-bearing mosquito. Twenty years ago, 145 gambusia were brought from Italy and placed in the Transcaucasian rivers. Very soon a new verb was added to the Russian language—to gambuse. Many of the rivers of the Caucasus and Central Asia have now been "gambused." In places on the Tejen, say, this foreign fish is now common. It has multiplied and its numbers are now enormous.

Ladoga and Chudskoye (Peipus) whitefish have been taken to Armenia and bred in the mountain lake, Sevan. Amur carp has been placed in Lake Baikal, where it never lived before. Bream are bred in the lakes of Byelorussia.

During the Great Patriotic War many fish were bred in the lakes and reservoirs of the eastern parts of the country. Collec-

17—777

tive farmers build ponds with power stations or mills on the dams and with fish and waterfowl in the water.

The Soviet Government encourages this valuable enterprise. "Fish and waterfowl shall be bred in ponds and reservoirs," says the postwar five-year plan.

The reservoirs of big power stations and canals also cause changes in the geography of our fauna.

The dam across the Dnieper had no sooner been built and a new lake formed than Dreissena molluscs began to breed rapidly: they hung in clusters on the still living gorse bushes that lay under the water.

As soon as the Moscow Canal was built the red-finned Volga pike made its appearance in the Moscow rivers.

The "Rybinsk Sea," a huge reservoir formed by the dam of the Shcherbakov Power Station on the Volga, brought about a complete "revolution" in zoogeography. Numerous fish began to breed in this huge new lake—pike, perch, bream and especially roach. To those varieties of fish that formerly inhabited the Volga, Mologa and Sheksna, new sorts have been added: the lake whitefish has been brought from the northern waters—Lake Ladoga smelt, Byeloozero smelt, and the nelma, a northern whitefish.

The postwar five-year plan provides that "valuable breeds of fish shall be widely acclimatized in the Moscow Sea and the Rybinsk Reservoir, and their catching shall be organized."

Several railway carloads of carp, golden carp and ryapushka have already been placed in the new lake. Fishermen's cooperatives have been set up on the banks—they use nets and seines similar to those used at sea. Fishermen go out in motor boats for "deep-sea fishing" around the haunts of the main schools of the bigger fish. Canneries have already been built to handle over a thousand tons of fish a year.

On the shores of the "Rybinsk Sea" a new feathered world has come into being. During migration flocks of swans and snipe and huge flocks of duck stay on this sea for long periods. Loons have settled there and wild geese are beginning to nest.

For the first time in history the flocks of waterfowl have attracted the white-tailed and golden eagles to this district.

This new geography of the animal kingdom is one of the important features of the new geography of the Soviet Union.

RESERVATIONS

The changes in the geography of the animal kingdom and the regrouping of animals on large expanses of the country are facilitated by a chain of reservations or preserves.

There were reservations in old Russia too, but they were few and were intended for purposes far removed from science and economy.

The Byelovezha forest, in which bison, the last of the wild oxen of Europe, roamed, was declared a reservation. This, however, was not done in the interests of science—the forest was the scene of ceremonial royal hunts. There rare animals were preserved in order that they could be senselessly destroyed. It was forbidden to shoot wild boar, roe and other deer in the western valleys of the Caucasus—the tsar's family had its hunting grounds here.

The wealthy Falz-Fein set up his private reservation in the southern steppes of the Ukraine; and just before the revolution the Barguzin Reservation was established in Transbaikal. This is the complete list of the reservations that existed in pre-revolutionary times.

In the Soviet Union work for the protection of nature has developed on a gigantic scale. It was begun on the instructions of Lenin. The first Soviet reservation—at Astrakhan—was founded in 1919. Today the U.S.S.R. possesses dozens of reservations with a total area of 22,000,000 hectares, almost equal to the area of England. We have reservations in all geographical zones, differing in landscape and in their flora and fauna.

We have reservations in the Far North and in the Far South. On the rocky Seven Islands of the Barents Sea the

17*

eider duck breeds—there is nothing warmer than the down with which this bird lines its nest. In the Kizyl-Agach Reservation, on the southwestern shores of the Caspian Sea, millions of migratory birds from the Far North spend the winter. They are so numerous that they cover the whole ground in the region. A single shot could kill a score of birds, but they are not hunted. Bearing in mind the needs and interests of the Komi and the Nentsi, the peoples of the North, the Azerbaijanians take good care of the birds during their winter's stay in the South.

We also have reservations in the Far West and the Far East. In the Byelovezha forest, on the Polish frontier, the bison live in primeval surroundings. At Kamchatka, in the huge Kronotsky Reservation, where there are active volcanoes and geysers that send up fountains of hot water, there are sable, ermine and red fox.

We have reservations high up in the mountains and in the plains. Amongst the mountains and glaciers, dense forests and rushing rivers of the Caucasus Reservation live the rare aurochs, in the Altai Reservation there is the Siberian stag, and in the Alma-Ata Reservation—the snow panther. At Askania Nova on the Ukrainian plain, there are antelope and ostriches, Przhevalsky horses and African zebras.

In the Suputinka Reservation, in the Far East, actinidia lianas and wild grapes grow on Korean cedars, under the carpet of grass grows the rare jenshen root, and on the sands of the seashore the tracks of tigers are to be found. In the Darwin Reservation on the "Rybinsk Sea" there are new bays, new islands and new colonies of migratory birds. In the Voronezh Reservation are the dams and houses built by the beaver. In the Lapland Reservation there are herds of wild reindeer. In the Pechora-Ilych Reservation we find an animal called "kidas," a cross between a marten and a sable. In the Astrakhan Reservation the lotus blooms. In the Stolby Reservation, near Krasnoyarsk, there are colonnades of peculiar rocks.

And then there are the Teberda Reservation in the Cauca-
sus, the Kondo-Sosva on the eastern slopes of the Urals, the
Hassan-Kuli in Turkmenistan, the Ak-Su Jebagly-Su in the
Tien Shan Mountains, the Sihote-Alin in the Far East....

These are only the biggest reservations. There are many
other smaller ones: the Living Book near Moscow, the Cedar
Waterfall near Vladivostok, the Pine Grove on the Sura, Bo-
rovoye in the Kazakhstan steppes, Woods on the Vorskla, Tula
Forest Paths.

Reservations in the U.S.S.R. work on principles that differ
from those on which reservations abroad are based. We say
"work" advisedly, for our Soviet reservations work.

Their work is not passive study, but the active control of
nature. It involves not only observation but also experiment,
scientific work. Our reservations are not only places where
valuable plants and animals are protected, they are also scientific institutions that solve important economic problems.

For this reason their role in changing the geography of
the animal kingdom in our country is so important.

The Askania Nova Reservation works to improve breeds
of domestic animals and to acclimatize and domesticate wild
animals. It has developed new breeds of sheep and pigs and
a breed of bison that is very close to the wild type. Animals
very similar to the aurochs have also been developed.

The Seven Islands Reservation breeds the young of the
eider duck in incubators.

The Voronezh Reservation has, for the first time, learned
to breed beaver in captivity. These valuable animals are now
sent out from Voronezh to other reservations—from the Mor-
dovian Reservation on the Middle Volga to the Lapland Reservation beyond the Arctic Circle.

The reservations of the U.S.S.R. are centres for the rehabilitation and exploitation of the wealth of the animal kingdom.

The Soviet people are firmly taking surrounding nature
into their hands and compelling her more fully and effectively
to serve the cause of renewing and developing our country.

VII

NEW ROADS

STEEL THREADS

THE TRANS-SIBERIAN Express takes ten days to make its rapid journey across the U.S.S.R., so big is our country. On the passenger platform at Vladivostok there is a post with the figure 9,337 kilometres—such a milestone is not to be found anywhere else in the world. Placed end to end, Soviet railway lines would go three times round the world....

Distances are great in the U.S.S.R. and the importance of transport is equally great.

Motors and machine tools, instruments and footwear, fabrics and farm implements—a multitude of the most diverse commodities are produced in the factories of the U.S.S.R. The Soviet countryside sends millions of tons of grain, meat, milk, cotton, flax and wool to the towns. The whole of this enormous mass of products has to be distributed over the country, has to be transported, delivered to the consumer.

In no other country are the natural resources spread so widely over the face of the earth. Very often they are so located that they have to be transported over great distances. Timber is needed in the South, but the South is treeless. In the North dense forests stretch from the Baltic to distant Kamchatka. Leningrad needs coal, but coal lies well over a thousand miles away, at the Arctic end of the Urals. Oil has to get to Novosibirsk from the Volga or the Emba, while flour from the Ukraine goes to Murmansk. The distance from Magnitogorsk to the Kuznetsk Basin, whence comes the coal for coking, is over two thousand kilometres. All these places have to be firmly linked up by the steel threads of the railways.

People also travel—they go to work in new districts, they serve in the armed forces on distant frontiers, they go on visits to Moscow, or for their holidays to the South. . . .

Transport "corrects geography"—it brings distant places closer, it "reduces" space and time. It links the numerous regions of the Soviet Union into one whole. As Comrade Stalin said: transport in our country is of "great state significance."

The U.S.S.R. is a great railway power.

Old Russia had outstanding railway engineers and inventors, but in tsarist times the railways could not help being as backward as the national economy as a whole. Industry was weak, and the equipment of the railways was equally weak. The locomotives were low-powered. The freight cars were small, all four wheeled—they used to be called "boxes." When the train ran downhill the engine whistled and the brakemen on the train applied hand brakes.

And even of this rolling stock there was not enough. Pre-revolutionary Russia did not load more than twenty-eight thousand cars a day.

In the Soviet Union our entire national economy is growing, and with it our socialist transport is growing too.

Soviet industry has provided the railways with many thousands of locomotives, hundreds of thousands of cars, tankers and floats. Before the war Soviet railwaymen loaded more than a hundred thousand cars a day.

Railway transport has been completely reconstructed. Locomotives are more powerful and the cars are more capacious. At the beginning of the Third Five-Year Plan period about two thousand "FD" locomotives, the most powerful in Europe, were running on our Soviet railways. They hauled a third of all the loads. Electric and Diesel locomotives have made their appearance on the steel ways—these are the most up-to-date and economical locomotives. On many railways the old semaphores have been replaced by automatic signals. Hand brakes have been replaced by automatic brakes. Heavy rails have been laid over long stretches of line.

The speed of the trains has increased. The average speed of the trains over long stretches has been doubled.

New railway lines have been laid and the railway network of the U.S.S.R. grew to almost double its original size during the prewar years.

The length of the lines was doubled, but the goods transported, expressed in kilometre tons, increased more than six-fold. What does this show? It shows that the railways are working better under the Soviet government. Transport in the U.S.S.R. is organized on socialist principles and we make fuller and more rational use of every locomotive, of every car and of every kilometre of permanent way than the capitalist countries do. The U.S.S.R. carries more tons of goods per kilometre than the U.S.A., and now occupies first place in the world in this respect.

The railways were put to a hard strain during the war when the country and the front required the shipment of enormous loads. The Soviet railways, however, proved capable of coping with this difficult task.

Today, after the war, the railways are continuing their rapid growth; what was destroyed is being rehabilitated, and new railways are being built. The present five-year plan provides for the building of 7,230 kilometres of new line and 12,500 kilometres of second track on existing lines—which is the equivalent of building two Trans-Siberian Railways. Many new powerful locomotives and capacious cars will be put on the railways. The transportation of both goods and passengers will be greatly increased. In the last year of the present five-year plan about 2,000 million people will be carried by the railways. This is the equivalent of the world's population.

The U.S.A. is the only country which has a greater total length of railways than we have; but the length of our railways is increasing, whereas in the United States it is shrinking. Many railways in the U.S.A. have been unable to withstand the competition of automobile transport and have stopped running. The rails have been pulled up and sold as scrap. In the course of forty years the total length of the American railways has diminished by over forty thousand kilometres.

In the Soviet Union new railways are constantly being built, and these cause changes in the layout of the network. As the industrial and agricultural maps change, the railway map changes with them.

The whole life of our country is reflected in the work of our railways. A lot can be learned about the character of a country from the distribution of the railway lines on the map.

In old Russia nearly all the railways started from the Centre. The Centre had no raw materials or food of its own—it drew cotton and timber, grain and metal to itself with the aid of steel threads. Manufactured goods from the Centre flowed along the steel arteries to the outlying districts—the disposal of these goods enriched the merchants and factory owners.

The farther from the Centre the greater the distance between the railways; their rays became farther apart, until the distant outskirts were plunged into the gloom of a roadless existence. Only a few lines penetrated into the depths of the outlying regions—the Siberian, Central Asian and Caucasian Railways.

Railway lines from the grain-bearing Ukraine and Volga Basin stretched not only to the Centre, to the North, but also to the Northwest and the South, to the Baltic and Black Sea ports. The Western imperialists, bossing backward, agrarian Russia as if she were their colony, pumped her grain and raw materials out of her—this was confirmed by the geography of the railways.

Under the Soviet government the relations between districts have undergone a radical change. The Centre is no longer a metropolis that exploits the outlying regions like colonies; and the outlying regions are no longer colonies. The Centre ships to other regions not only cotton and woolen cloth, but also machinery. The socialist Centre does not hinder the industrial development of other districts, on the contrary, it accelerates it. The outlying regions no longer send away all their cotton, timber and metal—they work a great part of them up themselves.

The industrialization of the outlying regions of the country accelerated the construction of railways in the periphery. Railways appeared in new directions. Today, the steel threads not only connect the Centre with the periphery; they also connect peripheral regions with each other.

But the importance of the lines that radiate from the Centre has not diminished. On the contrary, it has increased.

Formerly the *entire* cotton crop was shipped from Central Asia to the Centre. Today only *part* of it goes to the Centre, but this part is bigger than the whole was before. The same is true of metal and timber. The processing of raw materials has been brought nearer to their source of origin: big industries have grown up in places that were colonies in tsarist Russia. Nevertheless, more raw material is being shipped from the periphery than formerly, because industry has grown in all the regions and republics of the U.S.S.R. and the central regions also demand increasing quantities of raw materials. Although these central regions account for a smaller share of the country's total industrial output than they did before, they use up ever so much more coal, metals, raw cotton and timber than they did before.

The powerful socialist Centre, to which the revolution gave a new social significance and a new economic structure, still remains the determining and the leading economic zone of the Soviet Union. Year after year the flow of goods from the Centre to all parts of our vast country increases. This industrial output is vitally necessary for the economic prosperity of every region.

All this increases the importance of the railways that connect the Centre with the periphery.

The increase in the traffic on the lines running from the outskirts of the country to the Centre has another reason.

Before the revolution St. Petersburg got all its coal from Great Britain. Today we are no longer dependent on foreign countries. Leningrad uses Soviet coal. St. Petersburg also imported a lot of metal from abroad. Today Leningrad's metal comes from the Ukraine and the Urals. Moscow formerly imported part of its raw cotton from the United States. Today the Moscow mills weave cloth from the cotton of the Transcaucasus and Central Asia.

The work of the short, western lines running to the frontier has been relatively reduced, while the importance of the long lines connecting the outskirts of the country with the Centre and Leningrad has increased. What we formerly imported we now make ourselves. Most of what we formerly exported we are now using within the country.

This created the need of new lines running to the Centre. The plan foresaw this need and the lines were built.

During the period of the Stalin five-year plans the Moscow-Donets Basin main line was built. Two-thirds of the line—from Moscow to Valuiki—follows the old route, but it has been radically reconstructed. The remainder, from Valuiki to the Donets Basin, has been newly built: "FD" locomotives, travelling at the former speed of passenger trains, pull train after train of freight along this route. Coal and metal from the Donets Basin; pit props and manufactured goods to the Donets Basin.

In recent years railway connection was established between the Centre and the new coal field at Pechora. The freight traffic on this line, built quite recently through taiga and tundra, is almost as heavy as that of the other main lines. The Pechora main line has already carried to Leningrad over three million tons of coal mined beyond the Arctic Circle. After heavy winter snows the trains have to run through a corridor of snow, the white walls of which are sometimes higher than the locomotive.

The Centre is improving its communications with the East, with the Urals and Siberia. Under the Soviet government a line has been built from Kazan to Sverdlovsk. Another new line runs from Gorky to Kotelnich. The postwar five-year plan provides for the electrification of the Chelyabinsk-Ufa line, the heavily loaded section that goes across the Urals. A second track is being added to the existing line over the tremendous stretch from Omsk, through Sverdlovsk and Kotelnich, to Gorky. The Ural Mountains will be crossed by a fourth transverse line in the South. New steel threads are being woven into the fabric of the country.

During the First World War a railway was hurriedly and roughly built to the Kola Peninsula: the trains travelled practically through swamps; water splashed up from under the sleepers. During the period of the five-year plans this railway was completely rebuilt, and today the Kirovsk Main Line is one of the best in the country. It connects the Centre with the ice-free port of Murmansk—a gateway to the ocean that is open all the year round.

Thus, the rays that converge at the Centre are increasing in number.

The greatest number of new railways, however, are being built in the East. In the Soviet period, distant and formerly backward regions have been awakened to life. New industries are growing up there and new lands are being cultivated. New railways are being built in the once roadless periphery. Out of the 7,230 kilometres of new railways to be built under the postwar five-year plan, 3,550—half—will be built in Siberia.

Freight traffic in the Centre has greatly increased, but in the East the increase has been considerably greater. In 1937 the amount of goods carried for the whole country was four times that of 1913, for the Far East it was thirteen times, for Kazakhstan, fourteen times and for Siberia more than twenty times.

The new economic geography means a new freight traffic geography: Goods travel in new directions, and more goods are transported in the old directions than was formerly the case. This means that old roads must be improved and new roads built.

Look at the map of Kazakhstan. The area of this republic is equal to that of half of Western Europe. Before the revolution Kazakhstan was crossed by only one railway line, from Orenburg, through Aktyubinsk, to Tashkent; in the North the Siberian Railway just touched the republic at Petropavlovsk. The interior of Kazakhstan had no railways at all: the country was rich in cattle, but the animals were driven to market towns, losing weight on the way.

In the Soviet period new industrial centres have been built in Kazakhstan and new railways have been laid to them.

Railways connect the Karaganda coal field with the Siberian Railway and with the South Urals. A railway has been built to the shores of Lake Balkhash for the copper of Kounrad, and another to the Ulu Tau Mountains, in the heart of Kazakhstan, for the copper of Jezkazghan. The oil of Emba, the complex ores of the Altai, the phosphorites of the Kara Tau, the lead ore of Tekeli and the coal of Lenger have all attracted railways. In the Soviet period the backbone of a new railway system has been built up in Kazakhstan—railway lines of a total length of nine thousand kilometres have been laid where before the revolution they scarcely reached the two-thousand-kilometre mark.

The Ural Mountains run from south to north. This is also the direction of the main freight traffic of the Urals, and along this route, in addition to existing lines a new railway line has been laid from Chelyabinsk to Serov, via Kamensk. The last stretch of this line, from Sosva to Alapayevsk, was opened after the war. In the South, the Ural railways have been extended as far as Kandagach in Kazakhstan, and in the North they will be extended to Vorkuta.

The extension of North-South connections in the Urals will continue during the postwar five-year plan period; the Ufa-Ishimbai line will be extended to Yermolayevo in the south, and a new line from Magnitogorsk to Baimak will be laid. In the near future it will be possible to travel the whole length of the Urals, from Karpinsk in the North to Chelyabinsk in the South, by electric train. Electric traction will increase the traffic capacity of the railways by fifty to a hundred per cent. Thus, the electrification of the Karpinsk-Chelyabinsk line will be the equivalent of an additional meridional railway down the Urals.

In this way the backbone of the railway network in the Urals is being strengthened.

In Western Siberia the main freight traffic follows the parallels of latitude and not the longitudinal meridians—this route is being constantly improved. In the very First Five-Year Plan period an additional route was laid from Sverdlovsk to Kurghan. Later, a second latitudinal line was begun and is being built in sections—this is the South Siberian Railway. Today, the Siberian Railway has ceased to be the only latitudinal line in the western part of Siberia.

During the first months of the war, the Kartaly-Akmolinsk line, in Northern Kazakhstan, was opened; it will be an important link in the future South Siberian main line. New sections of it are being built now, and by the end of the present five-year plan period a new line will run from the Volga to the Yenisei—it will start at Kuibyshev, cross the Urals and reach Magnitogorsk, cross the steppes through Akmolinsk, Pavlodar and Barnaul, emerge at Kuzbas, plunge into the mountains again, cut across them and descend into the valley of the Yenisei and reach Abakan. This new steel artery will serve as the channel for incalculable wealth—ores from Bashkiria, steel from Magnitogorsk, grain from the trans-Urals, Kazakhstan and Altai steppes, salt from Kulunda, coal from Ekibastuz and Kuzbas, and timber and ore from Kuznetsk Ala-Tau.

This is the biggest piece of railway construction provided for in the present five-year plan. It is not an easy job. In amount of earth to be shifted alone it is the equivalent to digging a canal from the Baltic Sea to the Black Sea. The most difficult section is Kuznetsk-Ala-Tau, with its steep crags, avalanches and winter torrents, which sometimes carry down as much as ten thousand cubic metres of snow in one drop. It will entail the tremendous work of levelling the track and building an embankment, bridges, galleries and tunnels....

The old Siberian Railway is also being renovated. There have been no semaphores on its Western section for a long time—automatic block signalling was installed during the period of the five-year plans. The postwar five-year plan will introduce further changes; steam locomotives will be removed from the Ural section right up to the Kuzbas; their place will be taken by electric locomotives which will haul heavy trains at great speed across the trans-Urals plain. Soviet Siberia will have the longest electric railway in the world.

In old Russia, the outlying regions from which raw materials came were connected by rail with the Centre, but they were not connected with each other. In the Soviet Union all regions are in a state of harmonious growth; industry is developing in all of them and they maintain lively intercourse with each other. The former disconnected regions are now connected by rail.

There were maps before the revolution with a dotted line indicating the track of the Turkestan-Siberian Railway (Turksib). The need for railway connection between Siberia and Central Asia was anticipated and was considered desirable, but under the old regime it was impracticable.

At the end of 1926 Comrade Stalin proposed that the building of the Turksib Railway be commenced. Work was started in 1927, and in May 1930 the builders, moving from the North and South, met at Aina-Bulak. The dotted line on the map became a firm line indicating a fact: the Turksib Railway was built. The builders who moved from the North successfully crossed the broad Irtysh and the shifting sands of trans-Balkhash. And those coming from the South successfully crossed the difficult Chokpar Pass in the Chu-Ili Mountains.

A line nearly 1,500 kilometres long linked Siberia with Central Asia. Siberia began to supply Central Asia with what it lacked—coal, grain and timber. Central Asia, in its turn, supplied the new textile mills in Siberia with raw cotton.

But it was not only a matter of transportation. The Turksib Railway awoke to life the whole of the eastern part of Kazakhstan. On reaching Alma-Ata, the capital of Kazakhstan, the verdant city at the foot of snow-capped mountains, the railway, as it were, took it out of its roadless cul-de-sac and placed it on the great highroad of our country. It provided an outlet for the riches of fertile Semirechie, brought it new varieties of agricultural crops and helped it to develop the ore deposits of Jungar Ala-Tau and the Kalbin Range.

During the period of the Stalin five-year plans new railways crossed former desert and roadless country and laid the foundations of industry and high-level agriculture in former wild and neglected territories.

The newly-built Murmansk Railway facilitated the economic development of the Kola Peninsula and the riches of Khibiny. The new industrial centre beyond the Arctic Circle could not have developed without the Pechora Railway.

By penetrating the distant, non-Russian regions, railways facilitate their economic and cultural growth. The Turksib Railway not only brought new freights into being; it also accelerated the cultural development of Kazakhstan. Big urban centres sprang up along its route. Former nomad herdsmen became engine drivers, traffic managers and station masters. A branch line of the Turksib Railway linked the city of Frunze, the capital of Kirghizia, with the railway network of the country, and this branch line runs to Lake Issyk-Kul, far into the interior of the Republic.

The capitals of other non-Russian republics—Stalinabad, Sukhumi, Stalinir, Yoshkar-Ola, Cheboksary, Cherkessk and Abakan, have also received railway connection.

Under the Soviet government many regions of the country that were formerly disconnected became connected to their mutual benefit. Formerly, communication in the Volga region was poor. When the Volga froze in the winter, the direct road

Diesel train, runs between Baku and Tbilisi

Electric locomotive hauling train of oil cisterns

The Northern Sea Route. A caravan of ships

that connected the districts of the middle and lower reaches of the river was cut. To travel from Syzran to Saratov, one had to change at Penza. During the Great Patriotic War a thousand-kilometre railway was laid along the right bank of the Volga from Sviyazhsk near Kazan, through Syzran and Saratov, to Ilovlinskaya, near Stalingrad. On the left bank Pugachev was linked with Chapayevsk, thus forming an uninterrupted route from Kuibyshev right to Astrakhan. From Astrakhan a road was laid along the Caspian coast to Kizlyar—the Volga region was linked with the Caucasus. Freight can now be carried along the Volga also in the winter. There is no need now to travel from the Urals to the Caucasus via Moscow—there is a shorter and more direct route.

After the revolution, the South Urals were for the first time connected with the trans-Volga region through Troitsk-Orsk. A line now runs from the Karelian Isthmus to Petrozavodsk, bounding Lake Ladoga on the north. The Crimea has been linked with the lower reaches of the Dnieper by a line that runs across the Perekop Isthmus. A straight line now runs from the region of Baku to Armenia via Minjevan; it is no longer necessary to go the roundabout way via Tbilisi.

And the journey to Tbilisi from Moscow is now most often made not through Baku, but through Sochi and Sukhumi, there is no need to go round the wall of the Caucasian Range from the east along the Caspian coast; the Black Sea Railway has been laid, which reduces the journey by nearly twenty-four hours.

There is another big "curve" in Kazakhstan. As the crow flies, the distance from Alma-Ata to Karaganda—from the capital of the Republic to its biggest industrial centre—is only seven hundred kilometres, but one has to travel over three thousand kilometres—via Barnaul, Novosibirsk and Omsk. Soon, however, this "curve" will be removed. In conformity with the postwar five-year plan the Mointy-Chu line is being built. It will run through the waterless and uninhabited Bet-Pak-Dal Desert, go round Lake Balkhash on the west and link Alma-Ata with the meridional line that runs from Balkhash, through Kara-ganda, to Petropavlovsk on the Siberian main line. This will be a second "Turksib."

A railway is being built from Charjou to Kungrad. It will run across the sands of the Kara Kum Desert and over the irrigation canals of the lower Amu Darya, and link the boun-teous Khoresm Oasis with the central regions of Central Asia. Later on it will be extended along the Ust-Urt plateau to the trans-Volga region and will be a link in the new Central Asia-Centre line.

Rivers, in their own way, "participate" in the choice of rail-way routes. Railways were laid to the Volga in order to pick up that river's freights, but these lines did not cross the river at all points; there was no bridge at Kostroma, at Gorky or at Saratov. The lines were cut short at the riverbank; locomo-tives reached the water's edge and turned back again. There was the Syzran Bridge at Batraki, where the lines from the Centre, Siberia and Central Asia converged, but there was al-ways a "jam."

During the five-year plan periods many new bridges were built on the Volga. The line from Moscow to the Urals runs across the new bridge at Gorky. A line runs to Galich from the Kostroma bridge. Crossing the Volga by the new Saratov bridge, a continuous line links the southern trans-Volga region with Moscow. Bridges have "repaired" geography.

Railways intercross in big cities. For example, seven rays converge in Sverdlovsk and eleven converge in Moscow.

Formerly, railway junctions arose without any plan. They were hemmed in by new blocks of houses that sprang up in the towns. It is difficult to sort out cars in congested marshal-ling yards with a confused tangle of sidings; as a consequence, the cars were held up in them.

Soviet railway engineers are unravelling this tangle. Tim-ber from the North going South, and coal from the South going North, pass through Moscow. To prevent these through freights from blocking the Moscow junction, the "Moscow Eastern Semi-circle" was built in the period of the Stalin five-year plans. This is an arc running round Moscow from Alexandrov to Zhilev, via Kurovskaya and Voskresensk, about fifty kilometres from the capital. Thus, these timber and coal freights are enabled to give the congested Moscow junction a wide berth. During the Great Patriotic War the "semi-circle" was converted into a circle by the construction of the Big Circle Railway, which runs through Stolbovaya, Kubinka and Yakhroma. No through freights now congest the Moscow junction.

A circle was also built at Novosibirsk. Another is being built at Chelyabinsk.

These circles and arcs on the map serve as additional evidence of planned intervention in the railway geography of our country that took shape spontaneously in pre-revolutionary times.

The bane of the railways in Russia in the past was the one-way flow of freights. Loaded trains would reach their destination and go back empty. This was the effect of the division of the country into industrial and agricultural-mining regions.

Uneven distribution of freights still exists on many railways in the U.S.S.R. Moscow, for example, receives bulky freights— timber, coal and oil—and sends out freights which, though of greater value, are of smaller bulk—machinery, machine tools, instruments and books.

Under our planned system of economy, however, we are in a position to reduce this underloading of freight trains. Every region in the Soviet Union is developing both industry and agriculture. We no longer have any regions engaged solely in supplying raw materials—manufacturing industry is developing everywhere. The industrial regions are developing their own food supply bases. Consequently, the unevenness in freight movements is being smoothed out. For example, before the revolution the volume of freight carried from Moscow to Kursk was one-seventh of that carried from Kursk to Moscow; in 1937 Moscow-Kursk freights amounted to two-fifths of Kursk-Moscow freights.

18*

In the Soviet Union inter-district industrial combines are being formed which are interconnected not only by railways but also by a common plan of production. Trains carry coal from the Kuzbas to the Urals and on the return journey they carry iron ore. True, the flow of ore is less than that of coal, but for all that, a considerable number of cars are used that would otherwise go back empty. Formerly, trains carried ore from Krivoi Rog to the Donbas and went back empty. In the period of the Stalin five-year plans the iron and steel industry was developed in Krivoi Rog, and trains returning from the Donbas carry coal for this industry.

Uneven traffic is diminishing. And so is uneconomic transportation.

ROAD AND AIR TRAFFIC

There were few automobiles in Russia before the revolution, and those that were available rarely left the city streets. Today, automobiles carry passengers and freight not only from street to street.

For relatively short distances goods are transported by motor truck and not by train. On the main roads outside of Moscow trucks and cars race along in an almost continuous stream. The maps of the environs of our cities show close networks of automobile roads.

Motor trucks link the collective farms deep in the country with railway stations and river wharves, from which automobile roads radiate in different directions. This is a new feature on the map of our country.

But automobiles do not make only short journeys. Motor highways are beginning to link city with city in our country.

Such a highway, for example, has been laid from Moscow to Minsk—a broad, smooth ribbon with no steep inclines, sharp turns or intersecting railway traffic. Cars do not merely roll along it, they fly.

Motor highways of this kind bring cities "nearer" to each other and thereby alter the geography of the country. The landscape changes and becomes more cultured—the strip of asphalt running through woods or between fields, newly planted trees on the roadside, the pretty houses of the road-maintenance men and repair shops.

Among the other highways now being laid is that from the Centre to the Crimea. There will be a filling station at every hundred kilometres and a hotel at every three hundred kilometres. People from Moscow, Leningrad and Kharkov will be able to travel to the southern seaside in their own cars.

Automobiles are particularly needed in the mountain regions where no railways have been built yet. In many districts the motor road serves as a substitute for a railway.

Formerly, a narrow pack-horse track wound its way up over the Pamirs in the pellucid air and awesome stillness of the wilderness. There was scarcely a caravan that did not lose a camel or two on the way; the skeletons of animals, gnawed clean by jackals, shone white among the crags—the last remains of unfortunate wayfarers who had strayed from the path.

Today an automobile road runs through the whole of the Pamirs. The rocky crags were blown up and cleared away. Automobiles leave Osh, run through the Alai Valley—a highland pasture—zigzag up to the "Roof of the World," cross the bare, flat, yellowish-grey Pamir valleys and then over the mountain passes, race along the ledge in the deep and narrow gorges and reach Khorog, where, at giddy heights, the footpaths, flimsy shelves fastened to stakes driven into the steep crags, used to hang.

Stalinabad and Tashkent are linked by a motor road that within a short distance crosses three mountain ranges—the Hissar, Zeravshan and Turkestan, each of which is nearly of the same height as the Caucasus.

Automobile transport is continuing to develop in all parts of our country. The Moscow, Gorky and Yaroslavl automobile plants that were built in Soviet times are supplying it with hundreds of thousands of excellent cars and trucks. Several new automobile plants are in course of erection, and the old ones are being enlarged.

By the end of the present five-year plan period our industry will have an output capacity of 500,000 cars and trucks per annum. There will be twice as many automobiles on our Soviet roads as there were before the war.

* * *

The airways in the U.S.S.R. stretch for tens of thousands of kilometres.

Our civil aviation was built up almost entirely in the period of the Stalin five-year plans. It is employed for the most diverse purposes.

Supposing somebody in a remote settlement, on an exploring expedition, or in Arctic winter quarters, falls dangerously ill. The medical aviation service will be informed by telegraph or radio and an aeroplane will be despatched with the necessary medical supplies, or a medical specialist, and, if need be, the patient will be taken to the nearest hospital.

In Central Asia the sand dunes, shifted by the winds, threaten to invade the fields. Aircraft are sent over these moving dunes to scatter the seeds of sand-binding plants over them.

Lightning may cause a forest fire. There is nobody in the deserted forest to combat the flames and the fire may easily spread. It is checked by aircraft equipped with the necessary fire-fighting implements.

The forests in the Soviet North are immense. Aircraft soar over the impenetrable taiga, take photographs from the air and calculate the reserves of timber.

In the depths of Yakutia, on Chukotka, in the Arctic, there are stretches of practically unexplored territory. Aircraft fly over this territory and make surveys of it from the air.

But the chief function of civil aviation in the U.S.S.R. is transportation. Aircraft carry passengers, freight and mail.

Our country is a land of immense distances. It takes days to travel from one end of the country to another by train, but a fast aeroplane can do it in hours. Distance is overcome by speed; hence, the importance of fast air communication in a vast country like ours is enormous.

Aircraft fly all over our country, which is covered by a close network of airways. The airways map of the U.S.S.R. is crisscrossed with numerous lines of regular aircraft services. Every such line on the map is a record of the skilful work of the airman, of high flying, of struggle against the elements in the air. The airways map is a chart of daily, inconspicuous feats of heroism.

The villages in the Western Pamirs, hemmed in by narrow gorges, were almost cut off from the rest of the country. Only foot travellers and a rare horseman climbed the mountain tracks. Mail and goods were carried by pack horse. Today, these villages are connected with the rest of the country by airways. The first wheels that the inhabitants of these remote villages saw were the landing wheels of an aeroplane. The pilot flies his craft over snowy pinnacles and steers through mountain corridors so narrow that the tips of his wings almost touch the rocky walls.

In the Far East, aircraft link Khabarovsk with Sakhalin and Kamchatka. Fog forces the aeroplane down to the surface of the sea or else presses it close to the rugged shore.

In many places where airways cross the taiga, hydroplanes are used because the only available landing places are rivers. When a hydroplane flies from one river to another it has nothing but boulders or treetops beneath it.

WATERWAYS

The U.S.S.R. is a land of mighty rivers, some of them being among the biggest in the world. The Ob, together with the Irtysh, is 5,200 kilometres long, the Lena 4,264 kilometres, the Amur 4,354, the Yenisei 3,807 kilometres and the Volga 3,688 kilometres. For total length of rivers the U.S.S.R. holds first place in the world.

Before the revolution there were few ships on the river-ways in Russia, and they were poorly equipped. The technical backwardness of the country prevented the development of its internal water transport system. Often river transport could not compete with the railways. Steel rails robbed the water of its freight.

In the Soviet Union there is no competition between the different forms of transportation; together, they constitute the country's united transportation system and perform the functions prescribed for them in the plan. The steamship and automobile cooperate with the train.

Today there are numerous new ships on our rivers, more up-to-date and faster than the old ones. The river beds have been deepened. Cranes and other freight-handling equipment have been installed at the wharves.

Although river transportation is not yet developed to the extent that it could be considering the possibilities created by the biggest river system in the world, it, nevertheless, plays an important role. It is growing year after year; the volume of river-carried freight is increasing.

Oil barges, immersed almost up to their decks, float up the Volga. Down the river come tugs hauling rafts of timber. On the northern rivers timber floats in an unending stream. Both in the North and the South freights are carried from the railways to their destinations along the rivers of Siberia.

The small rivers, which are so numerous in our country, are also being opened for freight traffic. Big rivers serve as substitutes for railways. The cost of transporting a ton of oil from the Caucasus to Moscow by the Volga is only two-fifths of what it costs to carry it by rail. The small rivers serve as substitutes for horse and truck transport; transportation by river costs on the average one-seventh of the costs of transportation by truck.

The River Tsna, between Tambov and Morshansk, is becoming a local freight carrier of this kind. Dams and locks raise the level of the river, and small tugs haul barges loaded with grain, building materials and firewood.

The changes in the economic geography of the U.S.S.R. have affected river transportation; traffic on the eastern river basins has grown at a more rapid pace than that of the western basins. River freight traffic has appeared for the first time in the formerly backward remote regions.

Ships on the River Pechora cross the Arctic Circle. Ships now ply on the formerly deserted Kura in the Caucasus. A fleet has appeared on Lake Issyk-Kul, which lies among the snow-capped mountains of Kirghizia. Traffic has been opened on the rivers of Northern Siberia.

This is how the natural waterways are being developed. At the same time artificial waterways are being created.

Huge canals have been dug in our country under the Soviet government.

Between the White Sea and the Baltic Sea lies a rocky watershed furrowed by an ancient glacier and now covered by a conifer forest.

There was only one freight route across this watershed---a much overworked railway. The water route, which was cheaper and could carry more, was five thousand kilometres long, i.e., by sea, around the Scandinavian countries. It could run straight across the watershed and thus become ever so much shorter. And so, the Stalin White Sea-Baltic Canal was built in 1938. A strip of water 227 kilometres long was stretched across the watershed at a height of 108 metres. It linked Sorokskaya Bay in the White Sea with Povenetskaya Bay in Lake Onega, which was already linked with the Baltic Sea by a system of rivers. The Scandinavian Peninsula became an "island." Timber, apatite and building stone began to be carried along the canal.

The entire geography of the northeastern part of the Karelo-Finnish Republic was changed. Former river courses dried

up, new ones formed. The River Povenchanka disappeared.
Lake Vyg, the water level of which was raised six metres,
washed out scores of islands. Dams formed an enormous reservoir of an area equal to that of Lake Sevan in the Caucasus.
Villages were removed to new sites. The railway was shifted
back. New industrial centres sprang up in the canal zone—
Byelomorsk, Segezha, Povenets and Medvezhegorsk.

During the war the southern part of the canal was in the
area of hostilities and the canal structures were wrecked. When
Dam No. 20 was blown up, a tremendous flood of water
rushed down into Lake Onega, sweeping everything before it,
and formed a new course fifteen metres deep.

Our Soviet people set to work to repair the damage caused
by the enemy and the canal was restored as early as 1946, in
the very first summer after the war.

The Moscow River gave its name to a great city, but when
the city grew the river could not supply it with sufficient water. The capital of one-sixth of the globe stood on the banks
of a diminishing river. In the spring it gave up three-fourths of
its annual flow in the course of one month, but in the summer
there was scarcely any flow at all. Half the river's water was
used up by this huge industrial city.

The big river courses avoided Moscow. The Volga by-passes
it on the north and the Oka on the south. Only small vessels
could reach the city by the shallow Moscow River. The river
port of Moscow handled a negligible amount of freight compared with that handled by the Moscow railway junction.
Bulky freights—timber and building stone—were carried from
the Volga to Moscow by rail, instead of by cheap water transport.

This anomaly has now been removed. On Comrade Stalin's
proposal a canal was built which linked the Moscow River with
the Volga. This canal takes its name from the city of Moscow.

A dam built at Ivankovo, on the Upper Volga, raised the
river's water level seventeen metres and a huge lake, known
as the "Moscow Sea," 327 square kilometres in area, was

formed. The site on which the town of Korcheva stood was flooded. Part of the water that was raised by the dam flowed into an artificial course that ran in deep hollows in some places and between high dykes in others.

There is an eminence between the Moscow River and the Upper Volga. Through it a canal was dug 128 kilometres long. Electricity compels the water to run upstream instead of down; five automatic stations fitted with powerful propeller pumps force the water over the watershed. During the past ten years 9,000 million cubic metres of water have been pumped across the hilly Klin-Dmitrov ridge to Moscow! An "electric river" equal to twelve former Moscow Rivers now flows to Moscow.

To raise the water of the Volga thirty-eight metres an enormous amount of power is needed; but part of this is compensated, for as the water flows down to Moscow it passes through the turbines of hydroelectric stations and thus helps to produce the needed power.

The load carried by Moscow's electric power network is uneven; in the evening the city and its factories and the towns around the city need more electricity than in the day-time and late at night. The power stations on the canal send electricity through the network during the peak hours when the city and towns need most power, while the pumps that raise the water to the canal work in the daytime, when the require-ments of Moscow and its environs are less and there is power to spare. In this way the canal straightens the curve of the Moscow electric-power supply.

The influx of Volga water raised the water level of the Moscow River within the precincts of the city by three me-tres and thus made the river navigable. Day and night steam-ships, motorships, refrigerators, boats and barges, self-propelled and tugged, pass through the canal. Three-decker river boats now pass freely from Moscow to the Volga and along that river right to the Caspian Sea. The capital now has a deep channel that links it with the principal waterway of our country.

Half the water taken from the Volga is kept in a forest reservoir for a hundred days to allow the silt to settle and is then pumped into the Moscow water-supply system.

New bridges have been built across the canal, new trees have been planted along its banks. In place of the old villages that were flooded by the canal new ones have been built in its vicinity, and their economy and way of life are new.

As far back as the beginning of the last century, in 1810, the Volga was given an artificial outlet to the Baltic Sea through the Mariinskaya System, which became a waterway leading to St. Petersburg. But the Mariinskaya System remained narrow and shallow. The River Vytegra was intersected by no less than twenty-six locks on a stretch of only thirty kilometres. There was a shortage of water. The wooden chambers of the locks rotted and were washed away. Caravans of barges carrying grain from the Volga to St. Petersburg travelled two summers, being held up in the winter at Rybinsk.

The postwar five-year plan provides for the complete reconstruction of the Mariinskaya System. Along its course, from the Volga to Lake Ladoga, eight large locks will be built to take the place of the present forty-one locks. The Mariinskaya System will be converted into the deep, Volga-Baltic, heavy traffic waterway that will link Leningrad by water with the interior of our country.

From the Azov Sea to the Caspian Sea stretches the Manych Hollow, a small chain of diminishing lakes and small rivers. It is regarded as the borderline between Europe and Asia.

This hollow is to be converted into a canal with locks. Its construction was started before the war, and part of the waterway, from the Don along the Manych, is already finished.

When this canal is extended to the Caspian Sea it will become a marine canal. The courses of the rivers Kuban and Terek will be altered and part of their waters will flow into the new canal. Freights from Central Asia and Azerbaijan will be able to reach the Azov Sea by water. The steppe will be irrigated and become populated.

Soon the water of the Kuban will flow into the Manych via the new Nevinnomyssk Canal; the diversion of the water of the Terek, however, is a matter for the future.

The Dnieper Dam raised the level of the Dnieper high above the rapids and converted the river into a waterway navigable from end to end. Byelorussia thus obtained an outlet to the Black Sea.

Just before the outbreak of the Great Patriotic War, soon after the reunion of Western Byelorussia with the Byelorussian Soviet Republic, the Dnieper-Bug Canal was restored, or rather built anew. It linked the River Pripyat with the River Bug and thereby formed a waterway between the Dnieper and the Vistula basins.

To prevent the Germans from utilizing the canal, the Byelorussian partisans set fire to the locks. These have now been restored, the bed of the canal has been cleared and the canal is functioning again. Ships are again plying its whole length from Pinsk to Brest.

Thus, our Soviet people are linking the river basins of our country with each other and are changing the geography of our rivers.

Big projects are contemplated for the future. A canal at Stalingrad will link the Volga with the Don; Donets coal will be carried to the Volga and Volga timber to the Don by water. The Volga region will be linked with the Azov and Donbas regions, and this will bring about a change in our transport geography almost equal to that which would be made if coal were discovered on the Volga and if large forests were to spring up in the South.

In the future we will link the Dnieper with the Volkhov and the Western Dvina by a waterway, the course of which will follow the ancient route "from the Varangians to the Greeks."* It will be possible to travel by water from Kiev

---

* The ancient trading water route from the Baltic countries to Byzantium.—*Tr*.

to Leningrad and Riga. We will link the upper reaches of the Kama, the Pechora and the Vychegda; the Oka with the Dnieper and the Don; and the San with the Dniester. . . .

Perhaps we will cut a waterway through the Urals range, from the European to the Asiatic part of our country. Already Sverdlovsk, which is beyond the range, drinks the water of the River Chusovaya which flows on the western side of the Urals. Recently, part of the water of the upper reaches of the Chusovaya was diverted to Iset, and the water of the Volga and Ob basins mingled in the city reservoirs of Sverdlovsk.

THE NORTHERN SEA ROUTE

The Soviet Far North. Taiga, which passes into tundra. Tundra encircling the Arctic Ocean. Continuous day in summer, continuous night in winter.

The Far North is rich in minerals, fish, fur-bearing animals and marine animals. But how to reach these roadless regions of the Far North, on the coast of the Arctic Ocean, barred on the south by impenetrable forests and impassable swamps? It is possible to reach them by river, but the easiest way is by sea.

Formerly, merchant ships, few and far between, reached the mouth of the Ob from the West and the mouth of the Kolyma from the East. There was no sea route from the Ob to the Kolyma. The ice and other, unknown, dangers kept mariners away. Only a few vessels of scientific expeditions rounded Cape Chelyuskin, the northernmost point of Siberia.

After the revolution a caravan of ships sailed from the West every summer to the lower reaches of the Ob and Yenisei, bringing manufactured goods and carrying away timber. In 1924, icebreakers led three ships through the ice of the Kara Sea. Subsequently, four, five, six, eight, twenty-six and fifty ships were escorted in this way.

The "Kara Expedition" became a regular steamship service. A regular service was also inaugurated on the Vladivostok-Kolyma route. Finally, our navigators learned how to reach the Lena from the East and the West.

There remained the task of linking the western and eastern gaps, of establishing a through route along the whole of the Arctic coast, of linking the Pacific with the Atlantic.

The distance from Leningrad to Vladivostok via the Suez or Panama canals is twenty-three thousand kilometres. Travelling via the Northern Sea Route, the distance is only sixteen thousand kilometres. From Murmansk to Vladivostok by this route the distance is still shorter—eleven thousand kilometres, equal to the distance by rail. This is due to the spherical shape of the Earth.

Mariners and scientists had dreamed of a Northeast Passage for centuries. Europeans vainly sought here a route to China as far back as the sixteenth century.

Only three navigators succeeded in crossing this route—Nordenskjöld, Vilkitsky and Amundsen; but all were obliged to winter on the journey, and wintering robs the Northern Route of practical significance.

Soviet Arctic navigators undertook to travel from ocean to ocean in the course of a single summer.

In 1932 the icebreaker *Sibiryakov* put out from Archangel bound for Vladivostok. In the Chukotsk Sea the vessel broke its screw. Winter set in. The sea froze. The crew broke up the ice with explosives and the ship reached the Pacific under sail.

In the following year the *Chelyuskin* followed the track of the *Sibiryakov,* but she was caught in the ice in Bering Strait. The ice dragged her back to the Chukotsk Sea and crushed her there. Soviet airmen rescued the crew from the ice.

In the year after that the icebreaker *Litke* made a successful voyage from Vladivostok to Murmansk by the Northern Route.

And then, in 1935, ordinary merchant ships travelled by the Northern Sea Route.

In 1939, ten ships made a through voyage over the whole of the Northern Route from west to east. And in that same year the flagship of our Arctic Merchant Fleet, the *Joseph Stalin,* a new icebreaker, the most powerful in the world, performed the voyage there and back.

Special ships are being built for the Northern Sea Route. Depths are being sounded. Lighthouses are being built. The charts are being corrected. Every year scientific ice forecasts are made.

Formerly, passages in the ice were spied out by the ship's bo'sun perched in the "crow's nest," a barrel lashed to the mast top. Today, the track is indicated by radio stations and air scouts.

Before the revolution there were six scientific stations in the Russian Far North; now there are far more. The weather in the U.S.S.R. is largely influenced by the weather in the Arctic. Hence, the Arctic stations help our meteorologists to study and forecast the weather not only in the North, but also in the southern regions of our country.

The Great Northern Sea Route has been laid. This means that the Soviet Arctic has been opened for us, newly discovered, as it were. A waterway has been opened from the midland regions of our country to the Far East. This passage runs entirely within Soviet waters.

The postwar five-year plan sets the task of converting the Northern Sea Route into a normally functioning navigable waterway by 1950.

Our country borders on the open sea at several points: the Black Sea Coast, the Baltic Coast, the Arctic Coast and the Pacific Coast. Formerly, these points were disconnected. Under the Soviet government they have all been connected with each other by the Dnieper-Bug canal, by the Volga-Baltic waterway which is being reconstructed in the present five-year plan period, by the White Sea-Baltic canal and by

The Electric Motorship *Rossiya*, moored to wharf in the
port of Odessa, May 1, 1948

Khimki Station on the Moscow Canal

A mountain road in Central Asia

the Northern Sea Route. A network of railways connects our seaports and transfers the handling of freights in the winter season to the ice-free ports.

The U.S.S.R's maritime transport is developing, growing year after year. New ports are being opened, the old ones are being equipped with powerful travelling cranes and other freight-handling machinery. New ocean-going ships are leaving the slips of our shipyards. Soviet ships make voyages to ports in all parts of the world.

The U.S.S.R. is becoming a great maritime power.

VIII

A GREAT RENOVATION

THE VOICE OF THE PEOPLE

A NEW country, inhabited by new people. They are prompted by new sentiments and new thoughts. . . .

Look at the map. It is dotted with the names of cities, towns, rivers and mountains. These names are eloquent, they speak with the eloquence of the people.

Many new names have been added to the map of the U.S.S.R. during the past thirty years. New islands have been discovered, new towns have been built, the foundations of new cities have been laid, and these were given names. But by the will of the people many of the old names were changed, and these new names have registered the spirit of the age we are living in, they express the thoughts of the people, they have breathed freshness and life into the nomenclature of geography.

Look at the map of the world. You will distinguish the Land of Soviets without picking out the frontiers.

Explorers had to give names to the newly-discovered islands off Severnaya Zemlya and they named them October Revolution Island, Bolshevik Island, Komsomolets Island, Pioneer Island. . . .

Look at the names of the newly-conquered mountain peaks—Stalin Constitution Peak, Komsomol Peak, Victory Peak, Lenin Peak, Stalin Peak. . . .

The hearts of the Soviet people are filled with infinite love for their leaders Lenin and Stalin, and this love is recorded in the names of numerous cities—Leningrad, Ulyanovsk, Leninsk, Leninogorsk, Port Ilyich, Leninabad, Leninakan. ... Stalino, Stalingrad, Stalinsk, Stalinogorsk, Stalinabad, Stalinir.

On the map which the people have drawn we find the names of the devoted colleagues of Lenin and Stalin, of the distinguished leaders of our Bolshevik Party and of our Soviet State—the cities of Molotov and Kalinin, Sverdlovsk and Dzerzhinsk, Voroshilov and Frunze, Kuibyshev and Shcherbakov, Kirovsk and Zhdanovsk, Kirov, Kirovograd, Kirovgrad, Kirovakan, Kirovabad. ... The names which the Soviet people have given their cities ring with love, reverence and gratitude.

Our people have perpetuated the memory of the heroes of the Civil War in the names of the towns Kotovsk, Chapayevsk and Shchors. They have honoured the memory of the heroes in the war against German fascism by renaming the town of Jarkent to Panfilov; Likhvin is now named after the Young Communist Leaguer, partisan Chekalin. Nor have they forgotten their airmen heroes; we have towns named Chkalov, Osipenko and Serov.

On the map we find the names of famous men of the past—Susanino, Pereyaslav-Khmelnitski, Suvorov, Pugachev; and also the names of scientists and explorers who have rendered service to the Russian people—the towns of Przhevalsk, Karpinsk and Michurinsk, the Shokalsky Strait and the Sedov Archipelago. We also find the names of popular authors—the towns of Pushkin, Gorky, Serafimovich, Furmanov, Jambul, Fort Shevchenko, Peak Mayakovsky. ...

During the course of their life and struggle under the banner of the Communist Party our people developed a new ideology. The emancipated people, the free masters of their own destiny, think and feel in a new way.

The minds of Soviet men and women are imbued with new, Communist ideas, the ideas of emancipated labour, collectivism, the fraternity of peoples. They are casting off the features engendered by capitalist society in which selfishness, egoism, greed for profit and the cruel, jungle right of

19*

the strong prevail. This renovation does not come of itself; it is achieved in the course of the stubborn conflict between the new and the old, in the relentless struggle progressive, Soviet ideology wages against the corrupting influence of the individualistic, private-property morality that prevails in those countries where capital still reigns. The great process of renewing human personality is promoted by the life-creating, transforming power of Bolshevik ideas which our Party propagates among the masses of the people.

The thoughts of the people flow in unison with the ascending curve of the course of history. Having built socialist society under the leadership of the Party of Lenin and Stalin, our people are now devoting all their efforts to the building of Communist society, which was once the remote dream of mankind, but which is becoming a palpable reality in our country. And the names of those who are leading us to this society, who are devoting all their strength to the good of our country and to the speediest achievement of this great and glorious aim, are inscribed forever in the hearts of the people.

We see this in the life that goes on around us. We see it when we look at an ordinary geographical map.

A MAP OF FREE NATIONS

The map reflects the political structure of our country, the Soviet way of life.

If you look at the old map of the Russian Empire you will not find the names of the nationalities inhabiting it mentioned there. Tsarism not only robbed the oppressed peoples of their human rights, culture and written language, it even robbed them of their proper names. It called the Kazakhs Kirghiz, and the Kirghiz Kara-Kirghiz; it called the Uzbeks Sarts, and the Nentsi Samoyeds. But even these names were not entered on the map. The territories inhabited by these peoples were not supposed to bear their names.

Government offices in Tbilisi, capital of the Georgian S.S.R.

Stalinabad, capital of the Tajik S.S.R.

Lenin Square in Erevan, capital of the Armenian S.S.R.

The Soviet Government not only restored the correct names of the different nationalities, it also entered them on the map. The names Kazakh S.S.R., Kirghiz S.S.R., Uzbek S.S.R., Nenets National Area, and others, are indications of the profound respect that is entertained in the Soviet Union for the national dignity of the peoples.

Not only do we see new names on the map, we also see a new arrangement of the administrative divisions.

In the eighteenth century Catherine II introduced a police division of the country into gubernias to facilitate the administration, the collection of taxes and the conscription of recruits for the army. Time passed, but the rigid gubernia divisions remained almost unchanged.

Sometimes, regions and even towns that constituted single economic units were divided by boundaries that had no justification whatever. For example, the boundary between the Moscow and Vladimir gubernias cut into halves Orekhovo-Zuyevo, a large industrial centre.

The territories of the non-Russian nationalities were artificially cut up by boundaries. The Tatars who live on the Volga were divided up among several gubernias. The Kholm Gubernia was deliberately formed to enable the tsar's officials to Russify the Poles.

After the Great October Socialist Revolution, when new principles were introduced in the life of the country, the old divisions on the map—which were evidence of police rule and national oppression—could not be allowed to remain. The revolution introduced a new administrative division based on the Lenin-Stalin national policy and economic expediency.

The time had passed when some court favourite could have a new gubernia carved out for him so that he could become a Governor—"guardian of the inviolability of the supreme rights of the sovereign."

Under the Soviet government the old gubernia divisions were obliterated not only from the map, but also from the people's memory. The map became aglow with the colours of the different Union republics, dotted with the names of the autonomous republics and regions and crisscrossed with the boundaries of the national areas.

Take, for example, Soviet Central Asia.

In the nineteenth century Central Asia was incorporated in the Russian Empire as a colony. The tsar's legislators penned the internal boundaries of this region on the map with the deliberate purpose of splitting up national and economic units in order to be better able to rule them. They tore the living body of the country to pieces. They, as it were, threw a net of border lines over the different nationalities that inhabit Central Asia.

A boundary cut up the Kirghiz people, part of whom came within the Turkestan Dominion and part within the Steppe Dominion.

Wedged into the Turkestan Dominion were the Emirate of Bokhara and the Khanate of Khiva, which retained a shadowy independence. They were inhabited by the same peoples that inhabited the contiguous localities.

The frontier between Bokhara and the Turkestan Dominion, which ran through the Kyzyl Kum Desert, was drawn in such a way as to ensure a water supply on the route the tsar's generals had chosen for their campaign against Khiva. The wells, the source of life in the desert, were left within the borders of the Russian Empire.

The frontier line ran through the Zeravshan Valley and cut up the irrigation system, which constituted one whole system; the upper reaches of the Zeravshan came within the Russian Empire and the lower within Bokhara. The Russian Governor-General controlled the water and was thus the actual ruler of the whole region. The Uzbek people who lived in the region of the Zeravshan were partitioned.

The different nationalities were deliberately either divided or mixed up. The tsar's government fomented strife among these nationalities, acting on the principle: "divide and rule."

After the revolution and the victorious termination of the Civil War, the peoples of Central Asia, including Bokhara and Khoresm (Khiva), expressed a wish to set up Soviet states in their territories, based on the national principle and affiliated to the Soviet Union. National demarcation lines were drawn in Central Asia and the peoples which had been disunited were reunited.

New border lines were drawn on the map.

The present map of Central Asia shows four Union Republics that are affiliated to the Soviet Union: the Uzbek Republic, which includes the Kara Kalpak Autonomous Republic, the Turkmenian Republic, the Tajik Republic and the Kirghiz Republic. This conforms to the distribution of the native peoples inhabiting Central Asia.

The Soviet system, the victory of Socialism in our country, and the national policy pursued by the Bolshevik Party, facilitated the rapid economic and cultural progress of the Central Asian states. Within the new frontiers the peoples of the U.S.S.R., led by the Party of Lenin and Stalin and assisted by the great Russian people, developed their own economy and culture. Strife among these peoples has been abolished forever.

Formerly torn up into three parts, Uzbekistan is now a large, united, socialist state with a population of over six million. It is a large cotton-growing country and at the same time an industrial country which manufactures steel, machines, chemicals and textiles.

Turkmenistan, which was once divided into three parts, one in Bokhara, one in Khiva and one in Russia, now constitutes a single national state, a flourishing socialist republic, a land of collective and state stockbreeding and cotton growing, a land of chemicals, oil and textiles.

Before the revolution Tajikistan was partitioned between Bokhara and Russia; it is now a united socialist republic which has not only introduced a new branch of agriculture, the cultivation of long-staple cotton, but has built up new industries— textiles and the mining of non-ferrous and rare metals.

The Kara Kalpak territory, which at one time was divided between Russia and Khiva, became an autonomous republic. Under the Soviet government it has made enormous economic and cultural progress. It is now a world-famous centre for the cultivation of lucerne (alfalfa) seed, and for the first time in its history has developed the fish-canning and cotton-ginning industries.

Divided between two dominions before the revolution, Kirghizia is now a Union Soviet Republic. It is the coal centre of Central Asia. Its agriculture has been reorganized on socialist lines, it has developed stockbreeding and has created new industries—the mining of oil and rare metals, and the manufacture of sugar and woolen cloth.

The delimitation of the boundaries on national lines in no way damaged the economy of the different republics. Economic units were left intact. As a rule, a whole irrigation system remained within the borders of a single state; the national factor was corrected by the economic factor. This is quite possible in a country where there is no strife between the different nationalities, where all the peoples work for the common interest of the Soviet state as a whole.

These new internal borders on the Soviet map are indicative of the immense social and political changes that have taken place.

The Soviet system gave all the peoples of our country, including those who had lived in a state of colonial bondage in tsarist Russia, the opportunity to develop their national sovereignty, to display their native talents, to create a new, socialist way of life. The Lenin and Stalin national policy has caused the economy and culture of every nationality in the U.S.S.R. to flourish. The non-Russian outlying regions are no longer economically backward; they now have their own socialist industry and agriculture, and are rapidly raising the cultural level of their inhabitants.

This is further confirmation of the great truth uttered by Comrade Stalin.

"It was formerly the 'accepted idea' that the world has been divided from time immemorial into inferior and superior races, into blacks and whites, of whom the former are unfit for civilization and are doomed to be objects of exploitation, while the latter are the only vehicles of civilization, whose mission it is to exploit the former. This legend must now be regarded as shattered and discarded. One of the most important results of the October Revolution is that it dealt this legend a mortal blow, having demonstrated in practice that liberated non-European nations, drawn into the channel of Soviet development, are not a bit less capable of promoting a *really* progressive culture and a *really* progressive civilization than are the European nations."[*]

Under the Soviet sun the culture—national in form and socialist in content—of all the peoples of our country is flourishing.

The culture of old Turkestan has changed so completely that it is practically a new country. In thirty years, equal in their significance to centuries, it has passed from the patriarchal-tribal system, blood feuds and the complete enslavement of women, from a nomad existence, universal illiteracy and colonial oppression to the socialist system, to socialist production and the socialist way of life.

Everywhere we see an unprecedented growth of culture.

In former times there was scarcely a single Uzbek who had received a higher education. Today, in Tashkent, there is the Academy of Sciences of the Uzbek Soviet Socialist Republic in which we find Uzbek Academicians and Uzbek Doctors of Science. Uzbek workers and engineers in the most up-to-date plants melt steel, build complex machines and machine tools, and by means of the electrolysis of water produce nitrates from the air for fertilizers. The country has changed, and the people have changed too.

In the past the ratio of literates among the Tajiks was one

---

[*] J. Stalin, *Problems of Leninism*, Moscow 1945, p. 201.

to two hundred. Today, in the new city of Stalinabad, which grew out of a tiny native village on the threshold of the Pamirs, Tajiks are studying in colleges and universities, are doing research work in laboratories, and regularly visit the Tajik Theatre, things they never had before. This is to be seen not only in the capital, in Stalinabad, but even in Khorog, in the very heart of the Pamirs, once reached by steep and narrow mountain tracks and to which there is now a regular aeroplane service. There, Tajik actors perform in their own language the plays of the classical Russian dramatist Ostrovsky—"Guilty, Though Innocent," for example. The country has changed, and the people have changed too.

Before the revolution there were only two Turkmenian schoolgirls in the whole of Turkmenistan; in the courts the testimony of one man carried the weight of the testimony of two women. Now in that country there are women Stakhanovites, women outstanding in the field of culture, women managers of large enterprises and women members of the Government. The country has changed, and the people have changed too.

The Kirghiz had no written language; they could neither read nor write in their own tongue. They had no literature, no science, no theatre, no intellectuals. Today, there are more secondary schools in the Kirghiz Republic than there were in all the rural districts of the Russian Empire put together. Today the Kirghiz people have their own writers, artists and scientists.... The country has changed, and the people have changed too.

The census of 1939 showed that the average number of persons attending school throughout the U.S.S.R. was equal to 223 per thousand of the population. The figure for the Turkmenian Republic was 291 per thousand, for the Kirghiz Republic 303, for the Uzbek Republic 330 and for the Tajik Republic 394 per thousand.

This shows that not only has the industrial and agricultural geography of our country changed under the Soviet government, but so has the cultural geography. The culture of the people has made tremendous progress. The great Russian people, the elder brother in the friendly family of peoples of the U.S.S.R., helped the non-Russian peoples inhabiting the outlying regions that were formerly colonies of Russian tsarism to accelerate their cultural development.

The relations between the peoples of our country have fundamentally changed under the Soviet government. By putting an end to the rule of the landlords and capitalists, the October Revolution put an end to colonial oppression. The time when the non-Russian peoples in Russia were disfranchised, were called "aliens," has gone, never to return.

Soviet government bestowed great rights upon all the peoples inhabiting our country. The place of the former "prison of nations" as the Russian Empire was called, has been taken by a Union State, in which the absolutely equal and voluntarily united peoples are bound by indestructible ties of friendship and brotherhood. No such state—the only type that is just and fruitful—exists, or can exist, in the capitalist world. The durability and vitality of the Soviet multi-national state based on the principles of Socialism are something to be envied by any other state.

The strength of the union and friendship of the Soviet peoples manifests itself everywhere.

We see it in the field of labour. The workers of Moscow build complex machines for all the Union Republics; they make these machines out of Ukrainian steel. The Ukrainian miners use pit props made from timber that comes from Lake Onega. The Karelian lumbermen haul this timber to the waterside with tractors run by fuel produced by Azerbaijan oil workers. The Azerbaijan people eat bread made from grain that comes from the Volga region, which receives coal mined by Kazakhs. . . . Cooperative effort to achieve a common purpose—to increase the might of our motherland, and the happiness and prosperity of our working people.

We all see the strength of this union and friendship of the peoples in the field of culture. Russian scholars helped to form a written language for the Moldavians. The melodies of Moldavian songs are heard in the land of the Byelorussians, the poems of Byelorussian poets are read in Georgia. The visits of Georgian theatrical companies are festivals in Moscow.... It is a common urge towards knowledge, towards light, towards the discovery of new talent.

We saw the strength of these vital bonds of fraternity on the battlefield. Turkmenians helped to liberate the Ukraine from the German invaders. Ukrainians shed their blood on the battlefield near Moscow. Moscow citizens fought on the frontiers of the Baltic countries.... All fought for their common motherland against a common foe.

We see the friendship, the fraternal unity and equality of the Soviet peoples everywhere.

And we find them reflected on the map—in the lines indicating the national borders, in the names of the republics, in the four letters that are so full of majestic meaning and significance: U.S.S.R.

THE CITIES OF SOCIALISM

The immense changes that have taken place in the life of our country are vividly reflected in the appearance of our cities. New cities have sprung up on the renovated land—cities of Socialism.

Let us return to the buzzing oases of Central Asia and look at their towns. Near the ruins of ancient cities, living monuments of Asiatic medievalism, near half-ruined Moslem schools and mosques of the time of Tamerlane, now stand factories, modern schools and tall apartment houses. Where formerly only the crowns of Turkestan poplar trees and minarets with storks' nests on their roofs reared to the sky, tower huge factory chimneys, electric cable pylons and the aerials of radio stations. The streets in which clouds of dust were formerly raised at every step are now covered with asphalt, the irri-

The State Opera and Ballet in Alma-Ata, capital of the
Kazakh S.S.R.

A cinema house on Kirov Prospect in Baku, capital of the
Azerbaijan S.S.R.

Navoi Street in Tashkent, capital of the Uzbek S.S.R.

Public garden in Frunze, capital of the Kirghiz S.S.R.

gation streams which formerly ran along the gutters are now encased in concrete, the ancient mule-drawn carts have been displaced by automobiles. And these outward features reveal the new face of the Central Asian city which has cast off the old rags of the feudal-tribal system and is rapidly assimilating the industrial culture of Socialism.

There is a profound and striking contrast between the new and the old in the appearance of the cities in Central Asia. Formerly, a broad irrigation canal divided Tashkent into two dissimilar parts. Two cities lived in one—the "old" and the "new." The "old" city was a teeming anthill composed of Asiatic, flat-roofed mud huts with blank exterior walls, a labyrinth of narrow, crooked streets—this was the quarter inhabited by the Uzbek poor. The "new" city had European buildings, wide, planned streets and squares lined with tall poplars; you heard the ceaseless gurgling of the irrigation streams and the clanging bells of the streetcars and saw the fine mansions of the tsar's officials and of the cotton merchants. Two cities—the two poles of colonial relationships, of colonial exploitation.

Let us take a stroll through the streets of modern Tashkent, now the capital of Soviet Uzbekistan.

The city is still intersected by the broad canal, which to this day divides the ancient core of Tashkent from that part which is of comparative recent date. But it is no longer a border line between two worlds, class and national, it is no longer a symbol of social inequality. On both sides of the canal the same life teems—the same in interests, thoughts and actions. The "new" city has become much more beautiful—the streets are being asphalted, fine buildings are going up, water mains have been laid. But these are not the privilege of the rich, not the preserve of capitalist "civilizers." The "new" city is inhabited by metal turners and physicians, spinning-mill workers and engineers, people of different professions and different nations—Uzbeks, Russians, Kazakhs and Ukrainians. Different, and yet the same, for they all have a common motherland, common aims and engage in common free labour.

Well, what about the "old" city? Has it remained unchanged?
The "old" city is changing more rapidly than the "new."
Wide, straight streets are pushing their way through ramshackle survivals of the past. Schools and big apartment houses
are going up, the streets are being lined with trees and new
streetcar lines are being laid. Navoi Street, the new street named
after the great Uzbek poet, is perhaps the finest in the whole of
Tashkent. Recreation clubs, hospitals, printing plants and an
Uzbek national theatre have been built. In the heart of this
renovated quarter towers a monument to Lenin—the creator of
the new, socialist way of life, the great teacher and leader.

This is how the cities of Central Asia are being reconstructed
and the traces of the former colonial past, of patriarchal backwardness and of class oppression wiped out.

But it is not only the cities of Central Asia that are changing; the cities in the Ukraine, Transcaucasia, the Urals, Siberia
and in the midland regions of the country are assuming an
appearance they never had before.

It would be no use seeking in old Tula, or in ancient Kiev,
a definite barrier like the canal in Tashkent that separated one
part of the city from the other, the slaves from the masters;
but in all cities before the revolution there had always been
not such an obvious, perhaps, but a no less definite division
according to wealth and class. There was an aristocratic
quarter with fine mansions, coats of arms on the gates, stables
and many other appurtenances. There was the merchants'
quarter with solidly-built houses, warehouses with heavy locks,
gardens with arbours and spiked fences. And there was the
working-class quarter—filthy slums, unpaved, muddy streets,
hovels, shacks made of rotten boards and rusty sheet iron, and
dram shops, dram shops everywhere.

Compare this customary scene in the pre-revolutionary
cities with that in any of the big Soviet cities of today. Soviet
workers—factory workers, office workers and intellectuals—
now live in the houses in which formerly the aristocracy and
the bourgeoisie lived. Many workers were transferred to them

from hovels and cellar dwellings. And in the former slums, where small, ramshackle wooden houses huddled together, the Soviet authorities have built light and spacious apartment houses with water supply, electric light and central heating. Comfortable apartment houses with balconies, and with shops on the ground floor, but without the well-appointed "first floor" for the owner, and without the apartments being divided into "low rent" and "high rent" categories. Houses like these have been built on the outskirts and in many cities the outskirts today are finer than the central part.

We still have much to do in the way of reconstruction and new construction in our cities; many houses have still to be built, but already the scene in our cities throughout the country is entirely different from that before the revolution. The main and decisive thing that is reflected in this change is the victory of the new social order, the victory of Socialism.

The time when the names of private owners figured in gold letters on a wire netting stretched over factory gates—the Ryabushinskys, Schröders, Prokhorovs, Putilovs and Zindels—has long passed away.... The names that appear over factory gates now are "Emancipated Labour," "Red Proletarian," "Paris Commune," and so forth. Where, as is often the case, personal names appear over the gates, they are the names of those who personify the ideas and strivings of the whole people, of those whom the people honour as their front-rank fighters, as their brave champions and leaders.

Gone also are the times when the working class of our country was an exploited and enslaved class. Life and labour in the factories that now belong to the people are entirely different from the old. After capturing political power the working class of our country, for the first time in history, obtained the joyous opportunity to work not for a master but for itself, for the socialist state which it created; and this most important feature of the Soviet system has made a deep impress upon the appearance of our cities.

Recall the towns and workers' settlements in the old

Donbas: Yuzovka, Gorlovka, Lugansk. . . . The black silhouettes of the blast furnaces and hot-air compressors, the tall pyramids of coke, the shrieking engines on the narrow-gauge lines, the long trains of trucks loaded with coal or ore. Thousands of men—rolling-mill workers, furnace men, mechanics, engine drivers—whose labour set this clanking, clattering mechanism of production in motion, who compelled the fiery bowels of the blast furnace to blaze.

And near these centres of the steel industry in the South huddled innumerable dingy hovels built of clay and brick, or roughly knocked together out of old planks. The workers' settlement used to cling to a steel mill as fungus clings to a tree. It grew and spread for decades and still looked like something temporary, hurriedly knocked together for a short space of time. And indeed, it was no more than an adjunct of the mill; it was not built as a human habitation, where people could live as decent human beings, but merely to exist in while working to enrich the millowner. The mill did not exist for the people, the people existed for the mill.

Let us stroll through the streets of present-day, Soviet Donbas. We pass apartment houses, several storeys high, and cosy cottages with gardens. The streets are asphalted and lit with electric light. There are public gardens, parks and palaces of culture. In old Yuzovka, now called Stalino, four thousand apartment houses have been built since Soviet government was established, and, in addition, thirty hospitals, dispensaries and maternity homes, and a hundred kilometres of streetcar line. New, socialist towns are growing up around the new, socialist industrial plants. The people are working for themselves, for society, and society is making the lives of the people brighter and more beautiful.

Here is a detail of the city scene that cannot be seen under capitalism. A red streamer is stretched across the wall of a factory building bearing the inscription: "Follow the example of the tool shop staff, which has finished this quarter's plan ahead of schedule"; and in the park next to the factory, or

Minsk. Government offices of the Byelorussian S.S.R., restored
after the war

Stalin Square, Kiev

An Udegei village reading room, Khabarovsk Territory, R.S.F.S.R.

New theatre, built after the war in Zugdidi, Georgian S.S.R.

along the path leading to the factory dining room, are displayed
enlarged portraits of the front rankers, the Stakhanovites, the
heroes of labour. In the land of victorious Socialism, labour
is a matter of honour and glory.

Here is another striking detail—posters on hoardings an-
nouncing that such and such a factory needs workers of such
and such specialities. There are no people in our cities wandering about in search of work and sleeping on benches in the
park at night. Crowds of unemployed at factory gates—an inevitable feature of town life in capitalist countries—have long
vanished from the scene in our Soviet land.

Let us read the announcement that workers are wanted.
In the long list of professions called for we see engineers, cost
accountants, bookkeepers, technicians.... Never has the
country's demand for more and more brain workers grown so
rapidly. In the old Hughes' plant in Yuzovka, in the Donbas,
only twenty-nine members of the staff had a higher or secondary education. There were thirteen engineers on the staff; of
these, six were foreigners. The entire plant was reconstructed
and enlarged, and just before the Great Patriotic War 660
engineers and technicians were employed there. A numerous
intelligentsia—a new, socialist, people's intelligentsia—has
grown up in our country.

Culture has strongly permeated the life of our socialist
country. There are more cultural institutions in our towns and
cities than in those of capitalist countries; and many of them,
such as our workers' recreation clubs, Palaces of Culture, and
Young Pioneers' Halls, cannot be conceived of in capitalist
countries. Nor were there any such institutions in tsarist Russia.

Formerly, the Lyceums were for the aristocracy, the commercial schools for the merchant class and the "city" schools
for the children of the "lower classes." The students at the
Lyceums used to ride up in carriages with pneumatic tyres,
the pupils of the "city" schools had to run to school with their
books tied up with a piece of string. And they did not have
to run for long; poverty at home compelled them to leave

20—777

ST. MARY'S
COLLEGE LIBRARY
CALIFORNIA

school early in order to go to work and supplement the family earnings. Now there are schools all over the town or city; all children must attend school. You can tell a school building at once—it is newly built, has wide windows, and a spacious playground planted with young trees. In every town of any size there is a college and certainly a secondary vocational school; and students are enrolled not according to class, classes have long ceased to exist in our country, but according to proficiency. There were ten universities in Russia before the revolution, now there are thirty-one, and the total number of higher educational establishments has increased ninefold. We now have 788 colleges with a total of 670,000 students.

Formerly, a performance of an amateur theatrical company at the Merchants' Club was quite an event in a town. The "common people" were, of course, not admitted. Today, there is a theatre with a permanent company nearly in every town, and every evening there is a bustling crowd at the brightly lit entrance, and long before the performance starts a notice is put up at the box office window: "House full."

In the United States it is rare for a theatre to have a permanent company; no more than two hundred throughout the country have them. In tsarist Russia there were 150 theatres. Today, however, a town without a theatre doesn't seem to be a town at all. There are about a thousand theatres in the Soviet land.

Formerly a town could boast of a tiny hospital with a single physician and two nurses, and an "alms house," an ordinary brick building with a cupola, like a church. Today, there is a whole network of outpatient hospitals, dispensaries, consulting rooms and kindergartens, housed either in new buildings or in mansions in which the rich lived formerly.

And how many more cultural institutions have appeared in the streets of our towns and cities that were inconceivable in the old days!—Party Study Rooms, District Children's Libraries, Teachers' Halls. . . .

Tall gates with fluttering flags, a white statue of a discus thrower, animated groups of young people—this is a stadium.

Strains of music, green lawns, people promenading on the sandy paths—this is a Park of Culture and Recreation.

These are inevitable features of the city scene in our country; and they testify to the solicitude the socialist state shows for the working people, solicitude for their work, health, and recreation. The socialist state spares no funds to satisfy, as far as possible, all the needs of the people, to create the best possible conditions of life for them; for in the Land of Soviets the people and the state are one. This is the profoundly new principle that lies behind the outward appearance of our towns and cities—behind the doors of the new theatres, the trees, lawns and flowers in our new parks, the asphalt in our new streets and the tall façades of our new buildings.

We also see features that tell us about the relations between the people and the armed forces. What could have been uglier than the old army barracks? The very term became synonymous with boredom, loss of individuality and monotony. And their outward appearance confirmed this: a large, colourless building behind a bare fence.

We have garrisons in our towns today, but their quarters are different from what they were in the past. They are quartered in "army settlements" within the town, but most often outside the town. You can tell a camp by the arch with a Red Star at the entrance, the straight gravel drive lined with trees and flower beds, and amidst abundant foliage the well-furnished quarters. In addition to their military training the men have facilities for improving their education, reading rooms called "Lenin Corners," and recreation clubs. Large garrisons have "Officers' Clubs" which are large cultural institutions with a theatre and concert hall, a library, lecture rooms, etc. The people's state provides its protectors with the best possible conditions of life and all facilities for their all-round development, with the result that the Bolshevik-trained Soviet Army is not only a fighting but also a cultural force.

There are still other touches that express the love the people entertain for the armed forces which performed such

20*

wonderful feats in fighting to defend our Soviet motherland. The honour bestowed upon the fearless sons of our hero people, the liberator of mankind, is visible and palpable. In conformity with our laws, bronze busts of those who have been twice awarded the title of Hero of the Soviet Union are mounted in the public square at their place of birth, and the busts of those who have been awarded that title three times are mounted in addition in the capital of our country—Moscow.

The traces of the storm of war that raged in our country have not yet been wiped away. The scars on the bodies of our towns and cities in the Ukraine, the Moscow Region and Byelorussia are still visible. . . . The charred skeletons of wrecked buildings, the iron trestle tank obstacles accidentally left on the roadsides, and the anti-tank ditches still visible in the environs of our cities, all remind us of those stern days when our Soviet warriors, in conjunction with the whole people, defended our land from the fascist hordes. The entire people assisted the army—metal workers forged arms, women weavers dug trenches, school children kept guard on roofs.

And so the names of hero-cities have gone into the history of our motherland—Sevastopol, Stalingrad, Odessa, Leningrad and Moscow. . . . Cities of Socialism—victor-cities, living images of our people, who can create and can win victory.

All that is best in any of our towns and cities, as well as all over the country, is the result of the solicitude of our Soviet Government and of our Bolshevik Party. It is to them that our towns and cities are indebted for their beauty and their might; and the people reciprocate with the profound love and gratitude they entertain for our Party and our Government. You feel and see this in any town you go to. The biggest and finest building in any city is the House of Soviets. The main street is usually called "Lenin Street," or "Soviet Street."

In the finest spots in town or city you will see statues of the great leaders of our Party and Government—Lenin and Stalin.

There is not a town in our country that has not grown and

become more beautiful during the thirty years of Soviet government.

The importance of the towns in our country has grown
tremendously. Being the centres in which our glorious working
class is concentrated, they have become powerful levers for the
social, technical and cultural renovation and reconstruction of
our country.

The proportion of the urban population to the total population of the country has grown. Before the revolution the
rural population constituted eighty-two per cent of the total
population. Socialist industrialization increased the urban population. Formerly, one in every five or six of the population
lived in a town, now the ratio is one to three.

City life in capitalist countries is subject to the caprices of
the social elements. When a crisis breaks out and there is a
glut of goods on the market, unemployment becomes rife; the
city becomes poverty stricken and deteriorates. We remember
what happened in the Austrian town of Steyr during a crisis:
the automobile plant in that town stopped production and the
schools in the town were closed, light was cut off. The result
of the collapse of the Chile nitrates market was that the town of
Caleta in Chile actually went out of existence and was dismantled.

This cannot happen to any Soviet town.

Knowing no crises, the development of Soviet industry is
continuously expanding our towns.

The reconstruction of our cities, which was interrupted by
the war, has now been resumed.

The renovation of our cities, the centres of socialist industry and culture, is continuing. Tremendous building operations
are in progress in Chelyabinsk. Novosibirsk is growing, and
recently a huge theatre, one of the largest in the world, was
completed there. Archangel, which grew up on a bog, has em-
barked upon a general drainage of its soil. Ashkhabad is prospecting for new water-supply sources. In Erevan new streets
are being built.

Glorious Leningrad is laying out new parks, laying down

gas pipe lines, building an underground electric railway and healing the wounds inflicted by the enemy.

The traces of the war have to be wiped out in hundreds of towns.

Destruction was part of the Hitler generals' strategic design. They planned the destruction of our towns with the same care that they planned their battles. Artillery bombardment of residential quarters, square by square. Thousands of incendiary bombs dropped on the roofs of towns that were of no military importance whatever. A charge of explosives in the basement of every abandoned house....

Wrecked, burned and blown-up towns on a vast territory— from Novorossiisk to Petrozavodsk, from Minsk to Stalingrad.

What a scene our beloved Sevastopol presented when the Germans were expelled! The white city overlooking the blue sea had turned grey. Bare, shapeless heaps of limestone, roofless walls, empty window frames, heaps of rubble. The railway station was gone. The tops of the poplar trees on the platform had been shot away by artillery shells. The roof of the rotunda in which the panorama of the famous siege of Sevastopol was housed was just a jumble of twisted supports. The statues of the Russian soldiers on the monument in the Historical Boulevard were riddled with shell splinters. In Lenin Street the sea could be seen through the battered houses. Staircases dangling from wrecked houses. Streetcar rails torn up. The people huddled in basements. A metal tube protruding from the ground in the middle of the Esplanade with a wisp of smoke curling from it.

The cities are being resurrected. Kiev, Minsk, Stalingrad as well as Sevastopol are being rebuilt, but they will not be what they were before. Everything is being done to make them better, more convenient, more beautiful.

First-class architects are working on plans for the regeneration of these cities and are directing the rebuilding of their streets and public squares. All their plans are based on the most progressive ideas of town planning.

Spacious, bright dwelling houses, wide, asphalted streets. Extensive transportation services. Industrial enterprises outside the city limits. A dense network of cultural institutions: schools, Palaces of Culture, theatres. Extensive parks.

The cities are expanding. The area of Sevastopol will increase by fifty per cent, that of Murmansk will almost be doubled.

New streets will be laid out. A new prospect, or avenue, will run through the upper part of Kiev at right angles to Kreshchatik, the main street. Two new wide thoroughfares will run through Murmansk.

Towns which formerly stood with their backs to river or sea will now face them. The inhabitants of Rostov, one might say, did not see the Don. Boulevards are now being laid out along the riverbank. The embankments of the River Volkhov in Novgorod are being cleared of wharves and warehouses. Novorossiisk will turn round and face the sea.

All the advantages afforded by the localities will be utilized. In Smolensk, cottages will be built on the slopes of the hills facing the Dnieper, and this will add to the picturesqueness of the city. The central part of Oryol will be beautifully laid out on the high bank of the Oka, and Kalinin will spread out on both banks of the Volga.

Gardens will be laid out among the city blocks; and Kursk, in addition to gardens and boulevards, will have bungalow and sanatorium districts.

The glorious traditions of the towns will be worthily noted. The ancient buildings in Novgorod and Pskov will be restored. A new bronze statue of Peter the Great is to be cast for Voronezh to replace the one the Hitlerites destroyed.

Everywhere monuments will be erected to perpetuate the memory of the Great Patriotic War. Obelisks and arches will beautify the cities. Monuments will be erected in honour of Stalin, the organizer of Victory.

Stalingrad is in itself a monument to Victory. Soviet people are rebuilding that city with exceptional love.

The plan of the new Stalingrad includes the best features of the cities that have been built in Soviet times.

The city, which stretches along the Volga for forty kilometres, will constitute a single organism. Large parks will unite the links into a chain of districts. Magnificent, monumental buildings will be erected in the main streets and squares, while all around, amidst gardens, low, comfortable houses with balconies and verandas will be built; and unscreened by continuous rows of houses, the Volga in all its beauty will be seen down below. A wide avenue to be known as Stalin Prospect will run over the hills to the centre of the city. Another avenue, to be called Heroes' Avenue, lined with statues of the famous participants of the Battle of Stalingrad, will run down from the Square of Fallen Heroes in broad terraces to the Volga Embankment, which will be clothed in granite and foliage. On the Embankment, on the Square of Glory, a magnificent monument will be erected in memory of the Stalingrad Victory and in honour of the one whose glorious name this great victor city bears.

RENOVATED VILLAGES

Not only the industrial landscape, but the agricultural landscape too has changed in our country during the period of the Stalin five-year plans. Where the open field system with its tiny, separate strips formerly prevailed, vast stretches of unbroken field are now to be seen. Where the wooden plough once reigned, columns of machines, the towers of elevators and the new farm buildings of collective farms and state farms dominate the scene.

The appearance of the very villages has changed, and their new features show us what profound changes have taken place in the lives of our peasantry under the Soviet government.

The old countryside, where the landlords and kulaks ruled, has receded into the past, and it is with difficulty that we can

Monument to airmen heroes of Great Patriotic War on
Malakhov Kurgan, Sevastopol, the Crimea

Stalingrad. Restored apartment house in Tractor Plant District

LENINGRAD

ODESSA

recall the dismal scene it presented with all its contradictions and antagonisms.

On a high riverbank, in a wooded park, stands the squire's mansion, an old-fashioned house at the end of a long drive lined with lime trees. At the back of the house is the steward's office. There is a crowd round the office door—the steward is firing and hiring labourers. The squire himself appears wearing a hussar's tunic and officer's peaked cap. He gets into a droshky and drives to his fields to see how the work is going.

At the riverside there are clusters of willows, poles, called "cranes," with which buckets are dipped and raised from the well, and rows of huts—this is the village. In the middle of the village there is a house with fretwork ornaments and wooden gates with a heavy iron latch. This house is owned by a peasant, but he does not wear bast shoes and homespun clothes, he wears top boots and a large waistcoat over a sateen blouse. He is a kulak, grown rich by exploiting the labour of the poor peasants and lending them grain at usurious interest.

The kulak's house is roofed with sheet iron, some of the others with wooden boards, most of them are thatched with straw. The huts are lopsided, the foundations have sunk, the windows are almost level with the ground, the panes are broken and stuffed with sackcloth, the peasant cannot afford to buy window glass.

The huts are bare and squalid—a bunk with hay for a mattress and rags for covering. Half-naked children. On the bare, deal table a bowl of cabbage soup without meat and a loaf of rye bread.

In 1902, Dr. Shingarev visited the village of Novo-Zhivotinnoye, in the Voronezh Gubernia, to investigate the conditions of life of the peasants. He went from hut to hut and found nothing but poverty and squalor. The huts teemed with cockroaches. To his surprise he found some huts where there were no cockroaches and he enquired why this was so. He was told: "We are so poor that even the cockroaches can't find anything to eat."

This is how the peasants lived before the revolution—in slavery to the landlords and in bondage to the kulaks.

There have been no landlords in our countryside for a long time now; only those round about forty remember them.

And only a few of the features of the old rural scene have remained to remind us of those days—the old manor house, if it is still preserved, the park and the tree-lined drive, the pond and the service buildings of the manor. But these tell us something different now. Today, when you see a white house with a columned front standing on the hill amidst the trees you ask yourself: What is it—the village hospital, a sanatorium, a children's home, or a machine and tractor station? The cleanliness, the quietness and a woman in a white overall suggest to you that Soviet workers are receiving treatment or are convalescing here. The sound of merry voices and the flagstaff with a red pennant fluttering in the breeze tell you that it is a Young Pioneers' Camp. If in the courtyard you see cans of gasoline and machines of various kinds and hear the clang of metal, you know it is a machine and tractor station. We Soviet people are not surprised at this as a foreigner might be; our state uses state funds to help our working people to recuperate their health, to bring up healthy children and to obtain big crops in the fields. It is our people's state. We, the people, are the state.

The landlord has gone. So has the kulak. Where is the house with the fretwork ornamentation that stood in the middle of the village? It is not so easy to find. It is now one of many similar to it. Under the Soviet government the appearance of the village has changed. Many new houses have been built, and even the old ones look new. They look brighter, they have been straightened and given a coat of paint, they have cast off the imprint of degradation and poverty. Fine, solidly-built houses have long ceased to be a rarity, an exception, in the Soviet village.

The house with the sheet iron roof has a new master now. Not the kulak, but a working, collective-farm family lives in it now. Or perhaps it serves as the premises of the Village Soviet, or as the offices of the collective farm. And today the peasants, conscious of their dignity as Soviet citizens, go into this house, where they had formerly gone bowing and begging cap in hand, as full and equal members of their collective enterprise which knows neither bondage nor dependence.

Next door to the collective-farm office is the village recreation club, from which come the sounds of the radio and, in the evening, the low burr of the cinema apparatus. Then there is the crèche which has eased the life of the peasant women. The house with large windows is a school. Some villages have a stadium and even an amateur theatre organized by the young people of the village. Year after year the outposts of culture which the Soviet Government and the Bolshevik Party have pushed into the very depths of the country are increasing in number.

Go into one of the peasant huts. You will see electric light, a shelf lined with books, city furniture, and city clothes. The inhabitants of the village houses are living in a new way and, in many cases, are working at new professions formerly never heard of in the village—tractor drivers, electricians, librarians.

Another characteristic feature of the Soviet village are the collective-farm buildings. They have become an essential and inevitable feature of village life today. At the back of the rows of houses, nearer to the fields, are long buildings with small windows—these are the collective-farm cattle sheds. You see a structure with a sloping, earth roof with tall, wooden, chimney-like tubes—this is the storehouse for vegetables. Then there is the machine shed, a tall silo tower, and beyond, the extensive, continuous fields, cultivated by modern, large-scale methods which the old village with its individually-owned narrow strips of field never knew.

Today, after the war, we are faced with the task of building many villages anew. The fascist barbarians destroyed the fruit of our people's labour over a vast area; they razed to the ground over seventy thousand villages.

Before the war the collective farmers of the Ukraine, Byelorussia and the Smolensk Region left their small, isolated homesteads and moved into new, large and well-built villages. They had built these villages with loving care to well-considered plans with public buildings in the centre, with gardens and squares, and wide, straight streets and paved sidewalks along which ran electric cables suspended on tall poles.

These villages, which so strikingly demonstrated the advantages and might of the collective-farm system, the Hitlerites destroyed with exceptional ferocity. Compelled to retreat by the onslaught of our forces, they left men to go from house to house with lighted torches to set fire to and destroy everything.

New villages are now rising out of the ashes. The houses are gutted, the fields are scarred by trenches and pitted with shell holes, but the collective farms are alive. The new, growing way of life, engendered by the people themselves, is indestructible. Assisted by the Soviet state, the collective farms are rebuilding their villages. Collective-farm buildings, recreation clubs, schools, stadiums and parks are springing up again. With the assistance of the state and of the collective farms, the peasants are building themselves new houses.

For the first time the building of houses for peasants has become a national task. Special government departments have been set up to supervise collective-farm and village construction and special architects' offices are drawing the plans for this. In the Ukraine an institute has been established to train engineers for rural construction.

By the end of the postwar five-year plan period, the total number of new and rebuilt houses in the rural districts of the Soviet Union will reach 3,400,000. Two-thirds of these will be in the regions that had suffered from the German invasion.

The solicitude shown for the needs of the Soviet peasantry

by the Soviet Government, the Bolshevik Party and by Comrade Stalin knows no bounds, and it is introducing more and more new and striking features in the life of the Soviet village.

NEW HABITATIONS

New villages are being built not only on old sites, but also where there have never been any villages before. Soviet people are settling in new districts and are developing them by their labour.

Kishlaks (villages) are springing up in the newly-irrigated areas of Central Asia. The peoples of the North are moving from their small encampments in the taiga into large, new villages. In Armenia, villages are being built for Armenian immigrants returning from distant countries. Villages are being built in the newly-drained fertile areas of Colchis, and also in the Kaliningrad Region, in South Sakhalin and the Karelian Isthmus. Peasants from the Voronezh, Oryol and Tambov regions are migrating to the fertile lands of the Crimea.

Building is going on everywhere, everywhere you hear the whine of circular saws and see the whiteness of newly-sawn planks, and axes wielded by sure and skilful hands.

The largest number of new villages have sprung up in the East, beyond the Urals.

In old Russia too people migrated to the East. Russian peasants from the midland gubernias went beyond the Volga and beyond the Urals and there opened up new territory by their labour. They were prompted to do so by the desire to escape from land hunger, from constant starvation and poverty, and from landlord and kulak oppression. But bondage awaited them in the new lands. The fertile Siberian steppe enriched some but gave no happiness to others—and the latter constituted the majority.

Migration to the East has a different significance, a different object today.

The victory of the October Socialist Revolution, the transfer of the landlords' land to the peasantry, collective farming and the new methods of agriculture have abolished poverty in the rural districts forever. The policy pursued by the Bolshevik Party changed the life of the toiling peasantry, it brought them culture and prosperity. And migration today is not due to poverty, as it was in the past, but to the planned development of new territories. Collective farmers voluntarily move to more sparsely populated regions where nature is bountiful, but where there is a shortage of labour. There are such places in Siberia, Kazakhstan and the Far East.

In tsarist times migration was a ruinous business. The settlers travelled in freight cars marked "40 persons, 8 horses," and the journey took months. They hung around in filthy mustering centres, starved, fell sick, spent all their resources and at last, utterly worn out, arrived at the "place of immigration," with no means, no machines, without any assistance from the state, to meet strange and primitive conditions and the same kulaks and police officials they had tried to escape from in their "place of emigration."

Under the Soviet government the migration of peasants is organized by the state in a planned manner and with the utmost care. The state pays the cost of the journey, including food, and does everything to make the journey comfortable. Houses are provided in the place of settlement either free of charge or on the instalment plan. The settler receives temporary exemption from taxes and long-term credits for the purchase of a cow and domestic requirements.

With the assistance of the Soviet state and of the collective farms the newcomers soon become settled. New houses and sometimes whole villages spring up. The local collective farms receive additional workers and enjoy the gifts of bounteous nature to an ever increasing extent.

Migration today is not exclusively agricultural as it was in tsarist Russia, but also industrial. Not only are new fields broken in the new territories, but new factories are built too.

In fact, industrial migration exceeds agricultural migration in the U.S.S.R. The new construction that is going on in the as yet undeveloped areas is calling for people.

The more even distribution of industry implies a more even distribution of the population over the country. Industry is moving to the East, so people move to the East too. From 1926 to 1939 the population of our country as a whole increased sixteen per cent, but that of the Urals, Siberia and the Far East increased thirty-three per cent.

The industrial population of the East increased considerably during the war. The transfer of factories to new bases was not a temporary evacuation; the factories were not refugees, they did not try to go back to the places they came from at the first opportunity. Notwithstanding the swiftness with which it was achieved, the transfer was organized, well-considered and planned.

When the enemy was drawing near to Moscow, the Stalin Automobile Plant was removed to the East. Trainloads of equipment were despatched to five definitely indicated places across the Volga to the Urals, and in these five places they served as the nuclei of five new plants, including the one at Miass, known as the Urals Stalin Automobile Plant.

Part of the equipment, skilfully chosen, was left in Moscow, and the Moscow Stalin Automobile Plant continued to operate; not only that, it actually grew.

When the war ended we had six plants instead of one.

Part of the equipment that was evacuated during the war was sent back to where it came from, but part remained in the East. Part of the workers remained too. People from Moscow, Leningrad and Kharkov settled permanently on the Volga, in the Urals and in Siberia.

The Party and the Government see to it that the East should have increasing cadres of permanent workers. In the basic industries in the Eastern areas higher scales of wages are paid. The construction of dwellings is also being speeded up.

The productive forces—industry, agriculture and transport—

are distributed in a new way in our country. Hence, the chief productive force, that which sets the whole economy of our country in motion, and for whose benefit it is set in motion, viz., the people, are also distributed in a new way.

The October Revolution brought about a rise in the level of the material and cultural conditions of life of the people. As a result, the birth rate has greatly increased and the death rate has been reduced by nearly half. Our population is increasing at a much faster rate than that of capitalist countries where the toilers are crushed by exploitation and poverty, unemployment and uncertainty about the morrow. The average annual increase in the population of the U.S.S.R. in the period from 1926 to 1939 was 1.23 per cent; that of the U.S.A. was only 0.67 per cent, that of Germany 0.62, of Great Britain 0.36 and of France 0.08 per cent. . . . The population of our country is growing rapidly.

The Soviet people are working tirelessly to develop the wealth of their country. The new master is arranging and putting his house in order.

The new mineral wealth was discovered by the people. The new factories were built by the people. The new fields were ploughed up by the people. The new roads were laid by the people. And, in building the new factories, ploughing new fields and laying new roads the people distribute themselves over the country in a new way.

Our population has spread more evenly over the country in Soviet times. We are striving for the full development of the wealth of our country and, hence, for a more even distribution of the population. But this, of course, does not mean a mechanically even distribution—so many to the square kilometre. The density of the population need not be the same everywhere. It cannot be the same in, say, a developed coal area as in a cotton-growing area. Natural conditions of life in the rocky mountains of the Arctic differ from those in the southern black-earth plain. And the significance of the growth of the density of the population of the Far East and of the industrial regions of

Street in Krymskaya Stanitsa, Krasnodar Territory, R.S.F.S.R., restored after the war

New cottages for workers and technical and engineering staff of the Minsk Automobile Plant. Byelorussian S.S.R.

New electric power station at Politotdel Collective Farm, Uzbek S.S.R.

Siberia is incomparable with that of the Arctic tundra or the dense taiga in the lower reaches of the Yenisei and the Lena.

The difference in the density of population of different parts of the country remains; but the growth of the national economy all over the country stimulates the migration of people to new habitations.

The immense deposits of extremely valuable ores, the vast expanses of extremely fertile soil and the hundreds of new industrial construction jobs that are going on in the East are calling for more and more workers. There numerous new towns and villages will have to be built. The spaces of our socialist country are boundless, its natural wealth is inexhaustible. Our Soviet people have an immense field for constructive effort and immense opportunities for displaying initiative and daring in their efforts.

TOWNS WHERE THERE WERE NONE BEFORE

Soviet industry is conquering more and more formerly agricultural regions and giving rise to new towns there.

Nowhere have towns ever sprung up with such rapidity and in such great numbers as in our country. But rapidity and numbers are not all. Nowhere, except in our socialist country, have towns been built according to plan on a scientific basis. This is the chief thing.

We have special town-planning institutions in our country of a kind unknown in the capitalist world.

To plan a town is no easy task—it is a task for geologists, hydrologists, architects, engineers, economists and health specialists.

The number of inhabitants of a projected town is arrived at by an intricate calculation in which everything is taken into consideration: the size of the industry in connection with which the town is to be built, the auxiliary services, average size of families, seasonal fluctuations, etc. The site is very carefully

chosen, and this too is an intricate problem—will it be easy
for the workers to get to work, is the soil firm, is there enough
water; will the wind carry the smoke from the factory chimneys to the town? The types of houses to be built have to be
decided—how many large ones, how many small, their design,
what building materials are to be used. Then there is the question of where to locate the schools, recreation clubs, the theatre,
the park and stadium, so that the town should be convenient not
only for work, but also for study, sports, rest and recreation.

That is how a town is planned—how a new town arises.

A new town! But what is a new town? Only such a one
that has arisen on a vacant site? But many old towns have
been so reconstructed, have so expanded, that they are unrec-
ognizable; they are practically new towns. Take the old towns
in the Donets Basin—Stalino, Makeyevka and Voroshilovgrad—
have they not been transformed into new towns in the course
of the five-year plan periods?

These towns have grown and changed, but on the whole
they have retained their former characters—coal, metallurgy,
machine building. But some towns have not only changed in
appearance, they have acquired a different character, their
development has taken a different turn. Chelyabinsk was once
a commercial and railway centre; it is now a big metallurgical
and machine-building centre. Kuznetsk, once a small, out-of-
the-way place, is now Stalinsk, a big centre of heavy industry.
At Krasnoyarsk, on the right bank of the Yenisei, so many
new, huge plants have sprung up, such as locomotive building,
harvester combines, mining machinery, oil well pumps, cement and hydrolytic processes, that the town is entirely different from what it was. Formerly it was a town of one-storey,
flat-roofed houses with no water mains and no greenery of
any kind; during the Great Patriotic War it became a centre
of large-scale industry, a sufficient water supply was found,
public gardens were laid out and fine, large houses were built—
is it not really a new town?

Some old towns "yielded" as it were to the new ones which

have sprung up in their neighbourhood, threw in their lot with them, so to speak, adopted their names and became renovated themselves. On the right bank of the Kama stood the ancient town of Usolye, with log-lined shafts of salt mines, merchants' warehouses, and the old-fashioned houses that belonged to the wealthy Stroganovs. During the Stalin five-year plan periods the huge Berezniki Chemical Plant rose up on the other bank of the river, opposite Usolye, and beside the plant the town of Berezniki sprang up. The new town of Berezniki absorbed the old town of Usolye. Workers and engineers employed at the chemical plant live on both sides of the river. On the Dnieper, near the Dnieper Hydroelectric Power Plant and the factories which use its power, the new town of Zaporozhye was built during the period of the Stalin five-year plans. The old town of Alexandrovsk merged with the new one and adopted its name.

Many old towns have undergone such an immense industrial growth that the new, rapidly-developing life overflowed the brim, splashed into the surrounding countryside and gave birth to new towns, which now cluster around the old centres. Perovo, Babushkin, Lyublino, Mytishchi, Kuntsevo and Khimki are a close cluster of new towns around Moscow. By the side of Kuibyshev, on a nameless waste the town of Novy (New) Kuibyshev has grown up during the past five or six years, and from old habit this new town is still sometimes called Bezymyanka (Nameless). A new, first-class town with scores of streets and broad avenues now stretches for many kilometres along the Volga. This new town is growing so rapidly, and on such a wide scale, that it has even created its own building industry, including the largest tarred-paper and rubberoid factory in our country. Several new towns have sprung up near Tashkent—Chirchik, a centre of electric power, chemicals and machine building; Angren, a coal-mining town; Yangi-Yul, which has grown immensely and has eight large plants: cotton ginning, oil presses, sugar refinery, fruit and vegetable canning, and others. Near Baku, on the north coast of the Apsheron, the town of Sumgait is being built, and, among other things,

21*

it will supply its "elder brother" with piping and chemicals for the oil industry.

Karaganda, the centre of our third largest coal field, is quite a new town itself, but already new towns are teeming near it. Not far away, where a whole group of new pits are being sunk into the rich coal deposits, the town of Saran is spreading. On the shore of the reservoir that was built on the River Nura the huge Karaganda Power Station has been erected, and near it a new town has been built—Temir-Tau (Iron Mountain). In this town on the shore of a huge lake there are already several industrial plants, including the first steel mill in Kazakhstan. Tall apartment houses have sprung up in place of the adobe huts of the township of Samarkand.

That is how new, satellite towns come into being.

In many cases new towns grow out of workers' settlements. When a given district is drawn into the powerful stream of industrial development, the workers' settlements grow, expand and assume the features of a town, and at a definite moment they officially acquire the status of a town.

The numerous mining villages in the Kuzbas underwent a rapid process of conversion from settlements into towns. Just before the Great Patriotic War the total population of the new towns in the Kuzbas—Kemerovo, Anzhero-Sujensk, Prokopyevsk, Leninsk-Kuznetsky and others, amounted to a million, and during the war it grew still further.

During the war an exceptionally large number of workers' settlements grew into towns in the Urals. The industrial towns that grew up along the Ural range were the forts on the "Stalin line" which bore the main brunt of the economic war against fascism. The Ural front was reinforced in the centre by the towns of Talitsa, Rezh and Miass, and at the same time it stretched very much further to the north and south.

In the North Urals, the settlement known as Turynsk, where Popov, the inventor of the radio, was born, grew into the town of Krasnoturynsk. It was brought into being by the Bogoslovsky Aluminium Plant which was built in the taiga during the war and produced its first consignment of metal on VE Day. It has asphalted streets, houses with balconies, over twenty schools, a technical school and a streetcar service.

At a short distance from here, on the site of the settlement of Petropavlovsk, the town of Severouralsk has arisen, inhabited by the miners who mine the bauxite at the "Red Riding-hood" mine. Here, too, has grown up the town of Karpinsk, formerly the workers' settlement of Bogoslovsky.

On the other flank of the Urals, in the South, a group of new towns have appeared around Orsk, which can itself be called a new town: Khalilov, where iron is mined; Mednogorsk, where copper is refined; and Novo-Troitsk, where a steel plant is going up. Five years ago there was a settlement with sixteen cabins where Novo-Troitsk now stands.

Quite a number of towns have sprung up on the sites of villages where there was no industry before.

Machine building and oil refining was started before the war in the village of Chernyakovka, close to Ufa. During the war the volume of output here increased almost tenfold, and the village of Chernyakovka grew into the city of Chernyakovsk.

The oil industry transformed the village of Ishimbayevo into the town of Ishimbai, and the Altai Tractor Plant transformed the village of Rubtsovka into the town of Rubtsovsk. Begovat, the first metallurgical centre in Uzbekistan, is growing out of a kishlak.

Komsomolsk, the city that was built on the Amur fifteen years ago, was built on the site of the fishing village Perm-skoye that was inhabited by the descendants of ancient settlers from the Urals. A string of dingy huts, barns, the broad river in front and virgin forest at the back. In 1932, Young Communist Leaguers from Moscow, Leningrad and the Ukraine arrived here on the steamer *Columbus* to build the new industrial giants of the Far East. Here they laid the foundations of this magnificent city on the Amur—City of Youth.

The walls of steel mills, machine-building plants, oil refineries and shipyards rose up, one after another streets were

laid out, tall brick apartment houses were built. On the riverbank the ramshackle huts were living their last days, but they
too served the newly-growing town; before the apartment
houses were ready, workers lived in these huts. Thus, the old
served as the springboard for the new.

Komsomolsk now has a population of over a hundred thousand. It consists of large apartment houses of a hundred apartments each, and suburbs of cosy cottages, public squares, broad
avenues. The pioneer builders who lived in dugouts and huts—
navvies, lumbermen and carpenters, are now foremen, technicians and engineers, managers of departments and of whole
plants.

We have seen a large number of towns spring up not out
of old centres, workers' settlements or villages, but on vacant,
totally uninhabited sites.

Some of these towns have arisen at the terminals of newly-
developed waterways.

Near the spot where the Lena flows into the Arctic Ocean,
where river steamers from Yakutia, after coming down the
Lena, arrive to meet the ships that have crossed the Northern
Sea Route, Port Tiksi was built, and this brought a new town
into being.

On the lower Yenisei, at the point that seagoing vessels
can reach, the new town of Igarka has been built, one of the
biggest sawmill centres in Siberia. It has a permanent theatre,
and vegetation, cultivated here for the first time.

To the north, also on the waterside, the new town of Magadan has been built, on the northern shore of the Sea of
Okhotsk, near Nagayevo Bay. It has a fine wharf, blocks of
large apartment houses, a Hall of Culture ornamented with columns and sculptures, cinema theatres, factories, a Park of
Culture and Rest, and a museum. Beyond the last house of the
town stretches the taiga.

Most of the towns that have been built on vacant sites are
connected with the mining of useful minerals. The points indicating these towns on the map are symbols of the triumphs

achieved by our geology and industry. These points are dotted all over the map, and each of them indicates where our Soviet people have conquered coal, oil and ore.

In the extreme Northwest of the U.S.S.R., in the heart of the Kola Peninsula, are Kirovsk and Monchegorsk with their natural wealth. Six weeks of Arctic night, six weeks of continuous daylight. The new points lie where formerly the map bore the mournful legend: "Limit of human habitation."

In the extreme Northeast of our country stands Okha, in Sakhalin, and the forest of oil derricks near it seems to be more dense than the surrounding taiga, which trails off into the tundra....

In the extreme South, in Turkmenistan, there is Nebit Dagh, which is growing in spite of the desert storms which pile sand dunes among the derricks.

In the heart of Kazakhstan, on the shore of a desert lake, stands Balkhash, teeming with life; it is the centre of a huge copper-mining and refining industry. Near Moscow there is Stalinogorsk, which grew up in the region of large coal deposits. Bauxitogorsk, near Leningrad, owes its existence to the large deposits of the raw material for aluminium that lie there.

Magnitogorsk, which sprang up on the left bank of the River Ural only fifteen years ago, has become a huge industrial centre. With its new apartment houses and cottages, it has already spread across to the right bank of the river.

Kirovsk, Balkhash, Karaganda, Stalinogorsk and Magnitogorsk—we call them new cities. This is correct, of course. They were not on the map before. They are our pride, they came into being and grew under our very eyes.

But are they so new? They are each fifteen years old, and in our country fifteen years is quite a long space of time. They can now be called "old new towns," for beside them newer and much younger towns are growing up.

Ishimbai is a new town, but it is already being overtaken by the town of Oktyabrsky, which arose only two or three years ago near the Tuimazy oil fields, in the same Bashkir Republic.

Okha brought into being in its vicinity the Ekhabi oil fields, and there a town has grown up, the prospects of which are no less favourable than those of Okha itself.

Kirovsk is a new city in the north of the European part of Russia, but the town of Vorkuta which grew up there during the war is already rivalling Kirovsk in size and scale of cultural development. In the Pechora region, beyond the Arctic Circle, in the permafrost zone, numerous dwelling houses have been built; Vorkuta already has a theatre for drama and opera, a cinema theatre named "Victory," a Party Education Centre with a library and lecture hall, a Hall of Pioneers and School Children, a mining technical school and a "Dynamo" stadium. In the central square of the town stands a statue of Kirov—the great man who inspired the workers in our Soviet Arctic.

But even Vorkuta is an old town compared with Inta, which sprang up only recently....

These towns which sprang up only recently are growing with enormous rapidity, and this confirms the continuity and increasing rate of our progress.

ANCIENT AND YET YOUNG

Our capital, Moscow, is eight hundred years old. And yet, Moscow is the youngest, the newest city in our country.

The ancient city commenced its new life with the revolution. The national centre of the Russian people, the city which united the lands of Rūs in a single state, became the capital of the first socialist state in the world, the metropolis of the fraternal federation of the Soviet peoples.

Moscow proudly bears the banner of the new era, of the new social order, of life-creating, Soviet democracy.

Moscow is dear to the hearts not only of our multi-national country, but of the working people of all countries.

Here is concentrated all the best of what progressive mankind is striving for.

The Kremlin, Moscow

Columns marching through Red Square, Moscow, during the celebration of
the thirty-first anniversary of the Great October Socialist Revolution

Here is the light and wisdom of our age.

Here is Stalin.

Moscow is the herald of the emancipation of toiling mankind from capitalist slavery, the herald of the struggle for permanent peace and friendship among the peoples.

In this historical role Moscow faces the world as the most eloquent expression of the ideas and aspirations of our people, of the whole of our boundless Soviet land.

Moscow has become the symbol of the new, socialist world, the vehicle of the progressive ideas of our age. Hence, the outward appearance of Moscow should conform to this great mission.

The Bolshevik Party, which guides the whole life of our country, organized and carried through the renovation of Moscow. The lines on which the capital was to be reconstructed were indicated by the great Stalin.

The plan of the reconstruction of Moscow is being successfully carried out.

No other city is changing so rapidly. Moscow already looks entirely different from what it was before.

The dull-red tones of brick and dark-brown tones of timber are giving way to the light-grey colour of concrete and yellowish-grey facing. First one and then another tall apartment house is built, and gradually the whole street lines up with new buildings. In many cases tall, new buildings stand back a good way from the rest and we guess that it indicates the "red line," along which the whole street will be widened. In many parts of the city the main streets have already been widened and for the first time the citizens of Moscow saw fine vistas that were formerly hidden by narrow and crooked streets. The expansive vertical planes of the new houses, relieved by rows of balconies and windows, harmonize with the smooth, horizontal planes of the asphalted streets.

The chain of kerbstones, the green strip of grass in the gutters and the rough cobblestones have gone. Only the side-streets are now paved with stone, and then not all. The droshky has given way to the automobile and the draycart to the motor truck. But even the number of motor trucks seen in the streets is diminishing; more and more goods are being carted at night. Trolley buses have shifted the streetcars to the outskirts of the city. Street traffic has acquired not only a new tempo, but also a new rhythm, which old Moscow did not know; the traffic lights hold up cars at street crossings one moment and release them in batches at another.

The Moscow River, having been raised three metres by the influx of the water of the Volga, now has a level which it formerly reached only during the spring floods. It is now higher than the beds of its tributaries, the mouth of the pipe through which the Neglinka flowed into the Moscow River is no longer visible. In width and length the new bridges across the river are like new streets. The Bolshoi Krasnokholmsky Bridge is three-quarters of a kilometre long. The new bridges with their high, slightly arched spans stretch across the river and both its embankments, which have been converted into speedways. Four hundred new schools have been built in all parts of the city and have become a common feature of the Moscow scene. Finely laid out parks of culture and rest have become organic parts of the city.

Our people have renovated our capital and are continuing to renovate and improve it in conformity with the plans of the great Stalin. During the post-war five-year plan period, Moscow will receive new dwellings amounting to a total floor space of 3,000,000 square metres, which is equal to 600 seven-storey apartment houses. The foundations have already been laid of several extra tall buildings, including a 26-storey building on the Lenin Hills. These buildings will harmonize with the magnificent Palace of Soviets which in the future will rise up on the bank of the Moscow River in the middle of the city. In this same five-year plan period 200,000 apartments will be supplied with gas from Saratov. The capacity of "Mosenergo," the Moscow electric power plants, will be doubled. The existing radial lines of the Metro will be linked up by a big circle line, and the whole Metro system will conform to the historical development of Moscow—a star of radial roads linked by concentric rings.

Our glorious capital has been transformed and with it have changed the various districts of the city from the distant outskirts to the Red Square, right to the Kremlin.

Where there were waste lots on the outskirts there are now whole blocks of houses, streets and factories. The city has spread beyond the Circle Railway, has gathered within its precincts surrounding villages like Vorobyovo, Nagatino, Koptyevo and Kotly, and has populated them with workers and office employees.

Just as the "city gates" at Byely Gorod and Zemlyanoi Val have disappeared, leaving only a memory in the names of the present squares, so have the "bars" gone, and in their place are ordinary squares which are not at all distant in the opinion of the present-day citizen of Moscow.

The districts that were once regarded as distant suburbs have been, as it were, drawn nearer to the centre; by the Metro it is possible to get to Izmailovo, Sokol and Leninskaya Sloboda in a matter of fifteen or twenty minutes. The suburban districts have become urban in appearance too; the one-storey log houses have given way to tall apartment houses. In many parts "new towns" have sprung up, for example, at Usachovka, Dangauerovka, and beyond the Krasnopresnenskaya Zastava (Bar). There are schools, shops, cinema theatres, and dressmakers' and tailors' shops. There is now less need to "go down town."

There is a profound significance in these changes. The former division of the city into a comfortable "centre," and the squalid, poverty-stricken outskirts has gone. All districts are equal now, for Soviet citizens, builders, toilers, live in all of them.

A change has come over even those districts of Moscow which bore a specific social character right up to the revolution. Few now remember that the Rogozhskaya Zastava was the quarter inhabited by rich Old Believers, that Zamoskvorechye was the merchants' quarter where the playwright Ostrovsky found the characters for his comedies, that Sivtsev Vrazhek was the quarter of the shabby genteel, and that Povarskaya (now Vorovsky) Street, was the quarter of the rich factory owners and bankers. These districts have now merged with the city as a whole and their inhabitants differ in no way from those of the rest of the city.

The time when the rich lived in the fine houses in the central districts and the workers were huddled in tiny cubicles in factory barracks on the outskirts, beyond the Sadovaya Circle, has gone for ever. In the first years of the Soviet government hundreds of thousands of workers were removed from the slums and housed in the apartments of the bourgeoisie in the central districts. This changed the social character of the centre; the working-class suburbs changed too and began rapidly to catch up with the centre as regards city improvements.

This affected the distribution of the cultural institutions of the capital. Formerly, the theatres, museums and libraries were concentrated in the centre. Today, too, the principal institutions are located in the centre, which can now be conveniently reached from any district of the city. The Bolshoi Theatre, the Maly Theatre, the Art Theatre, the Lenin Museum and the Lenin Library are the property and pride of the whole country.... But under the Soviet government numerous cultural institutions have arisen in districts of Moscow far away from the centre. Thus, the Central Theatre of the Red Army, the Planetarium, cinema theatres, including the large Rodina Cinema House, and the Halls of Culture of the Stalin Auto Plant, the Sickle and Hammer Plant and of the Metro builders, are all outside the Sadovaya Circle. Cultural life has spread throughout the city. Culture has become accessible to all.

The city improvements in the working-class suburbs have kept pace with the industrial development of Moscow. Many new industrial plants have been set up in the capital under the Soviet government. Moscow has ceased to be a "calico" town; it is now a "city of metal." To the old textile centres, located

mainly on the Yauza, in the Presnya District and in Kozhev-
niki, were added new industrial centres, mainly machine building, which arose on the outskirts of the city. Many of the plants
that have grown into the industrial fabric of Moscow are so
large that each could itself serve as the nucleus of a town. Such
are the Stalin Auto Plant, the Ball-Bearing Plant, and the Cal-
ibre Machine-Tool Plant. They have firmly established for Moscow the status of the biggest industrial centre of the country.

Moscow sends its manufactures to all parts of the country
in ever increasing quantities. There is not a house or an industrial enterprise in our country which does not utilize articles
made in Moscow. The entire country is conscious of the assistance rendered by the capital.

Moscow not only supplies the country with its manufactures, but also shares with other cities its industrial experience
and skill. Workers from factories in all parts of the Soviet
Union come to those in Moscow to acquire knowledge and
practice, and in the remotest factories in the country there are
workers who obtained their industrial schooling in Moscow.

The citizens of Moscow are always in the vanguard, in the
front ranks of the Soviet people; they set an example to the
rest in the field of labour and in the field of struggle. The eyes
of the whole country are turned towards the capital, and the
whole country tries to keep in step with it.

Moscow is not only the industrial, but also the cultural
centre of our country; it is the centre of Marxist-Leninist
thought, the centre of Soviet science and art.

The cultural and political significance of the capital increases year after year. The works of Lenin and Stalin, the leaders of world science and the great creators of the new, socialist
world, are published in Moscow in millions of copies and from
here are sent all over the country. All the towns and villages
in the country receive Moscow newspapers and books, which
serve to educate our people and help them in the drive for
Communism.

Every year larger and larger numbers of young people from

all the nationalities that inhabit our boundless country come
to Moscow to receive their education in the Moscow University
and other higher educational establishments. The gatherings in
Moscow of workers in the field of art in the Union Soviet
Republics acquire increasing solemnity. Writers and poets,
actors and musicians from all the fraternal peoples of our
great Union bring their best works to Moscow, the capital of
our motherland, and Moscow crowns them with glory.

The entire country, all its regions and cities, daily feel the
organizing influence, the firm, guiding hand of Moscow. The
threads of the entire economic and political life of the U.S.S.R.
converge in the capital of our great Soviet State.

Once upon a time the ancient Kitai Gorod was the centre
of capitalist trade, finance and stock exchange speculation. Today it is the business centre of the Soviet capital and the location of many Ministries and their departments.

Here flow business bulletins and reports from all parts of
the U.S.S.R., and from here go out directives, instructions,
enquiries. Kitai Gorod, a district in which the central state institutions are concentrated, lives for the interests of the whole country, its life pulsates in unison with that of the whole country.

Between Kitai Gorod and the walls of the Kremlin stretches
the broad and magnificent Red Square. It has long ceased to
be an "outskirt in the centre." It is the point of concentration
of the new way of life. From here the Kremlin chimes are
wafted all over the country. Here, to the granite mausoleum
with the two sentries at the gate, come Soviet people from all
our republics, territories and regions to see the beloved features of Lenin. Here on solemn and joyous festivals come dem-
onstrations and processions, pouring through like a mighty
flood. And here, over the Red Square of the capital, golden
sheaves of sparks soar into the sky and the thunder of triumphant salvoes in salute of victory reverberates in the air.

There is no more thrilling spectacle than the scene in the
Red Square on popular festivals. The human flood that passes
through the Square grows in volume year after year. Hundreds

of thousands march past the ancient Kremlin walls and the
unceasing, heartfelt acclamation with which they greet their
beloved leader testifies to the indestructible unity of the Soviet
people, to their devotion to the ideas of Communism, to their
ardent love for their father and teacher—Stalin.

There is no more magnificent spectacle than a military
parade in the Red Square, when our Soviet warriors march
through in serried ranks and the formidable rows of fighting
machines roll past like an avalanche of steel. During those
hours our entire country, the whole world, receives a further
demonstration of the invincible might of Soviet arms, which
are crowned with the undying fame of victory.

Year after year the very appearance of the Moscow pa-
rades changes, and this reflects the general progress of our
country. Our men are supplied with more and more perfect
weapons, more and more powerful tanks rattle over the granite
blocks that pave the square, and more and more swiftly our
aircraft dash across the sky. . . .

This shows that our Soviet Army, the guardian and cham-
pion of our peaceful labours and the menace to aggressors and
warmongers, is growing stronger and stronger. It shows that
the Soviet State, which holds aloft the banner of peace and
friendship among the nations, is growing and gaining strength.

Towering above the Red Square, the ancient Kremlin—the
heart of our country and the heart of Moscow—has been rejuvenated, renovated. Its spires glitter with new gold. Its ruby
stars shine with unfading light. The scarlet standard flutters
proudly over the Kremlin.

This is the political centre of our glorious motherland, the
Headquarters of the Land of Soviets. Here, to the Supreme
Soviet of the U.S.S.R., our hero people send their chosen ones,
their finest sons and daughters. And here the elected of the
people adopt decisions of the greatest import.

The rays that bring our people happinesss radiate from
here. Stalin—the leader, friend, teacher and great architect of
the Land of Socialism—lives and works here,

IX

POSTSCRIPT

OVER a year has passed since the first Russian edition of this book appeared, and in this period the map of our country underwent further change. It records another step forward in our country's progress. I would, therefore, like to tell the reader about the latest changes that have taken place. Let this short narrative serve as a "new chapter" to a book already published.

The labour of our Soviet people in carrying out the postwar Stalin five-year plan makes the map of our country a living, constantly changing thing. As we look at the map we see how the country is growing.

In the South, in the North and in the East, in the territories conquered by collective labour, new industrial districts are springing up one after another—centres of socialist culture, bulwarks of our might, further and further steps towards the future.

At the same time, in the West, the industrial centres that were devastated by the enemy are rising out of the ruins, gaining strength and growing. They are being supplied with the most up-to-date machinery and technical appliances, and are being filled with new vigour, greater than they had before.

More and more new dots and lines are plotted on the map. The map is changing, and in this is reflecting the new great deeds performed by the people who, under the leadership of the Party of Lenin and Stalin, are transforming the country for the sake of their own happiness.

I turn over the leaves of the book.

A year ago the official map of the U.S.S.R. lay before me. I no longer saw "blank spaces" either in the region of the Pamirs or of Kara Kum. During the thirty years of Soviet government, the exploration of our country was practically completed and the formerly unexplored regions were plotted on the map. But in the Far North there was still a small "blank space" in the heart of the Taimir Peninsula. I wrote about it in my book.

But now, a year later, this is no longer the case. Distant Taimir has also ceased to be a "blank space."

In the case of a newly-discovered river, or mountain peak, it is enough to see and survey it to plot it on the map. But before a new town can be plotted on the map it has to be built. Last year there were 364 new towns on the map of the U.S.S.R. The number is larger now. Construction work is going on all over the country.

For example, there was the village called Rustavi, where the first steel mill in Transcaucasia is being built; now it is the town of Rustavi.

The appearance of new towns is evidence of the growth of industry. New towns are being built on the Zhiguli Hills on the Volga—here the oil industry is developing. New towns are coming into being in Central Asia and Kazakhstan—here the coal industry is expanding.

New circles on the map signify new coal pits, factories and ore mines. . . .

But not every new plant, of course, gives rise to a new dot on the map. Plants are also being built in old towns. The circles on the map remain unchanged, but they signify more than they did before.

Take Rostov. The agricultural machinery plant there, now restored, is turning out more harvester combines than it did before the war. Zaporozhye is again producing electrical energy, iron, steel and steel alloys. Rubtsovsk, in the Altai, is now producing not only tractors, but also tractor ploughs. Gori, in Georgia, is becoming a textile centre.

This is how the country is being changed by the will of the Party. And this is what the map tells us.

But here are some more changes on the map.

Last year, in my book, I mentioned two lines—one running to Leningrad and the other to Kiev. These lines indicated gas pipe lines, hundreds of kilometres long, that were then under construction. These pipe lines are now finished. Gas is now pumped to Leningrad from Estonia, and to Kiev from the foothills of the Carpathians.

There is something new in another place too—preparations are under way for supplying Tashkent with gas that will be piped from Angren.

Gas is flowing to towns. And so also is electricity. More and more new transmission lines are being traced on the map.

Many of these new lines start from hydroelectric power stations. Such stations are now being built on a wide front. Only a year' has passed—but how many revisions I must make in my book in this respect! Last year I wrote that the Farkhad Hydroelectric Power Station and the hydroelectric power station on the River Terek were under construction.... Both are now already in operation.

The Ozernaya Hydroelectric Power Station on the Sevan Cascade will shortly be started. As for the hydroelectric station now being built near Gorky on the Volga, I did not mention that at all in my book.

It is a hard job for a chartographer to keep pace with life nowadays.

For example, we now see on the map an entirely new artificial river, not for navigation, it is true, but for irrigation purposes. This river came into being in 1948. In my book I said that it was only in the course of construction.

But now its water is flowing for hundreds of kilometres,

leaping from one river basin to another. It fills dried up river beds and gives life to new orchards and fields.

I am referring to the Nevinnomyssk Canal, which diverts part of the River Kuban northward to the Manych.

This is a deathblow to drought in the Stavropol Territory.

But the offensive against drought did not commence only here. It was launched on an immense front, stretching from the lower reaches of the Danube to the Ural Mountains.

In the course of fifteen years this immense territory, five times the area of England and four times the area of Italy, will, in conformity with the decision of the Party and the Government's order adopted on Comrade Stalin's proposal, be covered with a network of tree shelter belts. Stalin's plan for the transformation of nature means high and stable crop yields; it means that our agriculture will flourish still more.

The "boundless steppe," the "distant horizon" will be things of the past. Geography tells us that the treeless steppe is the landscape zone of the globe, that it is something planetary, unchangeable.... But we are going to abolish the steppe as a treeless landscape zone in our country.

The plan to intersect the steppe with forest strips, to introduce the travopolye system, to dig ponds and reservoirs and to irrigate as much land as possible with local water resources, must take a number of years to carry out. But if we look at the 1948 large-scale map, at the map of the Central Black-Earth Belt, for example, we will already see the outlines of the new landscape.

In response to the call of the Party, the collective farmers in the Central Black-Earth Belt have begun, for the first time in this region, to practise irrigated farming.

Irrigation schemes are being planned, topographical surveys of the localities are being made, charts are being drawn and shelter belts are being planted. Hydrotechnical works are being planned and carried out—dams on small rivers and ra-

22*

vines, reservoirs, and an irrigation system. Hydroelectric power stations are being built, wind-driven motors and pumps are being installed. Motors, pipes and cast iron fittings are being unloaded at railway stations.

In 1948, water for the first time flowed across the fields of the Central Russian Plateau, where for ages the crops depended upon the rainfall.

It is not an easy matter to change habitual methods of farming. It is not an easy matter to calculate to a cubic metre the amount of water in the rivers, which is not so abundant here, and to distribute the water in such a way as to provide moisture for the largest possible area. Nor is it easy, in constructing reservoirs, to prevent the water from seeping through the chalk and sand deposits that are frequent here. It is a difficult matter also to arrange the flooding of lands so as to save as much valuable land as possible. But these problems must be solved, and with the help of the state, the collective farmers are solving them.

The waters of the River Don and its tributaries, the waters of the Oka and the Tsna, and the waters of innumerable small rivers will irrigate the fields—and the region that has always been distinguished for the instability of its crops will from its irrigated area, no matter what the weather is like, provide an abundance of cereals, sugar beets and vegetables. One can already picture the shady orchards and groves, the lights of electric power stations and the renovated, reconstructed villages....

Many decades ago the great Russian soil scientist and geographer Dokuchayev said: "There are no figures with which to appraise the strength and might of the king of soils, our Russian chernozem." Indeed, a threefold, fourfold yield—what figures are these? ... Only now, under the Soviet system, can the people fully appraise the riches they rightly own.

A close network of shelter belts will be planted in the course of fifteen years. But a vast number of trees have already been planted in 1948. And these trees are greatly changing the geography of various districts in our country.

"Green belts" have been planted around Samarkand, Karaganda, Begovat, and a number of other towns. Tens of thousands of trees have been planted along automobile and rail roads. The collective farmers of Turkmenia have planted mulberry trees and poplars along many of their big and small irrigation canals. Groves are being planted in the Crimea.

Various plants and trees are being cultivated in places where they have never been cultivated before—rice on the marshy riverbanks in Moldavia, lemons on the collective farms in the Vakhsh Valley, grapes near Moscow....

Michurinists in the Moscow Region have successfully grown grapes before. In the summer, get off the train at Pushkino, say, thirty kilometres from the capital, and after a five minutes' walk you will come to a "vineyard," two or three vines in a small garden. They were grown by a university professor, perhaps, or a schoolteacher, a factory worker or a doctor.

The geographical news of 1948 is that the border, not of amateur but of market grape growing, has been shifted to the latitude of Moscow. This year the collective and state farms in the Moscow Region have taken to grape growing.

The cultivation of melons has also spread to the Moscow Region, and even further north.

This changes not only the structure of farming in this region, but also the landscape. In 1948 we could see melon fields on the banks of the Oka near Kashira, or in places in the valley of the Pakhra.... Alongside of northern firs grow striped melons and yellow canteloupes that one would think could grow only near Kamyshin, or near Tashkent.

Thus, cultivation is transforming the North. It is also transforming the South.

Who would believe it—haymaking in the Kara Kum, water pipes in the Kara Kum, Diesel express trains running across the Kara Kum!...

Unfold the map of another desert—Muyun Kum. In 1948 many new conventional signs were entered on this map—"collective-farm centres," wells, cattle grazing routes....

The herds in Kazakhstan are growing rapidly and the collective farms need more pastures and more hayland. And so the collective farmers turned to the Muyun Kum, which hitherto had been a desert. Now, in the winter, thousands of head of cattle from the collective farms in the Jambul Region are driven here to graze.

And so cattle graze in the former desert, the herdsmen put up their yurtas, or tents, and permanent settlements are formed.

Soon the Muyun Kum will be overcrowded, and already the Kazakh cattle raisers are turning their gaze towards another vast desert which has not yet been developed—the Bet-Pak-Dala.

Now let us transport ourselves to another part of the country, to Kiev. The map of this part was also changed during 1948.

The capital of the Ukraine is bounded in the northwest by a small river called the Irpen. The land lying in the valley of this river was regarded as bad—heaving bog overgrown with alder brush and coarse grass. But under the sedge and rust-coloured stagnant water, soil of the most fertile kind was discovered. Now this soil is beginning to supply immense crops of potatoes and vegetables for the inhabitants of Kiev.

The collective farmers of this district, assisted by Young Communist Leaguers from Kiev, are digging drainage canals, uprooting stumps, putting up buildings for pumping stations, installing equipment and putting up high-voltage transmission lines. This new land is being ploughed with heavy tractor ploughs.

This soil is so fertile and collective labour is so fruitful that hundreds of collective-farm families from other parts of the Kiev Region are settling in the valley of the Irpen.

And so we look first at one and then at another part of the map of the U.S.S.R., and everywhere we see growth, changes, everywhere there is something new.

We will see something new in that which links up all these places that are scattered over the length and breadth of our country—the railways.

Here too I must make revisions in my book. An engine sounds its hooter on the new trunk line that skirts the mountain lake of Issyk-Kul; an electric train is ascending to the mines at Tkvibuli. The second track of the Moscow-Kharkov-Rostov line has been restored along its whole length. The first rails have been laid for the line to Khoresm. Very soon the South Siberian line will cut across the Salair Range.... All this was done in 1948....

Yes, everywhere there is growth. Literally everywhere. I have not told you all about this in my postscript, far from it. In fact I have told you only a little. But from what I have told you it is evident that there are no neglected regions in our country. Our country is inhabited by Soviet peoples who are all equal—and the entire country is growing.

V. M. Molotov put this splendidly in his address on the 31st Anniversary of the Great October Socialist Revolution when he said:

"Our country is taking a new ascent.

"This is evident from the labour enthusiasm and improvement in the lives of the common people of the Soviet Union, from the achievements of our men of science and art, from our achievements in socialist construction that we see daily, in which we all take part to the best of our ability and of which we have a right to be proud. Only yesterday our enemies tried to convert the vast territories of our country into a 'devastated area,' wrecking and destroying everything in the path of their hostile incursion. We have not yet healed many of the wounds of the war, we have not yet restored a number of cities, we have not built the premises and dwellings that we need in order to wipe out the consequences of the invasion of the fascist barbarians. But we are successfully proceeding with the work and are marching forward with increasing speed and confidence, leaving many of our prewar achievements far behind.

"On a great ascent is our country, in which the family of Soviet peoples, the numerous peoples inhabiting the Soviet Union, bound by friendship and joint labour for the benefit of their Motherland, are setting an example of cooperation and fraternity unprecedented in history."

Printed in the Union of Soviet Socialist Republics